Praise for *Coaching Youth Football*

"I first met Joe Galat at the age of 14 at the Cape Cod Massachusetts Football Camp. Getting the opportunity to learn the game the right way from Joe at a young age not only increased the chances of me being successful on the field but also increased my chances of staying injury free. Joe went on to coach in the NFL with the New York Giants and Houston Oilers. Joe coached a number of great players during his years in the NFL, including two Hall of Famers, Harry Carson and Elvin Bethea. In *Coaching Youth Football*, along with its online course, *Coaching Youth Football: The AYF Way*, Joe breaks down football fundamentals into simple, teachable techniques that are easy to grasp and execute and will be a great benefit to those serious about learning how to coach the great sport of football."

Howie Long
Football Analyst
2000 Pro Football Hall of Fame Inductee
Eight-Time Pro Bowl Selection

"I am proud to say that I have coached youth football for the past several years and have come to the realization that it involves far more than just Xs and Os. Promoting academic achievement, preparing for the season, ordering equipment, getting coaches to share a vision, coaching kids who are new to the game, and dealing with parents—the infrastructure of the organization alone can be a challenge to many rookie coaches. Joe Galat's *Coaching Youth Football* provides you with all the essentials to ensure your time spent with your kids and parents will be *prime* time."

Deion Sanders
NFL and MLB All-Star

"*Coaching Youth Football* by Joe Galat is the youth coach's playbook on the fundamentals of youth coaching. It provides essential information on coaching a youth football team—from the first day of practice to the final game of the season."

Jim Tressel
Head Football Coach
The Ohio State University

"Joe Galat was my linebackers coach when I was head coach of the New York Giants. Joe's insight on the basic fundamentals of the game detailed in this book will help everyone who is interested in teaching safe football techniques."

John McVay
Former NFL Head Coach
Former San Francisco 49ers Vice President of Football Operations
1989 NFL Executive of the Year

"Greater than my experience as one of Joe's Yale players in the early '70s is the fortune I've enjoyed for more than two decades through my marriage to Kathy Johnson, Olympic medalist in gymnastics. This relationship has reaffirmed for me the paramount lesson imbued by my dear old friend and coach: There is more to be gleaned from sport than mere winning and losing. Joe Galat's focus on fundamentals, team orientation, character development, and, above all, enjoying the process is completely consistent with the elements for enduring success long after the roar of the crowd has dimmed."

Brian Patrick Clarke
Actor and Former Yale Football Player

"Joe Galat's book and course on coaching football will assist football coaches and administrators at any level. It is a valued tool for developing players on the fundamentals of football so they may reach their potential on the field. More important, Galat's approach of using the values learned in football to teach life skills will be of great benefit."

Floyd A. Keith
Executive Director
Black Coaches and Administrators

Coaching Youth Football

FIFTH EDITION

American Sport Education Program
with Joe Galat

Endorsed by AYF

Human Kinetics

Library of Congress Cataloging-in-Publication Data

Coaching youth football / American Sport Education Program, with Joe Galat ;
endorsed by AYF. -- 5th ed.

    p. cm.

  ISBN-13: 978-0-7360-8566-3 (soft cover)

  ISBN-10: 0-7360-8566-1 (soft cover)

  1. Youth league football--Coaching. 2. Football for children--Coaching.
I. Galat, Joe. II. American Sport Education Program.

  GV956.6.R66 2010

  796.33207'7--dc22

2010009059

ISBN-10: 0-7360-8566-1 (print)

ISBN-13: 978-0-7360-8566-3 (print)

The Web addresses cited in this text were current as of April 2010 unless otherwise noted.

Content Provider: Joe Galat, American Youth Football President; **Acquisitions Editor:** Amy Tocco; **Managing Editor:** Laura Podeschi; **Copyeditor:** Patrick Connolly; **Permission Manager:** Martha Gullo; **Graphic Designer:** Nancy Rasmus; **Graphic Artist:** Francine Hamerski; **Cover Designer:** Keith Blomberg; **Photographer (cover):** Kevin Heitczman, © American Youth Football; **Photographer (interior):** Neil Bernstein, unless otherwise noted; photos on pp. 1, 11, 21, 37, 57, 75, 87, 137, 169, 189, and 203 by Kevin Heitczman, © American Youth Football; **Visual Production Assistant:** Joyce Brumfield; **Photo Production Manager:** Jason Allen; **Art Manager:** Kelly Hendren; **Associate Art Manager:** Alan L. Wilborn; **Illustrator:** © Human Kinetics; **Printer:** United Graphics

We thank Flamingo Park in Miami Beach, Florida, for assistance in providing the location for the photo shoot for this book.

Copies of this book are available at special discounts for bulk purchase for sales promotions, premiums, fund-raising, or educational use. Special editions or book excerpts can also be created to specifications. For details, contact the Special Sales Manager at Human Kinetics.

Printed in the United States of America   10 9 8 7 6 5 4 3 2 1

The paper in this book is certified under a sustainable forestry program.

Human Kinetics

Web site: www.HumanKinetics.com

United States: Human Kinetics
P.O. Box 5076
Champaign, IL 61825-5076
800-747-4457
e-mail: humank@hkusa.com

Canada: Human Kinetics
475 Devonshire Road Unit 100
Windsor, ON N8Y 2L5
800-465-7301 (in Canada only)
e-mail: info@hkcanada.com

Europe: Human Kinetics
107 Bradford Road
Stanningley
Leeds LS28 6AT, United Kingdom
+44 (0) 113 255 5665
e-mail: hk@hkeurope.com

Australia: Human Kinetics
57A Price Avenue
Lower Mitcham, South Australia 5062
08 8372 0999
e-mail: info@hkaustralia.com

New Zealand: Human Kinetics
P.O. Box 80
Torrens Park, South Australia 5062
0800 222 062
e-mail: info@hknewzealand.com

E4901

To my favorite coaches: Faye, Gregg and Tracy, Shane and Tracy, Joe and Diana, Adam and Jamie, and Jessica and Norman

To my children's children: Nic, Gabrielle, Abigail, Max, Gabriel, Grace, Isabella, Mia, and Aiden

Contents

FOOTBALL

Welcome to Coaching

Coaching young people is an exciting way to be involved in sport. But it isn't easy. Some coaches are overwhelmed by the responsibilities involved in helping athletes through their early sport experiences. And that's not surprising because coaching youngsters requires more than bringing the balls to the field and letting them play. It also involves preparing them physically and mentally to compete effectively, fairly, and safely in their sport and providing them with a positive role model.

This book will help you meet the challenges and experience the many rewards of coaching young athletes. You'll learn how to meet your responsibilities as a coach, communicate well and provide for safety, and teach tactics and skills while keeping them fun, and you'll learn strategies for coaching on game day. There are more than 70 drills and games included to help you with your practices. We also provide a sample practice plan and season plan to help guide you throughout your season. For access to some of this information online, visit the following Web site: www.HumanKinetics.com/CYFootball5E/ExtraPoints. Such materials are marked with this symbol in the text:

This book serves as text for two online courses developed by the American Sport Education Program (ASEP). *Coaching Youth Football: The AYF Way* is the official coach-certification course of American Youth Football (AYF). Coaches and administrators affiliated with AYF can visit www.AYFCoaching.com for more information or to register for the course.

The ASEP *Coaching Youth Football* online course is available to all youth sport organizations and coaches. For more information about this course or other ASEP courses and resources, please contact us at the following address:

ASEP
P.O. Box 5076
Champaign, IL 61825-5076
800-747-5698
www.ASEP.com

Welcome From American Youth Football

On behalf of the national staff and the many volunteers of American Youth Football (AYF), I welcome you to *Coaching Youth Football*.

This book, like all American Sport Education Programs (ASEP), details the most important components of participation, safety, and sportsmanship. In *Coaching Youth Football*, not only will coaches confirm their existing ideas on coaching, but they will also find many new ideas. Some of the techniques and drills will be familiar; others have been closely guarded by their inventors.

Football, one of the greatest team sports in history, is a laboratory of life's lessons. From AYF to the professional ranks, there are no shortcuts. Every fundamental technique a player learns helps to expand his knowledge of the complex sport of football, and repetition in practice is required to hone his skills at each position. The experience of seeing a young player learn a new skill because of your instruction is unforgettably rewarding. "A teacher affects eternity," and one of the highest levels of teaching is coaching.

I encourage the support staff of your association to also review this valuable and important resource. A successful team needs a community of volunteers, administrators, parents, trainers, and coaches working toward the goal of teaching football for its values and enjoyment.

Football is America's game. It is no coincidence that many community and national leaders have been former football players. Thanks to football coaches everywhere who provided us with a positive experience, we are now dedicated to giving back to our next generation. Nothing is more important than helping kids.

To those we call coach: Thank you!

Joe Galat
President
American Youth Football, Inc.

Drill Finder

> continued

> *continued*

Key to Diagrams

Offensive Positions

BC	Ballcarrier
C	Center
F	Flanker
FB	Fullback
G	Guard
HB	Halfback
O	Offense
OL	Offensive lineman
QB	Quarterback
RB	Running back
SE	Split end
T	Tackle
TB	Tailback
TE	Tight end
WB	Wingback
WR	Wide receiver

Defensive Positions

CB	Corner back
DB	Defensive back
DE	Defensive end
DL	Defensive lineman
DT	Defensive tackle
FS	Free safety
LB	Linebacker
MA	Middle linebacker, weak side (Mack)
MI	Middle linebacker (Mike)
S	Outside linebacker, strong side (Sam)
SS	Strong safety
W	Outside linebacker (Will)
X	Defense

Special-Teams Positions

FG	Field-goal team
H	Holder
K	Kicker
KR	Kickoff return team
LS	Long snapper
P	Punter
PC	Punt coverage team
PR	Punt return team
R	Returner
SS	Short snapper
SV	Safety valve

⟶	Player movement
�	Block
⊢	Tackle
⇢	Pass, snap, or handoff
CO	Coach

Stepping Into Coaching

1

If you are like most youth-league coaches, you have probably been recruited from the ranks of concerned parents, sport enthusiasts, or community volunteers. Like many rookie and veteran coaches, you probably have had little formal instruction on how to coach. But when the call went out for coaches to assist with the local youth football program, you answered because you like children and enjoy football and perhaps because you wanted to be involved in a worthwhile community activity.

Your initial coaching assignment may be difficult. Like many volunteers, you may not know everything there is to know about football or about how to work with children. In our society, anyone involved in football needs to have a high level of credibility. As a coach, you also have a significant responsibility to the sport of football and to the young people whom you will coach. *Coaching Youth Football* presents the basics of coaching football effectively. For access to some of this information online, visit the following Web site: www.HumanKinetics. com/CYFootball5E/ExtraPoints. Such materials are indicated by this symbol in the outside margin of the text:

To start, we look at your responsibilities and what's involved in being a coach. We also talk about what to do when your child is on the team you coach, and we examine five tools for being an effective coach.

Your Responsibilities as a Coach

Coaching at any level involves much more than designing scoring plays for offense or drawing up defenses that keep the other team away from your goal line. Coaching involves accepting the tremendous responsibility you face when parents put their children into your care. As a football coach, you'll be called on to do the following:

1. Provide a safe physical environment.

Playing football holds inherent risks, but as a coach you're responsible for regularly inspecting the fields and equipment used for practice and competition (see the "Facilities and Equipment Checklist" in the appendix on page 216).

Before the start of the season, make sure you explain to the players and parents that football is a contact sport. Everyone should understand that the players will experience the following during the course of the year:

- They will get bumps and bruises.
- They will be tired and will need extra rest.
- They will need to increase their fluid intake to stay hydrated.

Teach players and parents the importance of keeping their equipment in good working order (see chapter 3 for more information). You should reassure them that you will be teaching the safest techniques in order to help players avoid injury and that you have a safety plan in place (see chapter 4 for more information).

2. Communicate in a positive way.

As you can already see, you have a lot to communicate. You'll communicate not only with your players and their parents but also with the coaching staff, officials, administrators, and others. Communicate in a way that is positive and that demonstrates that you have the best interests of the players at heart (see chapter 2 for more information). Psychologists who study children have found that the level of a child's understanding varies with age. Reports indicate that the average age at which a child can safely navigate crossing a two-lane road is eight years. Most children think that an automobile driver can see them if they can see the driver (Whitebread and Neilson 1996). This implies that young players may not be capable of judging the angle needed for tackling a ballcarrier or the arch of a football on a long pass. A good coach will understand that the players perceive the game according to their age.

COACHING TIP Although it may take more thought and may require you to plan ahead, always explain to parents what you are trying to accomplish as a staff. In addition, explain to players what you want them to do rather than what they should not do.

3. Teach the fundamental skills of football.

When teaching the fundamental skills of football, keep in mind that football is a game, and therefore, you want to be sure that your players have fun. We ask that you help all players be the best they can be by creating a fun, yet productive, practice environment (see chapter 5 for more information). To help your players improve their skills, you need to have a sound understanding of offensive, defensive, and special-teams skills (see chapters 7 to 9 for more information).

The fundamental skills required for playing football can be better taught if you provide mental images and key words for the tasks you are teaching. Sport psychologists are employed by most professional sport teams. Although the relaxation techniques and mental rehearsal exercises used by professional teams are more sophisticated, we will introduce the basic learning concepts to you. In the following chapters, we provide some common images and key words used to teach football (e.g., "eyes up," "hit on the rise," "uncoil," "wrap up the ballcarrier," "drive the man," "snowplow him back," and "pancake him"). As a coach, you will soon develop your own fun vocabulary.

4. Teach the rules of football.

Introduce the rules of football and incorporate them into individual instruction (see chapter 3 for more information). Many rules can be taught in the first practice, including properly aligning the offense, avoiding illegal procedures, and handling being caught offside. Plan to review the rules any time an opportunity naturally arises in practices.

5. Direct players in competition.

Your responsibilities include determining starting lineups and a substitution plan, relating appropriately to officials and to opposing coaches and players, and making sound tactical decisions during games (see chapter 10 for more information on coaching during games). Remember that the focus is not on winning at all costs but on coaching your kids to compete well, do their best, improve their football skills, and strive to win within the rules.

6. Help your players become fit and value fitness for a lifetime.

We want you to help your players become fit so that they can play football safely and successfully. We also want your players to learn to become fit on their own, understand the value of fitness, and enjoy training. Thus, we ask you not to make them do push-ups or run laps as punishment. Make it fun to get fit for football and make it fun to play football so that your players will value fitness throughout their lives.

7. Help young people develop character.

Character development includes learning, caring, being honest and respectful, and taking responsibility. These intangible qualities are no less important to teach than the skill of blocking well. We ask you to teach these values to players by demonstrating and encouraging behaviors that express these values at all times. For example, in teaching blocking, stress to young players the importance of learning their assignments, helping their teammates, playing within the rules, showing respect for their opponents, and understanding that they are responsible for winning the individual battle on every play—even though they may not be recognized individually for their efforts.

You should also introduce your players to the concept of giving back to the community. Point out that many people within the community have helped make it possible for the players to participate in football; volunteers range from coaches to concession stand workers to various other positions filled by parents and community members. Players can learn to give back to their community through projects such as cleaning up a park, writing letters to support our troops, and participating in charity drives to help the homeless. These are some of the projects that have won the Giving Back to Community award, which is an award presented by American Youth Football (AYF) to those who help others.

These are your responsibilities as a coach. Remember that every player is an individual. You must provide a wholesome environment in which every player has the opportunity to learn how to play the game without fear while having fun and enjoying the overall football experience.

Coaching Your Own Child

Coaching can become even more complicated when your child plays on the team you coach. Many coaches are parents, but the two roles should not be confused. As a parent, you are responsible only for yourself and your child, but as a coach you are also responsible for the organization, all the players on the team, and their parents. Because of this additional responsibility, your behavior on the football field will be different from your behavior at home, and your son or daughter may not understand why.

For example, imagine the confusion of a young boy who is the center of his parents' attention at home but is barely noticed by his father (who is also the team coach) in the sport setting. Or consider the mixed signals received by a young boy whose skill is constantly evaluated at practice by a coach (who is also his father) who otherwise rarely comments on his son's activities. You need to explain to your child your new responsibilities and how they will affect your relationship when coaching. Take the following steps to avoid problems when coaching your own child:

- Ask your child if he wants you to coach the team.
- Explain why you want to be involved with the team.
- Discuss with your child how your interactions will change when you take on the role of coach at practices or games.
- Limit your coaching behavior to when you are in the coaching role.
- Avoid parenting during practice or game situations in order to keep your role clear in your child's mind.
- Reaffirm your love for your child, irrespective of his performance on the football field.

Five Tools of an Effective Coach

Have you purchased the traditional coaching tools—things such as whistles, coaching clothes, sport shoes, and a clipboard? They'll help you in the act of coaching, but to be successful, you'll need five other tools that cannot be bought. These tools are available only through self-examination and hard work; they're easy to remember with the acronym COACH:

C	Comprehension
O	Outlook
A	Affection
C	Character
H	Humor

Comprehension

Comprehension of the rules, tactics, and skills of football is required. You must understand the elements of the sport. To improve your comprehension of football, take the following steps:

- Read about the rules of football in chapter 3 of this book.
- Read about the fundamentals of football and the football plays in chapters 7 through 9 of this book.
- Read additional football coaching books, including those available from the American Sport Education Program (ASEP).
- Contact youth football organizations, including AYF (www.american youthfootball.com).
- Attend football coaching clinics.
- Talk with more experienced coaches.
- Observe local college, high school, and youth football games.
- Watch football games on television.

In addition to having football knowledge, you must implement proper training and safety methods so that your players can participate with little risk of injury. Even then, injuries may occur. And more often than not, you'll be the first person responding to your players' injuries, so be sure you understand the basic emergency care procedures described in chapter 4. Also, read in that chapter about how to handle more serious sport injuries.

Outlook

This coaching tool refers to your perspective and goals—what you seek as a coach. The most common coaching objectives are to *(a)* have fun; *(b)* help players develop their physical, mental, and social skills; and *(c)* win. Thus, your outlook involves your priorities, your planning, and your vision for the future. See "Assessing Your Priorities" on the following page to learn more about the priorities you set for yourself as a coach.

ASEP has a motto that will help you keep your outlook in line with the best interests of the kids on your team. It summarizes in four words all you need to remember when establishing your coaching priorities:

Athletes First, Winning Second

This motto recognizes that striving to win is an important, even vital, part of sports. But it emphatically states that no efforts in striving to win should be made at the expense of the players' well-being, development, and enjoyment. Take the following actions to better define your outlook.

Assessing Your Priorities

Even though all coaches focus on competition, we want you to focus on *positive competition*—keeping the pursuit of victory in perspective by making decisions that, first, are in the best interest of the players, and second, will help to win the game.

So, how do you know if your outlook and priorities are in order? Here's a little test:

1. Which situation would you be most proud of?
   a. *knowing that each participant enjoyed playing football*
   b. *seeing that all players improved their football skills*
   c. *winning the league championship*
2. Which statement best reflects your thoughts about sport?
   a. *If it isn't fun, don't do it.*
   b. *Everyone should learn something every day.*
   c. *Sport isn't fun if you don't win.*
3. How would you like your players to remember you?
   a. *as a coach who was fun to play for*
   b. *as a coach who provided a good base of fundamental skills*
   c. *as a coach who had a winning record*
4. Which would you most like to hear a parent of a player on your team say?
   a. *Mike really had a good time playing football this year.*
   b. *Mike learned some important lessons playing football this year.*
   c. *Mike played on the first-place football team this year.*
5. Which of the following would be the most rewarding moment of your season?
   a. *having your team want to continue playing, even after practice is over*
   b. *seeing one of your players finally master the skill of tackling*
   c. *winning the league championship*

Look over your answers. If you most often selected "a" responses, then having fun is most important to you. A majority of "b" answers suggests that skill development is what attracts you to coaching. And if "c" was your most frequent response, winning is tops on your list of coaching priorities. If your priorities are in order, your players' well-being will take precedence over your team's win–loss record every time.

- With the members of your coaching staff, determine your priorities for the season.
- Prepare for situations that may challenge your priorities.
- Set goals for yourself and your players that are consistent with your priorities.
- Plan how you and your players can best attain your goals.
- Review your goals frequently to be sure that you are staying on track.

Affection

Another vital tool you will want to have in your coaching kit is a genuine concern for the young people you coach. This requires having a passion for kids, a desire to share with them your enjoyment and knowledge of football, and the patience and understanding that allow each player to grow from his involvement in sport.

You can demonstrate your affection and patience in many ways, including the following:

- Make an effort to get to know each player on your team.
- Treat each player as an individual.
- Empathize with players trying to learn new and difficult skills.
- Treat players as you would like to be treated under similar circumstances.
- Control your emotions.
- Show your enthusiasm for being involved with your team.
- Keep an upbeat tempo and positive tone in all of your communications.

As the saying goes, "Children won't care how much you know until they know how much you care."

COACHING TIP   When players believe that you care for each of them as individuals, they will care about the team and will learn to play the game correctly.

Character

The fact that you have decided to coach young football players probably means that you think participation in sport is important. But whether or not that participation develops character in your players depends as much on you as it does on the sport itself. How can you help your players build character?

Having good character means modeling appropriate behaviors for sport and life. That means more than just saying the right things. What you say and what you do must match. There is no place in coaching for the "Do as I say, not as I do" philosophy. Challenge, support, encourage, and reward every youngster, and your players will be more likely to accept, even celebrate, their differences. Be in control before, during, and after all practices and games. And don't be afraid to admit that you were wrong. No one is perfect!

Each member of your coaching staff should consider the following steps to becoming a good role model:

- Take stock of your strengths and weaknesses.
- Build on your strengths.
- Set goals for yourself to improve on those areas that you don't want to see copied by your players.
- If you slip up, apologize to your team and to yourself. You'll do better next time.

COACHING TIP When you are successful as a coach, people will say that you are a master motivator. Motivation is a phenomenon that exists when repeated experiences of success occur. Winning will become a by-product of good coaching, and the team's motivation will grow with success. But the only lasting motivation must come from within. A true champion is always described as a self-driven individual of high moral character.

Humor

Humor is an often-overlooked coaching tool. For our purposes, humor means having the ability to laugh at yourself and with your players during practices and games. Nothing helps balance the seriousness of a skill session like a chuckle or two. And a sense of humor puts in perspective the many mistakes your players will make. So don't get upset over each miscue or respond negatively to erring players. Allow your players and yourself to enjoy the ups, and don't dwell on the downs.

Here are some tips for injecting humor into your practices:

- Make practices fun by including a variety of activities.
- Keep all players involved in games and skill practices.
- Consider laughter by your players to be a sign of enjoyment, not of waning discipline.
- Smile!

Communicating
as a Coach

2

In chapter 1, you learned about the tools you need for coaching: comprehension, outlook, affection, character, and humor. These are essentials for effective coaching; without them, you'd have a difficult time getting started. But none of the tools will work if you don't know how to use them with your players—and this requires skillful communication. This chapter examines what communication is and how you can become a more effective communicator.

Coaches often mistakenly believe that communication occurs only when instructing players to do something, but verbal commands are only a small part of the communication process. More than half of what is communicated is done so nonverbally. So remember this when you are coaching: Actions speak louder than words.

Communication in its simplest form involves two people: a sender and a receiver. The sender transmits the message verbally, through facial expressions, and possibly through body language. Once the message is sent, the receiver must receive it and, optimally, understand it. A receiver who fails to pay attention or listen will miss parts, if not all, of the message.

Sending Effective Messages

Young players often have little understanding of the rules and skills of football and probably even less confidence in their ability to play the game. So they need accurate, understandable, and supportive messages to help them along. That's why your verbal and nonverbal messages are important.

Verbal Messages

"Sticks and stones may break my bones, but words will never hurt me" isn't true. Spoken words can have a strong and long-lasting effect. And coaches' words are particularly influential because youngsters place great importance on what coaches say. Perhaps you, like many former youth sport participants, have a difficult time remembering much of anything you were told by your elementary school teachers, but you can probably still recall several specific things your coaches at that level said to you. Such is the lasting effect of a coach's comments to a player.

Whether you are correcting misbehavior, teaching a player how to catch the ball, or praising a player for good effort, you should remember several things when sending a message verbally:

- Be positive and honest.
- State it clearly and simply.
- Say it loud enough, and say it again.
- Be consistent.

Be Positive and Honest

Nothing turns people off like hearing someone nag all the time, and players react similarly to a coach who gripes constantly. Kids particularly need encouragement because they often doubt their ability to perform in a sport. So look for and tell your players what they did well.

But don't cover up poor or incorrect play with rosy words of praise. Kids know all too well when they've erred, and no cheerfully expressed cliche can undo their mistakes. If you fail to acknowledge players' errors, your players will think you are a phony.

An effective way to correct a performance error is to first point out the parts of the technique or tactics that the player performed correctly. Then explain—in a positive manner—the error that the player made and show him the correct way to do it. Finish by encouraging the player and emphasizing the correct performance.

Be sure not to follow a positive statement with the word *but*. For example, you shouldn't say, "Great handoff, Billy, but make sure you carry out your fake after handing the ball to the running back." This causes many kids to ignore the positive statement and focus on the negative one. Instead, you could say, "Great handoff, Billy. And if you set up after the handoff, the defense will not know it is a run. Also, you will be in a good position to throw our play-action pass. Great handoff. Way to go."

State It Clearly and Simply

Positive and honest messages are good, but only if expressed directly in words your players understand. Beating around the bush is ineffective and inefficient. And if you ramble, your players will miss the point of your message and probably lose interest. Here are some tips for saying things clearly:

- Organize your thoughts before speaking to your players.
- Know your subject as completely as possible.
- Explain things thoroughly, but don't bore your players with long-winded monologues.
- Use language your players can understand, and be consistent in your terminology. However, avoid trying to be hip by using their age group's slang.
- Use key words to describe the task you are striving to accomplish (e.g., "see the ball hit your hands"), and always try to paint a picture of what you want (e.g., "bend your knees, keep your back straight, and keep your eyes up, like a gorilla in the zoo").

Say It Loud Enough, and Say It Again

Talk to your team in a voice that all members can hear. A crisp, vigorous voice commands attention and respect; garbled and weak speech is tuned out. It's okay and, in fact, appropriate to soften your voice when speaking to a player individually about a personal problem. But most of the time your messages will be for all your players to hear, so make sure they can! An enthusiastic voice also motivates players and tells them you enjoy being their coach. A word of caution, however: Avoid dominating the setting with a booming voice that detracts attention from players' performances.

Sometimes what you say, even if stated loudly and clearly, won't sink in the first time. This may be particularly true when young players hear words they don't understand. To avoid boring repetition and still get your message across, you can say the same thing in a slightly different way. For instance, you might first tell your players, "Get an angle on the runner." If they don't appear to understand, you might say, "Try to meet and tackle the ballcarrier near or behind the line of scrimmage without letting him get by you for a touchdown." The second form of the message may get through to players who missed it the first time around. Remember, terms that you are familiar with and understand may be completely foreign to your players, especially beginning players.

Be Consistent

People often say things in ways that imply a different message. For example, a touch of sarcasm added to the words "Way to go!" sends an entirely different message than the words themselves suggest. You should avoid sending mixed messages. Keep the tone of your voice consistent with the words you use. And don't say something one day and contradict it the next; players will get their wires crossed.

You also want to keep your terminology consistent. Many football terms describe the same or similar skills or techniques. One coach may use the term *cutoff block* to describe blocking a defensive player lined up on the line inside of the blocker, while another coach may call the same technique a *down block*. Although both are correct, to be consistent as a staff, the coaches of a team should agree on all terms before the start of the season and then stay with them (see the glossary beginning on page 228 for common football terms).

COACHING TIP Your actions and voice should be calm and controlled. This will allow players to focus on your message rather than on what your personal feelings may be.

Nonverbal Messages

Just as you should be consistent in the tone of voice and words you use, you should also keep your verbal and nonverbal messages consistent. An extreme example of failing to do this would be shaking your head, indicating disapproval, while at the same time telling a player, "Nice try." Which is the player to believe, your gesture or your words?

Messages can be sent nonverbally in several ways. Facial expressions and body language are just two of the more obvious forms of nonverbal signals that can help you when you coach. Keep in mind that as a coach you need to be a teacher first, and any action that detracts from the message you are trying to convey to your players should be avoided.

Facial Expressions

The look on a person's face is the quickest clue to what the person thinks or feels. Your players know this, so they will study your face, looking for a sign that will tell them more than the words you say. Don't try to fool them by putting on a happy or blank "mask." They'll see through it, and you'll lose credibility.

Serious, stone-faced expressions provide no cues to kids who want to know how they are performing. When faced with this, kids will just assume you're unhappy or disinterested. Don't be afraid to smile. A smile from a coach can give a great boost to an unsure player. Plus, a smile lets your players know that you are happy to be coaching them. But don't overdo it, or your players won't be able to tell when you are genuinely pleased by something they've done or when you are just putting on a smiling face.

Body Language

What would your players think you were feeling if you came to practice slouched over with your head down and your shoulders slumped? Would they think you were tired, bored, or unhappy? What would they think you were feeling if you watched them during a game with your hands on your hips, your jaws clenched, and your face reddened? Would they think you were upset with them, disgusted at an official, or mad at a fan? Probably some or all of these things would enter your players' minds. And none is the impression you want your players to have of you. That's why you should carry yourself in a pleasant, confident, and vigorous manner. This posture not only projects happiness with your coaching role but also provides a good example for your young players, who may emulate your behavior.

Physical contact can also be a very important use of body language. A handshake, a pat on the head, an arm around the shoulder, and even a big hug are effective ways to show approval, concern, affection, and joy to your players. Youngsters are especially in need of this type of nonverbal message. Keep within the obvious moral and legal limits, of course, but don't be reluctant to touch your players, sending a message that can only be expressed in that way.

COACHING TIP When coaching at a practice or game, you should avoid wild hand gestures or standing with crossed arms or with your hands in your pockets. These postures can cause players to think that you are upset or indifferent about the actions of the team.

Improving Your Receiving Skills

Now let's examine the other half of the communication process: receiving messages. Too often, very good senders are very poor receivers of messages. But as a coach of young players, you must be able to fulfill both roles effectively.

The requirements for receiving messages are quite simple, but receiving skills are perhaps less satisfying and therefore underdeveloped compared to sending skills. People seem to enjoy hearing themselves talk more than they enjoy hearing others talk. But if you learn the keys to receiving messages and make a strong effort to use them with your players, you'll be surprised by what you've been missing.

Pay Attention

First, you must pay attention; you must want to hear what others have to communicate to you. That's not always easy when you're busy coaching and have many things competing for your attention. But in one-on-one or team meetings with players, you must focus on what they are telling you, both verbally and nonverbally. Be sure to establish and maintain good eye contact. You'll be amazed at the little signals you pick up. Not only will this focused attention help you catch every word your players say, but you'll also notice your players' moods and physical states. In addition, you'll get an idea of your players' feelings toward you and other players on the team.

Listen Carefully

How you receive messages from another individual, perhaps more than anything else you do, demonstrates how much you care for the sender and what that person has to tell you. If you care little for your players or have little regard for what they have to say, it will show in how you attend and listen to them. You need to check yourself. Do you find your mind wandering to what you are going to do after practice while one of your players is talking to you? Do you frequently have to ask your players, "What did you say?" If so, you need to work on your receiving mechanics of attending and listening. But if you find that you're missing the messages your players send, perhaps the most critical question you should ask yourself is this: "Do I care?" To show your concern as a coach, a good technique is to drop to one knee and look the player in the eyes. This gesture expresses your desire to communicate with the player as a person.

Providing Feedback

So far we've discussed sending and receiving messages separately. But we all know that senders and receivers switch roles several times during an interaction. One person initiates communication by sending a message to another person, who then receives the message. The receiver then becomes the sender by responding to the person who sent the initial message. These verbal and nonverbal responses are called feedback.

Your players will look to you for feedback all the time. They will want to know how you think they are performing, what you think of their ideas, and whether their efforts please you. You can respond in many different ways, and how you respond will strongly affect your players. They will react most favorably to positive feedback.

Praising players when they perform or behave well is an effective way to get them to repeat (or try to repeat) that behavior. And positive feedback for effort is an especially effective way to motivate youngsters to work on difficult skills. So rather than shouting at and providing negative feedback to players who have made mistakes, you should try offering positive feedback and letting them know what they did correctly and how they can improve. Sometimes the way you word feedback can make it more positive than negative. For example, instead of saying, "Don't run with the ball that way," you might say, "Run with the ball this way." Then your players will focus on what to do instead of what not to do.

Positive feedback can be verbal or nonverbal. Telling young players, especially in front of teammates, that they have performed well is a great way to boost their confidence. And a pat on the back or a handshake communicates that you recognize a player's performance.

Communicating With Other Groups

In addition to sending and receiving messages and providing proper feedback to players, coaching also involves interacting with members of the coaching staff, parents, fans, game officials, and opposing coaches. If you don't communicate effectively with these groups, your coaching career will be unpleasant and short-lived. So try the following suggestions for communicating with these groups.

Coaching Staff

Before you hold your first practice, the coaching staff should meet and discuss the roles and responsibilities that each coach will undertake during the year. Depending on the number of assistant coaches, the staff responsibilities can be divided into a head coach; offensive, defensive, and special-teams coordinators; a conditioning coach; and various position coaches. The head coach has the final responsibility for all phases of the game, but as much as possible, the other coaches should be responsible for their groups. During games, under the direction of the head coach, the coordinators will call the plays for the team on the field.

Before practices start, the coaching staff must also discuss and agree on terminology, plans for practice, schemes, game-day organization, and the method of communicating during practice and games. Although they should all bring individual strengths to the team, the coaches on your staff must present a united front and must speak with one voice; they must all take a similar approach to coaching, interaction with the players and parents, and interaction with one another. Disagreements should be discussed away from the playing field, and each coach should have a say as the staff comes to an agreement.

COACHING TIP As a head coach, you should enlist assistant coaches who work together and bring unique strengths to your staff. Avoid the trap of only having coaches who mirror the strengths you bring to the team.

Parents

A player's parents need to be assured that their son is under the direction of a coach who is both knowledgeable about the sport and concerned about their youngster's well-being. You can put their worries to rest by holding a preseason parent-orientation meeting in which you describe your background and your approach to coaching (see "Preseason Meeting Topics" on the following page).

If parents contact you with a concern during the season, you should listen to them closely and try to offer positive responses. If you need to communicate with parents, you can catch them after a practice, phone them, or send a note through e-mail or the U.S. mail. Messages sent to parents through players are too often lost, misinterpreted, or forgotten.

Keep in mind that parents can be a positive source of strength for your team, too. You can work to cultivate parent volunteers who may be able to assist with sponsorship or grant solicitation, as well as other needed functions.

Sponsors and Suppliers

Sponsor and supplier relationships can be a big advantage for your association. You should welcome the affiliation as a community resource that can help make equipment and facilities more affordable. By taking advantage of the sponsorships available in their surrounding communities, associations can provide safe, first-class facilities and quality equipment.

First, create an inventory of advantages you can provide to a sponsor—for example, space on a Web site, advertising in programs, signage on the field, PA announcements during games, coupon distribution, sample giveaways, naming rights of team awards, or guest of honor designation at banquets. After completing the inventory, list your expectations of the sponsor. Money may not always be your objective. You can benefit from bartering services or products as well.

Preseason Meeting Topics

1. Outline the paperwork that is needed:
   - Copy of the player's birth certificate
   - Completed player's application and payment record
   - Report card from the previous year
   - Participation agreement form (from the player's family physician; see the "Medical Clearance Form" on page 218 of the appendix for an example)
   - Parent contract (signed by the parent or guardian; see the "Minor Waiver or Release" on page 219 of the appendix for an example)
   - Team rules
2. Go over the inherent risks of football and other safety issues.
3. Inform parents of the date and time that uniforms and equipment will be handed out.
4. Review the season practice schedule, including the date, location, and time of each practice.
5. Go over the proper conditioning attire for the first days of practice, including accessories.
6. Designate certification day and list weight limits (see page 31 of chapter 3) for players.
7. Discuss nutrition, hydration, and rest for players.
8. Explain the goals for the team.
9. Cover methods of communication: e-mail list, emergency phone numbers, interactive Web site, and so on.
10. Discuss ways that parents can help with the team.
11. Discuss standards of conduct for coaches, players, and parents.
12. Provide time for questions and answers.

After you compile this listing in a clear, precise format, send it to all local merchants serving your community, including equipment, food and drink, medical and dental, and transportation suppliers. In addition, ask your local radio and TV stations to announce that sponsorships are available, and provide handouts to your players to distribute to their neighborhoods.

Once gained, sponsors need to feel that they are appreciated. You should always include them in your functions and provide a special seating area for them at games, banquets, and other related events.

Fans

The stands probably won't be overflowing at your games, which means that you'll more easily hear the few fans who criticize your coaching. When you hear something negative about the job you're doing, don't respond. Keep calm, consider whether the message has any value, and if not, forget it. Acknowledging critical, unwarranted comments from a fan during a game will only encourage others to voice their opinions. So put away your "rabbit ears" and communicate to fans, through your actions, that you are a confident, competent coach.

You must also prepare your players for fans' criticism. Tell your players that it is you, not the spectators, that they should listen to. If you notice that one of your players is rattled by a fan's comment, you should reassure the player that your evaluation is more objective and favorable—and the one that counts.

Officials

How you communicate with officials will greatly influence the way your players behave toward them. Therefore, you must set a good example. Greet officials with a handshake, an introduction, and perhaps casual conversation about the upcoming game. Indicate your respect for them before, during, and after the game. Don't shout, make nasty remarks, or use disrespectful body gestures. Your players will see you do it, and they'll get the idea that such behavior is appropriate. Plus, if the official hears or sees you, communication between the two of you will break down.

COACHING TIP Officials should be informed of any players with special needs. For example, if a child with autism is on your team, and this child shuts down when he is singled out, you should talk with the official before the game starts. Ask the official to avoid singling the player out by name or number if the player commits an infraction. Instead, the official can just indicate the infraction and then privately signal to you which child made the error.

Opposing Coaches

Make an effort to visit with the coach of the opposing team before the game. During the game, don't get into a personal feud with the opposing coach. Remember, it's the kids, not the coaches, who are competing. And by getting along well with the opposing coach, you show your players that competition involves cooperation.

Understanding Rules and Equipment

3

Football is a complicated game played by large teams divided into numerous positions.

The game is governed by a thick rule book. This introduction to the basic rules of football won't cover every rule of the game but instead will give you what you need to work with players who are 8 to 14 years old. In this chapter, we cover terminology, field size and markings, ball size, and equipment. We also describe specifics such as player positions, game procedures and scoring, and the rules of play. We wrap things up by discussing officiating and common officiating signals.

Field

In most youth programs, games are played on regulation high school fields, which are 100 by 53⅓ yards (see figure 3.1), but some programs may play on fields with 80 yards between goal lines and 40 yards between sidelines. Some programs start players on even smaller fields that are 60 yards by 30 yards. Most fields run north and south so that the sun does not shine directly in players' eyes. Stadiums may vary, but all fields are defined by the following:

- Endlines and sidelines serve as the outer boundaries of the playing field.
- A 10-yard end zone is located at both ends of the field; the end zone is used for scoring.
- A goal line at the beginning of each end zone determines scoring; to score, a player must be on, above, or over the opponent's goal line.
- Yard-line markers and hash marks are between the goal lines.
- A goalpost is used for field goals and points after touchdowns.

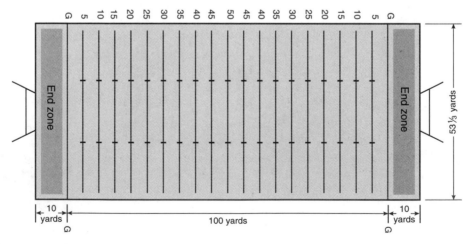

FIGURE 3.1 Regulation football field.

Football

Just as the size of the field is sometimes reduced to match players' development, so too is the size of the ball (see the examples from American Youth Football [AYF] shown in table 3.1). Your league will probably distribute to all teams a certain size and brand of ball to use throughout the season. The football should have a set of laces, and a leather surface is recommended. Check the air pressure of the inflated rubber bladder inside to make sure it is the same as the pressure designated on the ball's exterior.

Any junior- or youth-size ball is allowed. The smaller size lets players learn the proper techniques for throwing and carrying a football at an earlier age.

Table 3.1　Age Divisions and Ball Dimensions for AYF

Age group	Division	Football dimensions (inches)
7-9	Mighty Mites	10¼ to 10½ peewee ball
8-10	Junior Peewees	Junior ball
9-11	Peewees	Junior ball
10-12	Junior Midgets	10⅝ to 10¾ youth ball
11-13	Midgets	Youth ball
12-14	Junior Bantams	11 to 11½ (regulation)
14	Bantams	11 to 11½ (regulation)

Player Equipment

When choosing uniforms, leagues are best served by selecting lightweight jerseys so that players are able to withstand the heat. In cooler weather, layers of clothing can be worn. See page 44 in chapter 4 for more information regarding this topic.

The physical nature of football requires that players also wear protective gear. These items include a helmet, mouth guard, shoulder pads, girdle pads, thigh pads, knee pads, and cleated shoes, as shown in figure 3.2.

Examine the condition of each item you distribute to players. Also make sure that the pieces of equipment they furnish themselves meet acceptable standards. In addition, each piece of equipment must be fit to the player. Make sure that each player on your team is outfitted properly. To properly fit equipment to a player, see the "Player Equipment Checklist" on page 217 in the appendix.

COACHING TIP You may have to demonstrate to players how to put on each piece of equipment. Otherwise, expect some of them to show up for the first practice with their shoulder pads on backward and their thigh pads upside down.

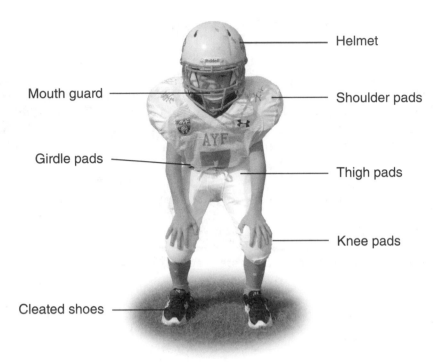

Helmet

Mouth guard

Shoulder pads

Girdle pads

Thigh pads

Knee pads

Cleated shoes

FIGURE 3.2 Protective football equipment.

Shaping a mouth guard is a mystery to most youngsters. Although these plastic mouthpieces come with easy-to-follow directions, your players may need further guidance. Take time to explain the heating and shaping process to the players' parents at the preseason meeting (see "Preseason Meeting Topics" on page 19).

The most important pieces of equipment are the helmet and shoes. Players' shoes must fit their feet appropriately and should include studs for better traction on the field. The helmet is the most commonly misused piece of football equipment. So before distributing helmets to your players, explain very clearly that a helmet is a protective covering, not a weapon. If you spot players using their helmet as a battering device, take them aside and demonstrate the correct, eyes-up technique (as discussed on page 143).

Player Positions

Give your young players a chance to play a variety of positions, on both offense and defense; then see where each player can best contribute on special teams. By playing different positions, the players will have a better all-around playing experience and will probably stay more interested in the sport. Furthermore, they'll have a better understanding of the many technical skills and tactics used in the game. They will also better appreciate the efforts of their teammates who play positions they find difficult.

Following are descriptions of the offensive, defensive, and special-teams positions for football.

Offensive Positions

The offensive team is responsible for moving the football down the field. The offense typically consists of 11 players (as in the split formation shown in figure 3.3) and is broken down into the following three segments:

1. The offensive linemen
2. The receivers
3. The offensive backfield, which includes the running backs and the quarterback

FIGURE 3.3 Offensive team alignment (split formation).

Following are the basic offensive positions with a short discussion of the skills and duties of each. Refer to chapter 7 for more information on the offense.

Offensive Linemen

Ideally, you'll put big, strong, and quick players into the center, guard, and tackle positions. These players, who typically begin each play at the line of scrimmage, must block and open up holes for ballcarriers to run through. When a pass play is called, the offensive linemen must protect the quarterback from opposing linemen.

Receivers

Another player who has important blocking duties is the tight end, a receiver positioned on the line of scrimmage next to (within 3 yards of) either tackle. The tight end must be strong enough to block a defensive end or linebacker yet speedy enough to get open on pass routes.

The two other receiver positions are the flanker and the split end, or wide receiver. Speed and agility, along with great catching ability, are the qualities to look for in filling these spots. The flanker can be positioned on either side of the line of scrimmage, whereas the split end is 8 to 10 yards outside the tackle (and up on the line) opposite the side of the tight end. The flanker is referred to as the slot when lined up on the same side as the split end.

Quarterback

Lined up directly behind the center to receive the snap, the quarterback is the field general of the offense. The quarterback calls the plays in the huddle, barks out the snap count at the line of scrimmage, and then, after taking the snap from the center, hands the ball off, runs with it, or passes it. For this position, you want a good communicator and good athlete who can handle many responsibilities. To complete your wish list, the quarterback will have an excellent throwing arm.

Running Backs

Most teams use a two-back set, either a split-back formation (like the one shown in figure 3.3) or an I-formation (as shown in figure 3.4). In an I-formation, the backs line up in a straight line behind the quarterback.

FIGURE 3.4   I-formation.

Often, one running back is called a fullback, and the other is called a halfback. The fullback has more blocking responsibilities and is expected to pick up short yardage when needed. Therefore, you want a strong, fairly fast, and dependable player at this position. The halfback (called the tailback in the I-formation) is the primary ballcarrier. Speed and agility to outrun and outmaneuver would-be tacklers are desirable attributes for a halfback.

Some coaches prefer to line up their teams in a three-back set, moving the flanker to a wing back position in the wing-T formation (as shown in figure 3.5) or to a second halfback position to form a wishbone formation (as shown in figure 3.6). Coaches typically use the wing-T and wishbone formations when they want their team to run the ball much more than pass it.

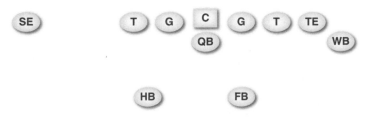

FIGURE 3.5   Wing-T formation.

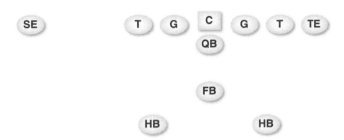

FIGURE 3.6 Wishbone formation.

Defensive Positions

The defensive players stop the opposing team from moving the football. Defensive alignments are usually identified using a two-digit number. The first number designates the number of defensive linemen in the game, and the second number designates the number of linebackers. Defenses can range from a 3-4 defense to a 7-1 defense and all the variations in between, but youth coaches typically use a 4-3 defense as shown in figure 3.7. Following are the basic defensive positions with a short discussion of the skills and duties of each. For further information on coaching the defense, refer to chapter 8.

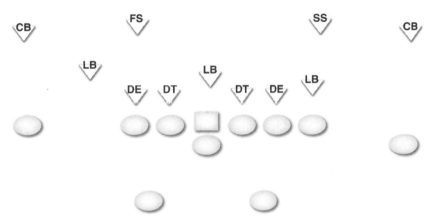

FIGURE 3.7 4-3 defensive alignment.

Defensive Linemen

Youth football coaches put four to six players up front on the line. The four-man front consists of two tackles and two ends. The five-man front adds a nose guard in the middle; the six-man front adds two ends, who may line up in an upright position much like outside linebackers (as discussed in the next section).

Defensive tackles and defensive ends are primarily responsible for defeating the offensive blocker, finding the ballcarrier, and then tackling the ballcarrier before he can gain yardage. The defensive linemen are also responsible for rushing the passer when the offense attempts to throw the ball. To carry out their assignments, defensive linemen need adequate size and strength as well as great quickness to fend off or avoid blocks by offensive players.

Linebackers

You will want two to four linebackers on defense, depending on the number of linemen you use. No matter how many linebackers you use, each should have a nose for the ball—that is, each linebacker should be able to read the offense's play and stop it quickly.

The standard three-linebacker set (as shown in figure 3.7) complements the four-man front nicely. In this alignment, you have a middle linebacker at the heart of the defense and two outside linebackers.

The middle linebacker should be one of your best athletes and surest tacklers. The outside linebacker on the tight end side, often called "Sam" to indicate that he plays on the offense's strong side, must be strong enough to fend off blocks but also fast enough to cover the tight end on pass routes. The weak-side linebacker, often referred to as "Will," must be able to stand his ground against blocks by linemen and backs to prevent the offense from running the ball successfully. This linebacker must also have the range to drop into zone coverage to the side of the split end.

Defensive Backs

The players responsible for preventing long runs and completed passes by the offense are the defensive backs. Again, depending on the alignment of your defensive front, the offense's set, and the game situation, you will have three to five defensive backs in the game. Safeties have responsibilities for the run and the pass. Cornerbacks cover the wide-outs on many pass coverages, but they must come up to play a running play to their side when the team is using a two-deep pass coverage.

All of these players must be agile and fast so that they can cover speedy receivers. The safeties must also be good tacklers in order to help linebackers stop the run.

Special-Teams Positions

Besides assigning players to the basic offensive and defensive spots, you will need to designate players for special-teams positions. *Special teams* refers to all members of the football team who participate in the kicking game. This includes the players involved in kicking the ball (the punt, kickoff, and field-goal and point-after-touchdown [PAT] teams), returning kicks (the punt and kickoff return teams), and blocking kicks (the field-goal and PAT block teams).

Following is a quick look at the key positions for each team. For further information on special teams, refer to chapter 9.

Punt, Kickoff, and Field-Goal and PAT Teams

The players on these teams are involved in the kicking phase of the game and must be taught the basic skills of blocking and tackling. They must also learn how to run down the field to cover the kick. These three teams require the following players—or specialists—with additional specialized skills:

- *Short snapper:* player who snaps the ball back 7 yards to the holder on the field-goal and PAT team; referred to as the center on the field-goal team
- *Long snapper:* player who snaps the ball back to the punter, who can be lined up 10 to 15 yards behind the long snapper depending on the ability of the long snapper; referred to as the center on the punt team
- *Holder:* player who receives the snap on field-goal attempts and places the ball on the tee for the kicker
- *Kicker:* player who kicks the ball off the tee during kickoff and field-goal attempts
- *Punter:* player who punts the ball

Punt and Kickoff Return Teams

Punt and kickoff return teams receive the punt or kickoff and try to move the ball down the field to gain advantageous field position for their offensive team. All of these players must learn the basic skill of blocking. These two teams also require the following players—or specialists—with additional specialized skills:

- *Kick returner:* player on the kickoff return team who is farthest from the kicker and ideally is the player who fields the ball and runs with it
- *Punt returner:* player on the punt return team who is farthest from the punter and ideally is the player who fields the ball and runs with it

How the Game Is Played

The game of football begins with a kickoff. A player on one team kicks the ball from a designated yard line off a tee toward the opponent's goal line. A player on either team can gain possession of the ball after it travels 10 yards downfield. If, as usually happens, a player on the receiving team gains possession, that player tries to advance the ball as far as possible toward the kicking team's goal line. The kicking team tries to tackle the ballcarrier, as close to the receiving team's goal as possible. When the returner is tackled or runs out of bounds, the officials whistle the ball dead and momentarily stop play.

The point where play resumes is called the line of scrimmage. The line of scrimmage stretches from one sideline to the other, passing through the point of the ball nearest the defense. The team with the ball is the offense; the opposing

Scoring

The primary objective of the offensive team is to score, although many coaches also want their offense to maintain possession of the ball for as long as possible. By doing so, they reduce the number of chances the opposing team's offense has to score.

The defensive team's main objective is to prevent the offense from scoring. In addition, the defense tries to make the offensive team give up possession of the ball as far as possible from the goal line it is defending.

Many strategic options for accomplishing these objectives are available to offenses and defenses. Read chapters 7 and 8 for information on how to teach your team basic offensive and defensive plays.

RULES

team is the defense. In 11-player football, the offensive team must begin each play with at least 7 players lined up on the line of scrimmage, facing the defense. Each play starts when one of these linemen—the center—snaps the ball to a teammate, typically the quarterback.

The offense is allowed four plays—or downs—to advance the football 10 yards toward the opponent's goal line. If successful, the offense is given a new set of downs and can maintain possession until it

- is stopped by the defense and has to punt, typically on fourth down;
- turns the ball over to the defense by means of a fumble, interception, or failure to gain 10 yards in four attempts;
- attempts a field goal; or
- scores a touchdown.

Rules of Play

Football rules are designed to make the game run smoothly and safely and to prevent either team from gaining an unfair advantage. Throw out the rules, and a football game quickly turns into a chaotic and dangerous competition where size, brute strength, and speed dominate.

Your league should already have rules concerning acceptable height and weight maximums and minimums for players. Even so, make sure your kids are matched up against opponents with similar physiques and skills. Discourage players from cutting weight to be eligible for your team, and if you spot a mismatch during a game, talk with the opposing coach to see if you can cooperate and correct the problem. Table 3.2 provides an example of league weight restrictions for the AYF National Division. In the AYF All-American Division, an open weight classification system exists from grades 4 to 9 (table 3.3). Eligibility is instead based on age and academic standing (players must have passing grades).

Table 3.2   Age–Weight Matrix for AYF National Division

Reminder: If you do not make the weight, you will not be allowed to participate.

Note: Any sweatdown or extreme weight loss used by a player to make weight will be grounds for immediate suspension for the player's own safety. Any coach, administrator, or team personnel found to have advised, encouraged, or tolerated any sweatdown or extreme weight loss techniques will be subject to immediate suspension. Suspension will be anywhere from one year to permanent depending on the severity. Head coaches will be held responsible for the actions of all team personnel.

Team	Age (as of July 31st)	Maximum stripped weight + uniform allowance = maximum dressed weight
Cadets	8, 9, and 10 O/L*	105 + 5 = 110 lb; 80 + 5 = 85 lb
Junior Peewees	10 and under, 11 O/L*	114 + 5 = 119 lb; 94 + 5 = 99 lb
Peewees	11 and under, 12 O/L*	129 + 5 = 134 lb; 109 + 5 = 114 lb
Junior Midgets	12 and under, 13 O/L*	144 + 6 = 150 lb; 124 + 6 = 130 lb
Midgets	14 and under, 15 O/L*	169 + 6 = 175 lb; 149 + 6 = 155 lb

*A player may be older if he is lighter in weight.

Pregame weigh-in must be conducted before each game.

Courtesy of American Youth Football, Inc. Source: www.americanyouthfootball.com/football.asp#AYF_Recommended_Team_Classification.

Table 3.3   Grade-Based / Age-Protected Matrix for AYF All-American Division

Grade maximum	Age range	Protected age	Protected age explanation
4th	8/**9**/10	10	10 in 4th grade cannot turn 11 on or before 12/31
5th	9/**10**/11	11	11 in 5th grade cannot turn 12 on or before 12/31
6th	10/**11**/12	12	12 in 6th grade cannot turn 13 on or before 12/31
7th	11/**12**/13	13	13 in 7th grade cannot turn 14 on or before 12/31
8th	12/**13**/14	14	14 in 8th grade cannot turn 15 on or before 12/31
9th	13/**14**/15	15	15 in 9th grade cannot turn 16 on or before 12/31

Grades can be combined.

Courtesy of American Youth Football, Inc. Source: www.americanyouthfootball.com/football.asp#AYF_Recommended_Team_Classification.

Your league will also specify the length of your games. Typically, youth football games consist of four 8- or 10-minute quarters. The clock is stopped when

- there is a change of possession,
- the ball goes out of bounds,
- an incomplete pass is thrown,
- the yard markers need to be advanced after a team gains 10 yards for a first down,
- a player is injured and officials call a time-out,
- a team scores, or
- a team calls a time-out.

You will be given two or three time-outs in each half. Use them wisely, not just for talking strategy. Remember, although the games may seem short to you, young players can easily become fatigued. So, besides substituting regularly, call a time-out when you see that your team is tired.

Rule Infractions

AYF and your local youth football program have rule books available for your use. Study them, learn the ins and outs, and then teach the rules to your football team.

Although no youth football team will perform penalty free, you should teach your players to avoid recurring penalties. For example, if a penalty occurs in practice, stop the play and briefly discuss the result of the penalty. By instilling this discipline, you'll help players enjoy more success, both as individuals and as a team.

Here is a brief list of common infractions that football players commit:

- *Offside:* defensive player in or beyond the neutral zone when the ball is snapped
- *Encroachment:* offensive player in or beyond the neutral zone before the ball is snapped
- *Illegal formation or false start:* failure of the offensive team to have at least 7 players on the line of scrimmage (in 11-player football); the offensive team having more than 1 player in motion or a player moving toward the line of scrimmage before the snap
- *Delay of game:* offensive team taking more than 25 seconds to snap the ball after the referee has marked it ready for play
- *Holding:* any player using the arms to hook or lock up an opponent to impede her movement; an offensive player extending the arms outside the body frame to grab an opponent

- *Pass interference (defensive):* defensive player making contact with an eligible receiver who is beyond the neutral zone with the intent of impeding the offensive player trying to catch a catchable forward pass

As you teach your players to play with discipline and to avoid these rule violations, remember that you are their model. Players will reflect the discipline that you display when teaching them in practices and coaching them from the sidelines during games. So show respect for the rules, and don't shrug off game infractions or personal misconduct. And provide a great example by communicating respectfully with the individuals who officiate your games.

Playing by the Rules

You are in a position to teach your players more than simply obeying the rules of the game. As a coach, you have a responsibility to teach players only those techniques that are safe.

For example, you must discourage spearing (tackling with the top of the helmet) on defense because it's against the rules. But you must also teach young players to never lead with their heads when blocking or running. Kicking or striking an opponent or jumping on the pile at the conclusion of a play is not acceptable. Also, teach your players not to grasp an opponent's face mask because doing so can cause serious neck injuries. If you fail to teach and enforce these rules, you are directly contributing not only to the next penalty one of your players commits, but also to the next injury one of your players or an opponent suffers.

Football is a contact, perhaps collision, sport. If participants play according to the letter and spirit of the rules, they can participate safely. Make certain that your players do. Proper football techniques for young football players are described in chapters 7, 8, and 9. Refer to "Football No-Nos" on page 35 for a list of the techniques that you should not tolerate.

Officiating

Football rules are enforced by a crew of officials on the field. In youth football, as many as seven officials or as few as two may work the games. Referees are the officials who control the game. A referee marks the ball ready for play; signals penalties, time-outs, and first downs; and communicates with team captains and coaches. See figure 3.8, *a* through *n*, on page 34 for common officiating signals.

If you have a concern about how a game is being officiated, address the referees respectfully. Do so immediately if at any time you feel that the officiating jeopardizes the safety of your players.

FIGURE 3.8 Officiating signal for *(a)* time-out, *(b)* touchdown or field goal, *(c)* personal foul, *(d)* illegal use of hands, *(e)* illegal contact, *(f)* delay of game, *(g)* offside or encroaching, *(h)* holding, *(i)* illegal motion, *(j)* first down, *(k)* pass interference, *(l)* incomplete pass, penalty refused, or missed kick, *(m)* failure to wear required equipment, and *(n)* roughing the kicker or holder.

Football No-Nos

It's inevitable that your players will violate minor rules during practices and games; even pros go offside now and then. But make clear to your players that some actions are unacceptable on the football field. Officials typically call unsportsmanlike conduct penalties or personal fouls for these actions:

- Tripping
- Face masking (grabbing an opponent's face mask)
- Blocking or tackling with a closed fist
- Spearing (tackling with the top of the helmet)
- Swearing
- Taunting
- Fighting
- Clipping (blocking a player in the back)
- Clotheslining (knocking a player down with a blow to the head or neck)
- Chop blocking (engaging a player high and then chopping the legs out from under him)

Promote good sporting behavior along with the use of proper fundamentals. Encourage players to help opponents up from the ground after a play. Ask ballcarriers to hand the ball to the referee or leave it on the ground where they were stopped. The official will appreciate this behavior and so will the players' parents, league administrators, and players' future coaches.

RULES

Providing for
Players' Safety

4

SAFETY

Your fullback breaks free through a huge hole in the line, and he appears to have daylight all the way to the end zone. Suddenly, a linebacker comes from nowhere and makes a crushing tackle on the runner. Although momentarily pleased with the yardage gained on the play, you quickly become concerned when you see that the ballcarrier is not getting to his feet. He seems to be in pain. What do you do?

No coach wants to see players get hurt. But injury remains a reality of sport participation; consequently, you must be prepared to provide first aid when injuries occur and to protect yourself against unjustified lawsuits. Fortunately, coaches can institute many preventive measures to reduce the risk of injury and ultimately the risk of a lawsuit (for more information, visit the risk management section at www.americanyouthfootball.com). In this chapter, we describe steps you can take to prevent injuries, first aid and emergency responses for when injuries occur, and your legal responsibilities as a coach.

Game Plan for Safety

You can't prevent all injuries from happening, but you can take preventive measures that give your players the best possible chance for injury-free participation. To create the safest possible environment for your players, you must address these areas:

- Preseason physical examination
- Physical conditioning
- Equipment and facilities inspection
- Player matchups and inherent risks
- Proper supervision and record keeping
- Environmental conditions

Preseason Physical Examination

We recommend that your players have a physical examination before participating in football. The exam should address the most likely areas of medical concern and identify youngsters at high risk. The player's doctor should then fill out a form similar to the "Medical Clearance Form" on page 218 of the appendix. We also suggest that you have players' parents or guardians sign a participation agreement form and an informed consent form to allow their children to be treated in case of an emergency. For a sample form, please see the "Minor Waiver or Release" on page 219 of the appendix.

Physical Conditioning

Players need to be in shape (or get in shape) to play the game at the level expected. They must have adequate cardiorespiratory fitness and muscular fitness, along with good warm-up and cool-down habits.

It is important to note that proper breathing is essential to efficient physical activity. Young players tend to breathe in through the mouth or even hold their breath while performing a physical act. However, breathing in through the nose and out through the mouth has been proven to be more beneficial. Remind players of this often until proper breathing becomes a habit. Start each meeting with a breathing session. Ask your players to take deep breaths, using the stomach muscles (diaphragm) to fill the lungs.

Cardiorespiratory Fitness

Cardiorespiratory fitness refers to the body's ability to use oxygen and fuels efficiently to power muscle contractions. As players get in better shape, their bodies are able to more efficiently deliver oxygen to fuel muscles and carry off carbon dioxide and other wastes. Football requires lots of running and exertion, usually in short bursts, throughout a game. Youngsters who aren't as fit as their peers often overextend in trying to keep up, which can result in light-headedness, nausea, fatigue, and potential injury.

Before full-pad workouts begin, you should instruct your youth players on the following fundamental running skills. This will give them a basis for cardiorespiratory training and lay the groundwork for advanced training later in their careers. Running is broken into several phases: the stance, the start, the stride, the burst, and the finish.

Stance   The entire body (feet, knees, hips, shoulders, arms, and head) is aligned toward the finish line. Telling the player to stay square is a common coaching point. For a good example of proper stance, observe a pro wide receiver as he lines up before the ball is snapped.

Start   This phase begins when the front leg pushes off as the back leg extends (the knee rolls toward the ground) and the back foot comes forward. A sprinter's start from the blocks illustrates this phase the best.

Stride   This phase consists of three basic movements of the legs:

1. Pushing off
2. Bringing the knee up
3. Reaching the leg out

Ask the player to imagine that his legs are on an axle, similar to a locomotive's wheels. As part of a warm-up to the stride, the player should do each of the three movements for 30 yards:

1. *Goose steps.* Reach out with one leg and then the other, with the knees locked (see figure 4.1*a* on page 40).
2. *High knees.* Alternate bringing each knee high while pumping the arms back and forth (the arm on the same side as the up knee should be back, as shown in figure 4.1*b*) for balance.
3. *Glute kicks.* Lean forward and alternate kicking the glutes with the heel of each foot (see figure 4.1*c*).

FIGURE 4.1   Stride warm-ups: *(a)* goose steps, *(b)* high knees, and *(c)* glute kicks.

Burst   At this point, the foot hits the ground, creating a burst of speed. Fast runners perfect the basic wheel motion of their legs with **short ground contact** time. Coach the player to square his entire body toward the finish line.

Finish   Runners need to run through the finish line. Younger players tend to stop at the finish line (or goal line) rather than continue through it, resulting in a marked difference in speed. Ask the player to imagine that the line is 5 yards beyond where it actually is.

Try to remember that the players' goals are to participate, learn, and have fun. Therefore, you must keep the players active, attentive, and involved with every phase of practice. If you do, the players may be able to attain higher levels of cardiorespiratory fitness as the season progresses simply by taking part in practice. However, you should watch closely for signs of low cardiorespiratory fitness; don't let your players do much until they're fit. You might privately counsel youngsters who appear overly winded, suggesting that they train outside of practice (under proper supervision) to increase their fitness.

Muscular Fitness

Muscular fitness encompasses strength, muscular endurance, power, speed, agility, and flexibility. This type of fitness is affected by physical maturity, as well as strength training and other types of training. Your team members will likely exhibit a relatively wide range of muscular fitness. Those who have greater muscular fitness will be able to run faster, jump higher, and throw farther. They will also sustain fewer muscular injuries, and any injuries that do occur will tend to be minor. And in case of injury, recovery is faster in those with higher levels of muscular fitness.

Let's look at two aspects of muscular fitness—speed and agility—along with ways to improve them.

Speed Speed training, which is used to improve a player's speed, has gained considerable acceptance throughout the football community. Make sure that your players practice proper fundamentals when speed training, because this type of training can cause greater impact on the players' joints. If done correctly, however, speed training is a great tool for improving muscular fitness. More advanced approaches to speed training include the following:

1. *Resistance running.* The player runs while pulling a sled of weights tethered by a belt around his waist (another method is to run in the sand at the beach).

2. *Reverse resistance running.* Two players are harnessed together while facing opposite directions. They take turns pulling while the partner resists.

3. *Stride lengthening.* The player runs on a downhill slope to force her to lengthen her stride.

Agility Agility is the ability to move quickly in any direction while remaining in control. This may be one of the most important qualities that a football player can have. The old adage of being quick within the confines of a phone booth (or a 5-yard square) describes what great players possess.

Agility is important to the football player not only when he is on his feet, but also when he is off balance or falling—whether he is being tackled, being blocked, or in the act of catching or throwing a ball. A young player may have a fear of being off balance or falling to the ground because he has had a bad experience. However, if a player's knees and arms are bent in position when being bumped by an opponent or falling to the ground, this extra give makes injury less likely. Most injuries from contact with an opponent or the ground occur when a player's limbs are locked.

The higher the level of skill, the more you will see a player who knows how to fall. Professional quarterbacks are the best at falling, unless they get their arms pinned to their sides with nothing to break the fall. Running backs learn early to make room for the ball by dropping to their side to prevent the ball from being jammed into the belly. Having both hands on the ball keeps the shoulders round and allows the ballcarrier to roll on his side.

Help players learn to move with arms and knees bent and shoulders rounded. Some ways of improving agility in order to avoid injury are as follows:

1. *Changing direction.* Players can improve their agility and balance by running around and between pylons placed 3 yards apart. This forces players to practice changing direction while remaining in control.

2. *Figure-eight roll.* Three players begin on their bellies, facing the coach. On the coach's command, the player on the right gets up and dives between the other two players on the ground; this player then rolls as the player on the left gets up, dives between the two players now on the ground, and rolls. This continues until the coach's whistle.

Warm-Up and Cool-Down

Two other components of fitness and injury prevention are the warm-up and the cool-down. Although young bodies are generally very limber, they can become tight through inactivity. The warm-up should address each muscle group and should elevate the heart rate in preparation for strenuous activity. Players should warm up for 5 to 10 minutes using a combination of light running, jumping, and stretching. Flexibility is improved in this manner. Remember that the muscles are like elastic bands and should be stretched by slowly extending a player's range of motion. As practice winds down, slow players' heart rate with an easy jog or walk. Then have the players stretch for 5 minutes to help prevent tight muscles before the next practice or game.

Equipment and Facilities Inspection

Another way to prevent injuries is to check the quality and fit of uniforms, practice attire, and protective equipment used by your players. No player can perform to his maximum ability without proper footwear. Slick-soled, poor-fitting, or unlaced football shoes are a knee or ankle injury waiting to happen. Make sure your players' shoes have appropriately sized studs, are the proper size for their feet, and are double tied to prevent self-inflicted "shoestring tackles." Players should wear their shoes weeks before their first practice. Two pairs of socks, one thinner than the other, can help prevent blisters. Putting Vaseline on areas where the shoe rubs is also an effective preventive measure.

The pants, pads, jerseys, and helmets that your players wear will probably be supplied by your local youth sport program. Check the quality of all equipment and uniforms before fitting them to the kids on your team. After distributing properly fitting equipment that is safe and in good condition, show players how to put on every part of their uniform.

Helmets are the most important piece of protective equipment. A helmet should be tight enough to allow for one finger to fit between the player's head and the helmet's padding; the helmet should never slide in any direction. The chin strap should always be kept snug. Never leave a helmet lying on the field; players may accidentally step in it, or worse, they may trip over it and injure themselves. Also, never allow players to sit on their helmet. Sitting on a helmet will compromise its shape, thus rendering it less protective.

Make certain that each player on the field has a mouthpiece in place at all times. And tell your players that chin straps should be fastened at all times. Finally, advise each of your players to wear an undershirt, such as a wick-away shirt, beneath their shoulder pads to reduce the chance of skin irritations. Staph infections must be closely monitored to prevent any infected area from coming in contact with other players.

COACHING TIP You are responsible for the safety of all your players. Always make your decisions regarding player equipment and field surfaces based on safety!

Remember to regularly examine the field on which your players practice and play. Remove hazards, report conditions you cannot remedy, and request maintenance as necessary. If unsafe conditions exist, either make adaptations to prevent risk to your players' safety or stop the practice or game until safe conditions have been restored. Refer to pages 216 and 217 of the appendix for the "Facilities and Equipment Checklist" and the "Player Equipment Checklist." These forms will guide you in verifying that the facility and player equipment are safe.

Player Matchups and Inherent Risks

We recommend that you group teams in 2-year age increments if possible. You'll encounter fewer mismatches in physical maturation with narrow age ranges. Even so, two 12-year-old boys might differ by 90 pounds in weight, a foot in height, and 3 or 4 years in emotional and intellectual maturity. This presents dangers for the less mature of the two. Whenever possible, you should match players against opponents of similar size and physical maturity. This approach gives smaller, less mature youngsters a better chance to succeed and avoid injury while providing more mature players with a greater challenge. Closely supervise games so that the more mature players do not put the less mature players at undue risk.

Although proper matching helps protect you from certain liability concerns, you must also warn players of the inherent risks involved in playing football, because "failure to warn" is one of the most successful arguments in lawsuits against coaches. So, thoroughly explain the inherent risks of football and make sure each player and his parents know, understand, and appreciate those risks. Some of these inherent risks were outlined in chapter 1; you can learn more about them by talking with your league administrators.

The preseason parent orientation meeting is a good opportunity to explain the risks of the sport to parents and players. After explaining the risks, have both the players and their parents sign waivers releasing you from liability should an injury occur. The waivers should be reviewed by a lawyer before presentation to parents. These waivers do not relieve you of responsibility for your players' well-being, but they are recommended by lawyers and may help you in the event of a lawsuit.

Proper Supervision and Record Keeping

To ensure players' safety, you must provide both general supervision and specific supervision. General supervision means that you are in the area of activity so that you can see and hear what is happening. You should be

- on the field and in position to supervise the players even before a formal practice or game begins,
- immediately accessible to the activity and able to oversee the entire activity,
- alert to conditions that may be dangerous to players and ready to take action to protect players,
- able to react immediately and appropriately to emergencies, and
- present on the field until the last player has been picked up after the practice or game.

Specific supervision is the direct supervision of an activity at practice. For example, you should provide specific supervision when you teach new skills and should continue it until your players understand the requirements of the activity, the risks involved, and their own ability to perform in light of these risks. You must also provide specific supervision when you notice players breaking rules or a change in the condition of your players. As a general rule, the more dangerous the activity, the more specific the supervision required. This suggests that more specific supervision is required with younger and less experienced players.

As part of your supervision duty, you are expected to foresee potentially dangerous situations and to be positioned to help prevent them. This requires that you know football well, especially the rules that are intended to provide for safety. Prohibit dangerous horseplay, and hold practices only under safe weather conditions. These specific supervisory activities, applied consistently, will make the play environment safer for your players and will help protect you from liability if a mishap occurs.

For further protection, keep records of your season plans, practice plans, and players' injuries. Season and practice plans come in handy when you need evidence that players have been taught certain skills, whereas accurate, detailed injury report forms offer protection against unfounded lawsuits. Ask for these forms from your sponsoring organization (see page 220 in the appendix for a sample "Injury Report Form"), and hold onto these records for several years so that an "old football injury" of a former player doesn't come back to haunt you.

Environmental Conditions

Most health problems caused by environmental factors are related to excessive heat or cold, although you should also consider other environmental factors such as severe weather and air pollution. A little consideration of the potential problems and a little effort to ensure adequate protection for your players will prevent most serious emergencies related to environmental conditions.

Heat

On hot, humid days the body has difficulty cooling itself. Because the air is already saturated with water vapor (humidity), sweat doesn't evaporate as easily. Therefore, body sweat is a less effective cooling agent, and the body retains extra heat. Hot, humid environments put players at risk of heat exhaustion and heatstroke (see more on these in "Serious Injuries," beginning on page 52). And if *you* think it's hot or humid, it's worse for the kids, not only because they're more active, but also because kids younger than 12 have more difficulty regulating their body temperature than adults do. To provide for players' safety in hot or humid conditions, take the following preventive measures:

- Monitor weather conditions and adjust practices accordingly. Figure 4.2 shows what equipment should be worn at specific air temperatures and humidity percentages.

- Acclimatize players to exercising in high heat and humidity. Players should first train without pads, adding them a few at a time, to help reduce the risk of heat illness. Players can adjust to high heat and humidity in 7 to 10 days. During this period, hold practices at low to moderate activity levels and give the players fluid breaks every 20 minutes.

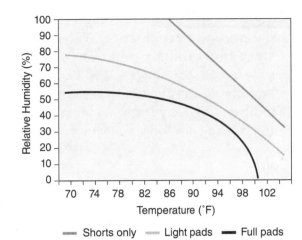

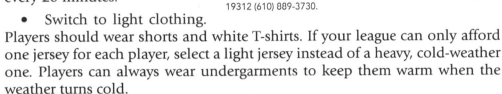

FIGURE 4.2 Warm weather precautions.

Adapted, by permission, from J. Kulka and W.L. Kenney, 2002, "Heat balance in football uniforms: How different uniform ensembles alter the equation," *The Physician and Sportsmedicine* 30(7): 29-39. *Physician and Sportsmedicine* is a registered trademark of JTE Multimedia, LLC, 1235 Westlakes Drive, Suite 320, Berwyn, PA 19312 (610) 889-3730.

- Switch to light clothing. Players should wear shorts and white T-shirts. If your league can only afford one jersey for each player, select a light jersey instead of a heavy, cold-weather one. Players can always wear undergarments to keep them warm when the weather turns cold.

- Identify and monitor players who are prone to heat illness. This would include players who are overweight, heavily muscled, or out of shape and players who work excessively hard or have suffered previous heat illness. Closely monitor these players and give them water breaks every 15 to 20 minutes. Use a weight loss chart to record the players' weights before and after practice.

- Make sure players replace fluids lost through sweat. Encourage players to drink 17 to 20 ounces of fluid 2 to 3 hours before each practice or game, to drink 7 to 10 ounces every 20 minutes during practice and after practice, and to drink 16 to 24 ounces of fluid for every pound lost. Fluids such as water and sports drinks are preferable during games and practices (suggested intakes are based on NATA [National Athletic Trainers' Association] recommendations).

- Encourage players to replenish electrolytes, such as sodium (salt) and potassium that are lost through sweat. The best way to replace these lost nutrients—as well as others such as carbohydrates (energy) and protein (muscle building)—is by eating a balanced diet. Experts say that additional salt intake may be helpful during the most intense training periods in the heat. Players may eat bananas to prevent cramping.

COACHING TIP Encourage players to drink plenty of water before, during, and after practice. Water makes up 45 to 65 percent of a youngster's body weight, and even a small amount of water loss can cause severe consequences in the body's systems. It doesn't have to be hot and humid for players to become dehydrated, nor is thirst an accurate indicator of dehydration. In fact, by the time players are aware of their thirst, they are long overdue for a drink.

Cold

When a person is exposed to cold weather, body temperature starts to drop below normal. To counteract this, the body shivers to create heat and reduces blood flow to the extremities to conserve heat in the core of the body. But no matter how effective the body's natural heating mechanism is, the body will better withstand cold temperatures if it is prepared to handle them. To reduce the risk of cold-related illnesses, make sure players wear appropriate protective clothing (such as gloves and dry-fit undershirts and tights), and keep the players active to maintain body heat. Also monitor the windchill because it can drastically affect the severity of players' responses to the weather. The windchill factor index is shown in figure 4.3.

Temperature (°F)

	0	5	10	15	20	25	30	35	40
Flesh may freeze within one minute									
40	-29	-22	-15	-8	-1	6	13	20	27
35	-27	-21	-14	-7	0	7	14	21	28
30	-26	-19	-12	-5	1	8	15	22	28
25	-24	-17	-11	-4	3	9	16	23	29
20	-22	-15	-9	-2	4	11	17	24	30
15	-19	-13	-7	0	6	13	19	25	32
10	-16	-10	-4	3	9	15	21	27	34
5	-11	-5	1	7	13	19	25	31	36

Wind speed (mph)

Windchill temperature (°F)

FIGURE 4.3 Windchill factor index.

Adapted from National Weather Service, 2009, NWS windchill chart. [Online]. Available: http://www.nws.noaa.gov/om/windchill/index.shtml [February 16, 2010].

Severe Weather

Severe weather refers to a host of potential dangers, including lightning storms, tornadoes, hail, and heavy rains, which can cause injuries by creating sloppy field conditions. Lightning is of special concern because it can come up quickly and can cause great harm or even kill. Practice or games must end immediately when any lightning is sighted. In addition to these suggestions, your school, league, or state association may also have rules that you will want to consider in severe weather.

Safe places to take cover when lightning strikes include fully enclosed vehicles with the windows up, enclosed buildings, and low ground (under cover of bushes, if possible). It's not safe to be near metal objects such as flag poles, fences, light poles, and metal bleachers. Also avoid trees, water, and open fields.

You should cancel practice when under either a tornado watch or warning. If you are practicing or competing when a tornado is nearby, you should get inside a building if possible. If you cannot get into a building, lie in a ditch or other low-lying area or crouch near a strong building, using your arms to protect your head and neck.

The keys to handling severe weather are caution and prudence. Don't try to get that last 10 minutes of practice in if lightning is on the horizon. Don't continue to play in heavy rain. Many storms can strike both quickly and ferociously. Respect the weather and play it safe.

Air Pollution

Poor air quality and smog can present real dangers to your players. Both short- and long-term lung damage are possible from participating in unsafe air. Although it's true that participating in clean air is not possible in many areas, restricting activity is recommended when the air quality ratings are lower than moderate or when there is a smog alert. Your local health department or air quality control board can inform you of the air quality ratings for your area and when restricting activities is recommended.

Responding to Players' Injuries

No matter how good and thorough your prevention program is, injuries most likely will occur. When injury does strike, chances are you will be the one in charge. The severity and nature of the injury will determine how actively involved you'll be in treating it. But regardless of how seriously a player is hurt, it is your responsibility to know what steps to take. Therefore, you must be prepared to take appropriate action and provide basic emergency care when an injury occurs.

Being Prepared

Being prepared to provide basic emergency care involves many things, including being trained in cardiopulmonary resuscitation (CPR) and first aid and having an emergency plan.

First Aid Kit

A well-stocked first aid kit should include the following:

- Antibacterial soap or wipes
- Arm sling
- Athletic tape—one and a half inches
- Bandage scissors
- Bandage strips—assorted sizes
- Blood spill kit
- Cell phone
- Contact lens case
- Cotton swabs
- Elastic wraps—three inches, four inches, and six inches
- Emergency blanket
- Examination gloves—latex free
- Eye patch
- Face mask removal tool
- Foam rubber—one-eighth inch, one-fourth inch, and one-half inch
- Insect sting kit
- List of emergency phone numbers
- Mirror
- Moleskin
- Nail clippers
- Oral thermometer (to determine if an athlete has a fever caused by illness)
- Penlight
- Petroleum jelly
- Plastic bags for crushed ice
- Prewrap (underwrap for tape)
- Rescue breathing or CPR face mask
- Safety glasses (for assistance in first aid)
- Safety pins
- Saline solution for eyes
- Sterile gauze pads—three-inch and four-inch squares (preferably nonstick)
- Sterile gauze rolls
- Sunscreen—sun protection factor (SPF) 30 or greater
- Tape adherent and tape remover
- Tongue depressors
- Tooth saver kit
- Triangular bandages
- Tweezers

SAFETY

Adapted, by permission, from M. Flegel, 2008, *Sport first aid*, 4th ed. (Champaign, IL: Human Kinetics), 20.

CPR and First Aid Training

We recommend that all coaches receive CPR and first aid training from a nationally recognized organization such as the National Safety Council, the American Heart Association, the American Red Cross, or the American Sport Education Program (ASEP). You should be certified based on a practical test and a written test of knowledge. CPR training should include pediatric and adult basic life support and obstructed airway procedures.

Emergency Plan

An emergency plan is the final step in being prepared to take appropriate action for severe or serious injuries. The plan calls for three steps:

1. Evaluate the injured player.

Use your CPR and first aid training to guide you. Be sure to keep these certifications up to date. Practice your skills frequently to keep them fresh and ready to use when you need them.

2. Call the appropriate medical personnel.

If possible, delegate the responsibility for seeking medical help to another calm and responsible adult who attends all practices and games. Write out a list of emergency phone numbers and keep it with you at practices and games. Include the following phone numbers:

- Rescue unit
- Hospital
- Physician
- Police
- Fire department

Take each player's emergency information to every practice and game (see the "Emergency Information Card" in the appendix on page 221). This information includes the person to contact in case of an emergency, what types of medications the player is using, what types of drugs the player is allergic to, and so on.

Give an emergency response card (see the "Emergency Response Card" in the appendix on page 222) to the contact person calling for emergency assistance. Having this information ready should help the contact person remain calm. You must also complete an injury report form (see the "Injury Report Form" in the appendix on page 220) and keep it on file for all injuries.

3. Provide first aid.

If medical personnel are not on hand at the time of the injury, you should provide first aid care to the extent of your qualifications. Although your CPR and first aid training will guide you, you must remember the following:

- Do not move the injured player if the injury is to the head, neck, or back; if a large joint (ankle, knee, elbow, shoulder) is dislocated; or if the pelvis, a rib, or an arm or leg is fractured.
- Calm the injured player and keep others away from him as much as possible.

Emergency Steps

You must have a clear, well-rehearsed emergency action plan. You want to be sure you are prepared in case of an emergency because every second counts. Your emergency plan should follow this sequence:

1. Check the player's level of consciousness.
2. Send a contact person to call the appropriate medical personnel and to call the player's parents.
3. Send someone to wait for the rescue team and direct them to the injured player.
4. Assess the injury.
5. Administer first aid.
6. Assist emergency medical personnel in preparing the player for transportation to a medical facility.
7. Appoint someone to go with the player if the parents are not available. This person should be responsible, calm, and familiar with the player. Assistant coaches or parents are best for this job.
8. Complete an injury report form while the incident is fresh in your mind (see page 220 in the appendix).

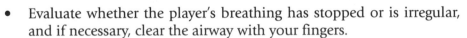

- Evaluate whether the player's breathing has stopped or is irregular, and if necessary, clear the airway with your fingers.
- Administer artificial respiration if the player's breathing has stopped. Administer CPR if the player's circulation has stopped.
- Remain with the player until medical personnel arrive.

Taking Appropriate Action

Proper CPR and first aid training, a well-stocked first aid kit, and an emergency plan help prepare you to take appropriate action when an injury occurs. In the previous section, we mentioned the importance of providing first aid to the extent of your qualifications. Don't attempt to "play doctor" with injuries; sort out minor injuries that you can treat from those that need medical attention. Now let's look at taking the appropriate action for minor injuries and more serious injuries.

Minor Injuries

Although no injury seems minor to the person experiencing it, most injuries are neither life threatening nor severe enough to restrict participation. When these injuries occur, you can take an active role in their initial treatment.

Scrapes and Cuts   When one of your players has an open wound, the first thing you should do is put on a pair of disposable latex-free examination gloves or some other effective blood barrier. Then follow these four steps:

1. Stop the bleeding by applying direct pressure with a clean dressing to the wound and elevating it. The player may be able to apply this pressure while you put on your gloves. Do not remove the dressing if it becomes soaked with blood. Instead, place an additional dressing on top of the one already in place. If bleeding continues, elevate the injured area above the heart and maintain pressure.

2. Cleanse the wound thoroughly once the bleeding is controlled. A good rinsing with a forceful stream of water, and perhaps light scrubbing with soap, will help prevent infection.

3. Protect the wound with sterile gauze or a bandage strip. If the player continues to participate, apply protective padding over the injured area.

4. Remove and dispose of gloves carefully to prevent you or anyone else from coming into contact with blood.

For bloody noses not associated with serious facial injury, have the player sit and lean slightly forward. Then pinch the player's nostrils shut. If the bleeding continues after several minutes, or if the player has a history of nosebleeds, seek medical assistance.

> **COACHING TIP**   You shouldn't let a fear of acquired immune deficiency syndrome (AIDS) and other communicable diseases stop you from helping a player. You are only at risk if you allow contaminated blood to come in contact with an open wound on your body, so the disposable examination gloves that you wear will protect you from AIDS if one of your players carries this disease. Check with your sport director, your sport league organization, or the Centers for Disease Control and Prevention (CDC) for more information about protecting yourself and your participants from AIDS.

Strains and Sprains   The physical demands of football practices and games often result in injury to the muscles or tendons (strains) or to the ligaments (sprains). When your players suffer minor strains or sprains, you should immediately apply the PRICE method of injury care:

P   Protect the player and the injured body part from further danger or trauma.

R   Rest the injured area to avoid further damage and to foster healing.

I   Ice the area to reduce swelling and pain.

C   Compress the area by securing an ice bag in place with an elastic wrap.

E   Elevate the injury above heart level to keep the blood from pooling in the area.

Bumps and Bruises Inevitably, football players make contact with each other and with the ground. If the force applied to a body part at impact is great enough, a bump or bruise will result. Many players continue playing with these sore spots, but if the bump or bruise is large and painful, you should take appropriate action. Again, use the PRICE method for injury care and monitor the injury. If swelling, discoloration, and pain have lessened, the player may resume participation with protective padding; if not, the player should be examined by a physician.

Serious Injuries

Head, neck, and back injuries; fractures; and injuries that cause a player to lose consciousness are among a class of injuries that you cannot and should not try to treat yourself. In these cases, you should follow the emergency plan outlined on page 49.

If you suspect that a player has received an injurious blow to the head, no matter how mild the symptoms, you should view it as a serious injury. If the player only has mild symptoms, such as a headache, call the parents and have them take the player to a doctor immediately. You should alert EMS immediately if the player has lost consciousness or has impaired memory, dizziness, ringing in the ears, blood or fluid draining from the nose or ears, or blurry vision. For more information, see the "Heads Up: Concussion in Youth Sports" fact sheet, provided by the Centers for Disease Control and Prevention (www.cdc.gov), on page 54. If you suspect that a player has a spine injury, joint dislocation, or bone fracture, do not remove any of the player's equipment unless you have to do so to provide life-saving CPR.

We do want to examine more closely, however, your role in preventing and handling heat exhaustion and heatstroke. Additionally, please refer to figure 4.4 for signs and symptoms associated with heat exhaustion and heatstroke.

Heat Cramps Tough practices combined with heat stress and substantial fluid loss from sweating can provoke muscle cramps commonly known as heat cramps. Cramping is most common during the early part of the season when the weather is the hottest and the players may be least adapted to the heat. The cramp, a severe tightening up of the muscle, can drop players and prevent continued play. Dehydration, electrolyte loss, and fatigue are the contributing factors. The immediate treatment is to have the player cool off and slowly stretch the contracted muscle. The player should also consume fluids with electrolytes in order to rehydrate. The players may return to play later that day or the next day provided the cramp doesn't cause a muscle strain.

Heat Exhaustion Heat exhaustion is a shocklike condition caused by dehydration and electrolyte depletion. Symptoms include headache, nausea, dizziness, chills, fatigue, and extreme thirst. Profuse sweating is a key sign of heat exhaustion. Other signs include pale, cool, and clammy skin; a rapid, weak pulse; loss of coordination; and dilated pupils.

A player suffering from heat exhaustion should rest in a cool, shaded area; drink cool fluids, particularly those containing electrolytes; and apply ice to the neck, back, or abdomen to help cool the body. If you believe that a player has heat exhaustion, seek medical attention. Under no conditions should the player return to activity that day or before regaining all the weight lost through sweat. If the player has to see a physician, the player shouldn't return to the team until he has a written release from the physician.

Heatstroke Heatstroke is a life-threatening condition in which the body stops sweating and body temperature rises dangerously high. It occurs when dehydration causes a malfunction in the body's temperature control center in the brain. Symptoms include the feeling of being extremely hot, nausea, confusion, irritability, and fatigue. Signs include hot, dry, and flushed or red skin (this is a key sign); lack of sweat; rapid pulse; rapid breathing; constricted pupils; vomiting; diarrhea; and possibly seizures, unconsciousness, or respiratory or cardiac arrest.

If a player experiences heatstroke, send for emergency medical assistance immediately and cool the player as quickly as possible. Remove excess clothing and equipment from the player, and cool his body with cool, wet towels, by pouring cool water over the player, or by placing the player in a cold-water bath. Apply ice packs to the armpits, neck, back, abdomen, and between the legs. If the player is conscious, give him cool fluids to drink. If the player is unconscious, place him on his side to allow fluids and vomit to drain from the mouth. A player who has suffered heatstroke may not return to the team until getting a written release from a physician.

Heat exhaustion	Heat stroke
Dizziness	Dizziness
Headache	Headache
Fatigue	Disoriented, combative, or unconscious
Dehydration	Dehydration
Profuse sweating	Hot and wet or dry skin
Mildly increased body temperature	Markedly increased body temperature
Nausea or vomiting	Nausea or vomiting
Rapid, weak pulse	Diarrhea
Diarrhea	
Muscle cramps	

FIGURE 4.4 Signs and symptoms of heat exhaustion and heatstroke.

Heads Up: Concussion in Youth Sports

What Is a Concussion?

A concussion is a brain injury. Concussions are caused by a bump or blow to the head. Even a "ding," "getting your bell rung," or what seems to be a mild bump or blow to the head can be serious.

You can't see a concussion. Signs and symptoms of concussion can show up right after the injury or may not appear or be noticed until days or weeks after the injury. If your child reports any symptoms of concussion, or if you notice the symptoms yourself, seek medical attention right away.

What Are the Signs and Symptoms of a Concussion?

SIGNS OBSERVED BY PARENTS OR GUARDIANS

If your child has experienced a bump or blow to the head during a game or practice, look for any of the following signs and symptoms of a concussion:

- Appears dazed or stunned
- Is confused about assignment or position
- Forgets an instruction
- Is unsure of game, score, or opponent
- Moves clumsily
- Answers questions slowly
- Loses consciousness (even briefly)
- Shows behavior or personality changes
- Can't recall events prior to hit or fall
- Can't recall events after hit or fall

SYMPTOMS REPORTED BY ATHLETE

- Headache or "pressure" in head
- Nausea or vomiting
- Balance problems or dizziness
- Double or blurry vision
- Sensitivity to light
- Sensitivity to noise
- Feeling sluggish, hazy, foggy, or groggy
- Concentration or memory problems
- Confusion
- Does not "feel right"

How Can You Help Your Child Prevent a Concussion?

Every sport is different, but there are steps your children can take to protect themselves from concussion.

- Ensure that they follow their coach's rules for safety and the rules of the sport.

- Encourage them to practice good sportsmanship at all times.

- Make sure they wear the right protective equipment for their activity (such as helmets, padding, shin guards, and eye and mouth guards). Protective equipment should fit properly, be well maintained, and be worn consistently and correctly.

- Learn the signs and symptoms of a concussion.

What Should You Do If You Think Your Child Has a Concussion?

1. **Seek medical attention right away.** A health care professional will be able to decide how serious the concussion is and when it is safe for your child to return to sports.

2. **Keep your child out of play.** Concussions take time to heal. Don't let your child return to play until a health care professional says it's okay. Athletes who return to play too soon—while the brain is still healing—risk a greater chance of having a second concussion. Second or later concussions can be very serious. They can cause permanent brain damage, affecting your child for a lifetime.

3. **Tell your child's coaches about any recent concussion.** Coaches should know if your child had a recent concussion in ANY sport. Your child's coach may not know about a concussion your child received in another sport or activity unless you tell the coach.

Reprinted from Centers for Disease Control and Prevention, 2007, Heads up: Concussion in youth sports: A fact sheet for parents. [Online]. Available: http://www.cdc.gov/concussion/pdf/parents_Eng.pdf [February 17, 2010].

Protecting Yourself

When one of your players is injured, naturally your first concern is the player's well-being. Your feelings for youngsters, after all, are what made you decide to coach. Unfortunately, you must also consider something else: Can you be held liable for the injury?

COACHING TIP You must trust your trainer or EMT in handling a player who needs attention. Do not overrule medical personnel, because this will create a liability issue.

From a legal standpoint, a coach must fulfill nine duties. We've discussed all but planning in this chapter (planning is discussed in chapter 11). The following is a summary of your legal duties:

1. Provide a safe environment.
2. Properly plan the activity.
3. Provide adequate and proper equipment.
4. Match players according to height and weight.
5. Warn of inherent risks in the sport.
6. Supervise the activity closely.
7. Evaluate players for injury or incapacitation.
8. Know emergency procedures, CPR, and first aid.
9. Keep adequate records.

In addition to fulfilling these nine legal duties, you should check your organization's insurance coverage and your own insurance coverage to make sure these policies will properly protect you from liability.

For a complete guide to liability and risk protection, visit the risk management section at www.americanyouthfootball.com.

Making Practices Fun and Practical

5

PRACTICES

In the past, we have placed too much emphasis on learning skills and not enough on learning how to perform skillfully—that is, how to use those skills in competition. The games approach (which is based on Alan Launder's book *Play Practice*), in contrast to the traditional approach, emphasizes learning what to do first, then how to do it. Moreover, the games approach lets kids discover what to do, not by your telling them but by their experiencing it. It is a guided discovery method of teaching that empowers your kids to solve the problems that arise, which is a large part of the fun in learning.

On the surface, it would seem to make sense to introduce football using the traditional approach—by first teaching the basic skills and then teaching how to use those skills in competition. But this approach has been shown to have disadvantages.

First, the traditional approach teaches the skills of the sport out of the context of competition. When executed without an opponent, the basic ball skills—passing, catching, punting, and kicking the football—are strictly biomechanical. When those skills are executed while facing competition, the X factors—including courage, timing, and coordination—that define the great sport of football come into play. For example, a player may learn the proper technique for kicking a field goal and may be able to place the ball between the posts every practice; however, this player may be unable to perform the same skill in a game situation. Players must be able to compete when the whistle blows and the game is under way.

Second, learning skills by doing drills outside of the context of the competition is downright boring. The single biggest turnoff in sports is overorganized instruction that deprives kids of their intrinsic desire to compete.

COACHING TIP We previously discussed the use of mental pictures and key words in teaching. Now, we not only want the player to visualize (mental picture) and hear the task (key word), but also to execute the skill while competing with others in a fun yet challenging way.

The games approach adapted for football can be described as a four-step process:

1. Stage a modified activity.
2. Help players understand the activity.
3. Teach the skills of the activity.
4. Practice the skills in another activity.

Step 1: Stage a Modified Activity

It's the first day of practice; some of the kids are eager to get started, while others are obviously apprehensive. Some have never played tackle football, most don't know the rules, and few know anything about the techniques used. What do you do?

Activities Development

When developing modified activities, here are a few questions that you should ask yourself:

- Are the activities fun?
- Are the activities organized?
- Are the players involved in the activities?
- Do the activities require the players to use creativity and decision making?
- Are the spaces used appropriate for the activities?
- Is your feedback appropriate?
- Do the activities involve football-specific skills?

PRACTICES

If you used the traditional approach, you would start with a quick warm-up activity, then perhaps begin teaching the fundamentals of passing, catching, blocking, and tackling. With the games approach, however, you begin by allowing players to participate in a modified activity that is developmentally appropriate for the level of the players and also designed to focus on learning a specific skill or approach to competition.

Modifying activities lets you emphasize a limited number of technical aspects. This is one way to guide your players to discover certain methods that will improve performance. Beginning on page 62 at the end of this chapter are examples of such football-specific challenges.

Step 2: Help Players Understand the Activity

As your players are participating in a modified competition, you should look for the right spot to freeze the action, step in, and ask questions about errors that you're seeing. When you do this, you help the players better understand the objective of the event, what they must do to achieve that objective, and what skills they must use.

Asking the right questions is a very important part of your teaching. Essentially, you'll be asking your players—often literally—"What do you need to do to succeed in this situation?" Sometimes players simply need to gain more experience, or you may need to modify the task further so that it is even easier for them to discover what they need to do. It may take more patience on your part, but it's a powerful way for players to learn. For example, if your players are playing the handoff game (page 68), you may need to interrupt the action and ask the following questions:

- What are you supposed to do in this activity?
- What do you have to do to hand off in an efficient manner?
- What happens to your emotions as your relay team falls behind?
- How do you respond after failed attempts?

COACHING TIP If you've learned the sport of football through the traditional approach, you'll be tempted to tell your players how to execute a skill rather than spend time asking questions. When using the games approach, however, you must resist this powerful temptation to tell your players what to do. If your players have trouble understanding what to do, you can phrase your questions in a way that allows the players to choose between two options.

Step 3: Teach the Skills of the Activity

Only when your players recognize the skills they need in order to be successful do you want to teach these skills through activities that are focused on specific football situations. In such cases, you should use a more traditional approach to teaching sport skills—the IDEA approach, which we will describe in chapter 6. This type of teaching breaks down the skills of the events. Key words and mental pictures (e.g., "When passing, keep the ball at ear level," "For a good spiral, your index finger is the last to leave the ball," or "When passing on the run, line the shoulders and hips to the target") should be implemented early in the season to help players as they begin attaining skills.

Step 4: Practice the Skills in Another Activity

As a coach, you want your players to experience success as they're learning skills, and the best way for them to experience this success early on is for you to create an advantage for them. Once the players have practiced the skill, you can then have them participate in another activity—this time slightly more challenging but with an advantage that will make it more likely that your players will be able to successfully reach the goal. For example, in the game Fourth and Goal (page 71), you can control the tackler or ballcarrier by positioning him with his back turned (this creates a delay in the actual time of contact), by telling the tackler or ballcarrier to lie on the ground (the player will have to get up before tackling or running across the goal line), or by asking the ballcarrier to take a handoff (the player must be sure of the handoff before attempting to go over the goal line). You can create a scenario where the ball is on the 1-yard line with just seconds to go and with a Super Bowl victory at stake. An exciting challenge is fun for the entire team.

As players develop and improve their skills, however, you may not need to provide an advantage. When this time comes, you can lessen the advantage, or you may even decide that the players are ready to practice the skill in regular competition. The key is to set up situations where your players experience success yet are challenged in doing so. This will take careful monitoring on your part, but having kids compete in modified activities as they are learning skills is a very effective way of helping them learn and improve.

And that's the games approach. Your players will get to be more involved and engaged in practice, and once they learn how the skills fit into their performance and enjoyment of the competition, they'll be more motivated to work on those skills—which will help them to be successful. Every child deserves to experience success. A good coach will design ways for each player to experience success and self-worth.

Gamelike Drills

The gamelike drills that follow are for use in your football program. As a youth football coach, you will want to use gamelike drills during practices—not only to help keep motivation and interest high and to keep the sport fun, but also to guide your players to discover various approaches that will better their performance on the field.

➤ DRIVE-THROUGH

The purpose of this drill is to use drive blocking to open holes for the ball-carrier. Play 3v2 or 4v3 in a 5-square-yard area. The offense and defense start opposite each other on one of the boundary lines. The game begins with the offensive line's first move. The offense gets one point every time it keeps the defense from tackling the running back, or ballcarrier. The defense gets one point each time it tackles the ballcarrier. Each team gets three consecutive plays. Because teams score based on whether or not the ball-carrier gets tackled rather than how many yards are gained, each play can begin where the other play ended. However, if players get close to the boundaries, flip the teams around and have the offense move down the field in the opposite direction. Rotate players to maintain the same number of blockers and defenders.

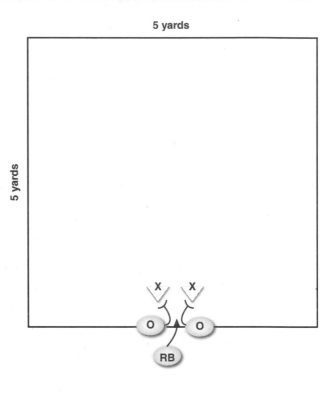

To make the game easier, widen the playing area or have the defense play at half or three-quarters speed. To make the game more difficult, narrow the playing area.

➤ PANCAKE

Players separate into pairs, and they line up on the goal line. Partners face one another; one partner is facing the end zone, and the other has his back toward the end zone. The paired-up players go to their knees and hold each other with one arm under and one arm over the other player's arms. On the whistle, each player tries to throw his partner on his back (pancake him) during a set time frame (e.g., 30 seconds). Neither player can leave his knees. Be sure to match players based on position and size. Players will also benefit from this drill by strengthening their obliques. To make the pancake drill more intense, try shortening the duration of the drill.

➤ PROTECTING THE QUARTERBACK

In this drill, the offense uses pass protection blocking to keep defensive players from getting to the quarterback. Play 2v1 or 3v2 in a 5-square-yard area using a quarterback and one or two offensive line players and one or two defensive line players. The offense and defense start opposite each other on one of the boundary lines. The coach stands behind the defense and signals the start count to the offense. On the count, the blocker or blockers move into pass protection blocking as the quarterback drops back to pass. The blockers must keep the defense from getting to the quarterback for at least 5 seconds. The offense gets one point for keeping the defense away from the quarterback. The defense gets one point for touching the quarterback.

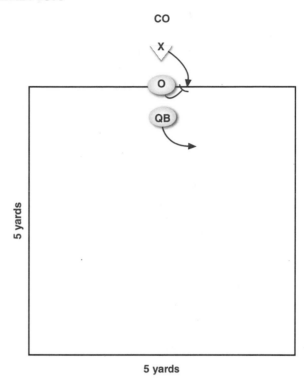

To make the game easier, give the defense only 3 seconds to touch the quarterback or play 3v1 or 4v2. To make the game more difficult, give the defense 7 seconds to touch the quarterback or play 2v2 or 3v3.

➤ SUMO

Inside a circle approximately 10 yards in diameter (usually a logo on the field), two players hold each other's right and left biceps. On the whistle, each player tries to push or pull the other player until one steps out of the circle. All players should concentrate on keeping their elbows in. They should avoid holding of any kind. This is a footwork drill that helps players learn proper body position and helps them develop quick feet. You will want to reduce the size of the circle when working with younger players.

➤ SCREEN DOOR

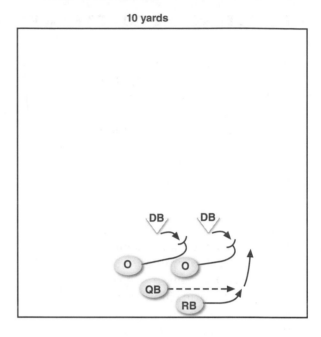

10 yards

The object of this drill is to use screen blocking to keep defenders from the ballcarrier. Play 4v2 in a 10-yard-wide playing area. A quarterback, running back, and two blockers will play offense; two defensive backs will play defense. The quarterback begins with the ball. On the quarterback's signal, the play begins and the running back receives a swing pass in the flat. The running back then follows his blockers and tries to elude the defenders. The offense gets one point each time the running back is able to elude the defenders by using the blockers. The defense scores one point each time it tackles the running back. Rotate players every three plays.

To make the game easier, widen the playing area or play 4v1 or 5v2. To make the game more difficult, narrow the playing area or play 4v3.

➤ THE ESCORT

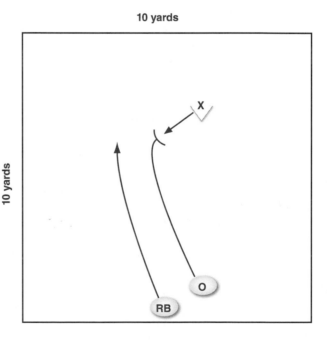

10 yards

10 yards

In this drill, the offense tries to gain yardage by blocking downfield for the ballcarrier. Play 2v1 or 3v2 in a 10-square-yard area. Blockers and defenders start at least 5 yards apart anywhere inside the playing area. The game begins with the blocker's first move. The offense gets one point every time it keeps the defense from tackling the running back, or ballcarrier. The defense gets one point each time it tackles the ballcarrier. Switch offense and defense after three plays, rotating players to maintain the same number of players on offense and defense.

To make the game easier, widen the playing area or play 3v1 or 4v2. To make the game more difficult, narrow the playing area or play 2v2 or 3v3.

➤ FOLLOW THE LEADER

In this drill, blockers are used as shields between the ballcarrier and defenders. Play 2v1 in a 10-square-yard area. The blocker lines up on one of the boundary lines and uses a hand behind the back to signal which way the ballcarrier should go and on what count. The running back stands behind the blocker and outside the playing area, holding the ball. The blocker's first move initiates the play. The offense gets one point each time it gains 10 yards in one play. The defense gets one point each time it stops the offense from gaining 10 yards. Rotate players after a running back has run three straight turns with the ball.

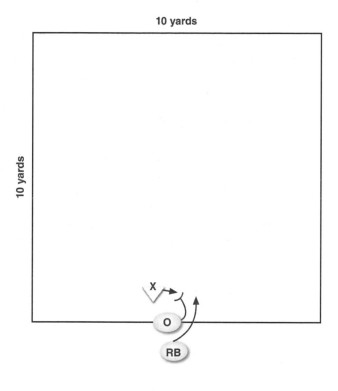

To make the game easier, widen the playing area. To make the game more difficult, narrow the playing area or play 3v2 or 4v3.

➤ CATCHING ON

Play 2v1 or 3v2 in an area 10 yards wide. You can vary the length of the playing area, but it should be at least 10 yards long and should probably not exceed 20 yards. The quarterback tells the receiver or receivers what route to run and the count to start on. Play begins on the count specified by the quarterback. The offense gets one point each time it completes a pass, and the defense, which includes a defensive back, gets one point each time it prevents a receiver from catching the ball. Rotate offensive players after three consecutive plays.

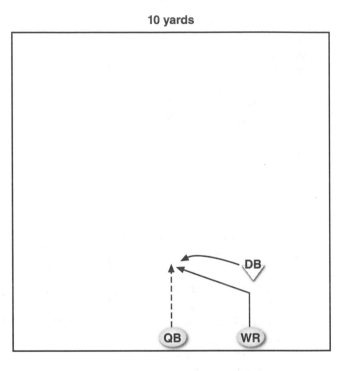

10 yards

To make the game easier, move the receiver closer to the quarterback or play 3v1 or 4v2. To make the game more difficult, move the receiver farther away from the quarterback or play 2v2 or 3v3.

➤ PASSING

Players are lined up sideline to sideline, facing each other. The first player begins to run from his designated sideline. He must pass the ball to the first player across from him when he reaches the hash mark, which will place the two players approximately 17 yards apart. The receiver then runs to the other side of the field and passes to the next player on his relay team when he reaches the hash mark. This drill is an excellent opportunity for your players to work on passing (honing in on their touch—not too hard or too soft) and receiving skills, while also benefiting from conditioning.

When receiving, have players concentrate on looking the ball in—watching it hit their hands. When passing, the players will work on their mechanics and will strive to achieve proper hip action. With younger players, shorten the distance for passing. If players are consistently throwing the ball too high during the passing drill, they may be releasing the ball too soon. Conversely, if they are throwing the ball into the dirt, you should check to see if they are overextending and thus having a delayed release.

➤ AIR BALL

Play 2v1 or 3v2 in a 20-square-yard area with goal lines at each end of the area and a 10-yard line across the middle of the area. The offense begins on the goal line. The quarterback tells the receiver or receivers what route to run. The play begins on the quarterback's count. Once the play begins, the quarterback drops back to make the pass, as shown in the figure. The offense gets three plays to advance the ball 20 yards to the opposite goal line; the offense gets one point for passing the 10-yard line in the middle of the area and an additional point for passing the 20-yard goal line. The defense gets one point if the offense doesn't get past the 20-yard goal line and two points if the offense doesn't get past the 10-yard line in the middle of the area. After a team advances past the 20-yard goal line or after three plays, switch offense and defense, rotating players to maintain the offensive advantage.

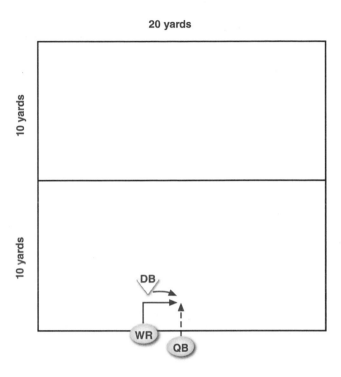

To make the game easier, widen the playing area to 30 yards or play 4v2 or 5v3. To make the game more difficult, play 2v2 or 3v3 or make the field 15 yards wide or 30 yards deep, or both.

➤ HIT THE HOLE

Play 4v3 in a 10-square-yard area with goal lines at each end of the playing area. Three defensive players are lined up inside the playing area 2 to 3 feet (60 to 90 cm) off the goal line. Three offensive players are lined up on the goal line, and a running back, with the ball, is lined up behind them and outside the playing area. The coach stands inside the playing area and behind the defensive players; without letting the defense see him, the coach signals to the offense where the ball is to be run by pointing to a specific spot in the playing area.

On the running back's signal, play begins. The

10 yards

10 yards

CO

X X X

O O O

RB

running back runs through the area where the coach pointed and attempts to gain as many yards as possible. The offense has three chances to score. The next play begins where the running back was tackled. If the offense can score within three plays, the offense gets a point. If the offense can't score, the defense gets a point. Switch offense and defense after the offense scores or after it runs three plays, rotating players to maintain the 4v3 offensive advantage.

To make the game easier, widen the playing area to 15 or 20 yards or play 4v2. To make the game more difficult, lengthen the playing area to 15 or 20 yards or play 4v4.

➤ HANDOFF

Beginning at one sideline, players carry the ball to the other sideline and hand off the ball to the next player, who then crosses the field to hand off to the next person. Players should concentrate on handing off the ball so that it is secure before they let go. The players handing off the ball should use their hand away from the player receiving the handoff to minimize the risk of fumbling the ball. The winning relay team should be rewarded for its efforts. For example, they may win the right to be first in line for a scheduled water break.

➤ HEADS UP

The purpose of this drill is to execute the proper front-on tackling form in tackling the ballcarrier. Play 1v1 in an area 3 yards wide by 6 yards long with a line of scrimmage across the middle of the playing area. A running back—or ballcarrier—and a defender line up facing each other; the defender is on the line of scrimmage, and the running back is on a boundary line at one end of the playing area. The running back's goal is to get past the defender and get to the other end of the playing area. In other words, the running back needs to gain 3 yards beyond the line of scrimmage. The defender's goal is to tackle the ballcarrier using proper form before the ballcarrier gains these yards.

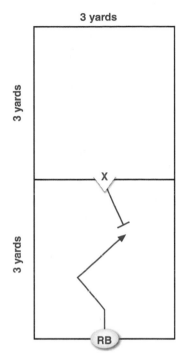

The play begins on the coach's command. Defenders get one point for keeping their eyes up, one point for wrapping their arms around the ballcarrier, one point for taking the ballcarrier down, and two points for stopping the runner from gaining the 3 yards beyond the line of scrimmage. The running back gets three points for gaining 3 or more yards. The running back should run three times and then switch positions with the defender.

To make the game easier, require the running back to gain 5 yards before you award the three points, or move the players closer together. To make the game more difficult, widen the playing area, move the players farther apart, or award the running back three points for gaining yardage. The game can be adapted for angle and open-field tackling by making the playing area larger and adjusting players' positioning

Note: Before the players begin, instruct all players to keep their shoulders up as they attempt to tackle and to slide their head to the outside just before making contact.

➤ NO-PASSING ZONE

Play 3v2 or 4v3 in an area 10 yards wide by 40 yards long with goal lines at each end of the area. To start, receivers are positioned on a goal line at one end of the area, and defensive backs are positioned inside the playing area. The quarterback is also positioned on the goal line and has the ball; the quarterback signals for the play to start. Receivers run straight down the field and run whatever pattern they want. The defensive backs can play either man-to-man or zone defense and must backpedal and break to the ball when it is thrown. The defense gets two points for intercepting a pass and one point for preventing a receiver from catching the ball or causing a receiver to drop the ball. If an offensive player catches the ball, the defenders must tackle the ballcarrier. After three plays, switch defense and offense, maintaining the same number of players on each side. If the offense is able to gain 40 yards (or more if they lost yardage and later picked it up), crossing the opposite goal line within the three plays, any points gained by the defense are wiped out.

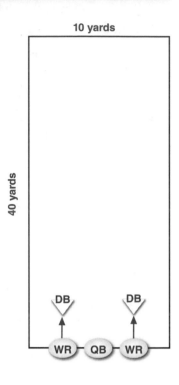

To make the game easier, lengthen the playing area or play 3v3 or 3v4. To make the game more difficult, shorten the playing area.

➤ AIRTIGHT D

Play 2v2 or 3v3 in an area 5 yards wide by 10 yards long with goal lines at each end of the area. The offensive players are positioned on a goal line at one end of the area, and the defensive players are positioned inside the playing area. Play starts on the offensive movement, which is initiated by a signal from the coach. The defense gets one point each time it prevents the offense from gaining yardage. The offense is allowed three downs to gain 10 yards and gets three points each time it does so. Rotate defense and offense when the offense gains 10 yards or when the offense has completed the three downs.

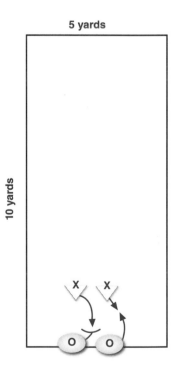

To make the game easier, lengthen the playing area to 20 yards or play 2v3 or 3v4. To make the game more difficult, widen the playing area to 10 yards or play 3v2 or 4v3.

➤ LARGE AND IN CHARGE

Play 2v2 or 3v3 in an area 5 yards wide by 5 yards long with goal lines on each end. The offense lines up approximately 3 yards from the goal. The defense lines up along the goal line. The defense gets two points each time it prevents the offense from scoring. The offense gets two points when it scores. Rotate defense and offense after four plays.

To make the game easier on the defense, give the offense just one down to score. To make the game more difficult on the defense, give the offense three downs to score.

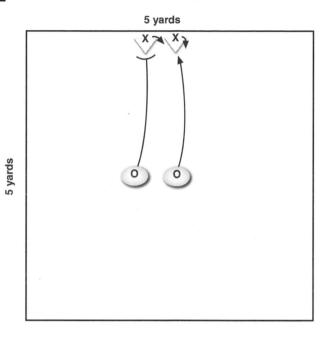

Note: For safety purposes, players should never run head-on from a distance of more than 3 yards.

➤ FOURTH AND GOAL

Two players match up near the goal line; one is a ballcarrier, and the other is a defender. On the whistle, the defender should try to prevent the ballcarrier from scoring a touchdown. A player's first experience at tackling or being tackled should be a good one. Place high-jump pads behind both players so they experience safe and pain-free landings. Never perform a tackling drill with the defender and ballcarrier starting more than 4 yards apart. Many rookie coaches do not understand the force of a player coming in full-speed contact with another player.

➤ FUMBLE RECOVERY

Players line up sideline to sideline, facing each other. The first player runs to the other side of the field and drops the ball on either side of the line, near the field numbers. The next player must recover the fumble and then cross the field and fumble to the next player lined up. Players will learn to pick up the ball while moving. Emphasize that players should come under control, clear their feet (so their feet are out of the way), and secure the ball.

➤ FIELD POSITION

The purpose of this drill is to gain better field position than the other team through returning punts and defending against returned punts. Play 3v3 in an area 15 yards wide by 50 yards deep. Team A lines up on the 10-yard line and punts to team B. Team B returns the punt as far as possible. Team B then lines up where the returner was tackled and punts the ball back to team A. Team A returns the ball as far as possible. Play continues until each team has made three punts. The team with the best field position wins the game.

To make the game easier for the offense and more difficult for the defense, widen the playing area or put an additional player on the receiving team. To make the game more difficult for the offense and easier for the defense, narrow the playing area or put an additional player on the punting team.

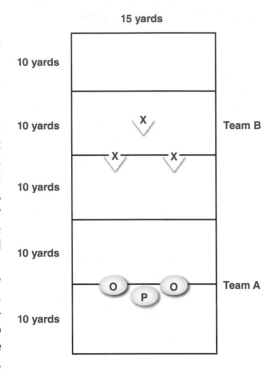

➤ TRIFECTA

Play 5v2 or 7v4 with the ball placed 13 yards from the goalposts. Defensive and offensive players line up on the 13-yard line. Play starts when the center hikes the ball to the placekick holder, who places the ball on the tee. The defensive players cannot hit the center, but they can attempt to block the kick. The kicking team gets three points for each successful kick. Each team gets three consecutive kicks.

To make the game easier, shorten the length of the kick or start play with the placekick holder moving to place the ball on the tee. To make the game more difficult, lengthen the kick, add another defensive player, or move the ball to the left or right rather than kicking from the center.

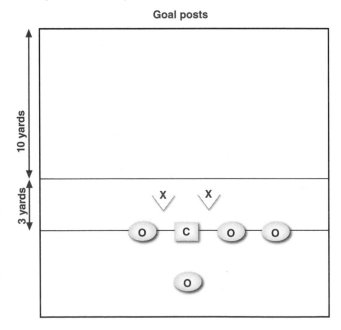

➤ KICKING INTO GEAR

The objective of this drill is to give your kickers an opportunity to kick from the tee in a gamelike situation. Play 3v3 in an area 15 yards wide by 50 yards deep. Team A lines up on the 10-yard line and kicks off (using a tee) to team B. Team B returns the kickoff as far as possible. Team B then lines up where the kick returner was tackled and kicks off to team A. Team A returns the ball as far as possible. Play continues until each team has kicked off three times. The team with the best field position wins the game.

To make the game easier for the offense and more difficult for the defense, widen the playing area or add a player to the receiving team. To make the game more difficult for the offense and easier for the defense, narrow the playing area or add a player to the kicking team.

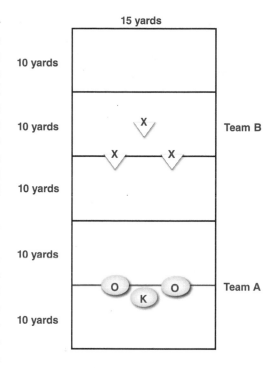

➤ TUG-OF-WAR

A large rope is used with a flag tied to the middle. Six players are on each end of the rope. When the whistle blows, the players tug until the rope's flag crosses over a designated line, such as the goal line. Players should avoid improper balance. This drill helps players improve arm strength and core strength, and it leads to better awareness of body position. You may even want to have the defense matched up against the offense.

When doing the tug-of-war game, be sure to use a rope that is large in diameter. Smaller ropes can cause rope burns more easily.

➤ FOOTBALL VOLLEYBALL

Have the players play volleyball (with or without a net) using a football. The height of the rope or net should be a little above head level, and the net may be set up at one of the goalposts. This game helps to improve eye–hand reflexes. It also helps players learn how to respond to unpredictable bounces. Players develop eye–hand coordination by keeping the ball from hitting the ground. This game takes teamwork as the players help others keep the ball off the ground.

➤ TANK

This is a communication game. Pair players together based on position. For example, you may pair a center and a quarterback together. Ideally, you want the offensive or defensive player who calls the plays paired with a key player whom she works with. One player is the tank (blindfolded with three tennis balls), while the other is her driver (her eyes). The driver tells the tank where to throw; the tank tries to eliminate the other players by hitting them with the balls. The driver can also direct her tank to pick up a ball that her tank or another tank has thrown. The last tank and driver win. To vary the game, you can change the number of balls that you provide to the players.

Teaching and Shaping Skills

6

SKILLS

Coaching football is about teaching kids how to play the game

by teaching them technique, fitness, and values. It's also about coaching players before, during, and after games. Teaching and coaching are closely related, but there are important differences. In this chapter, we focus on the principles of teaching, especially on teaching technical skills and tactics. But these principles apply to teaching values and fitness concepts as well. Armed with these principles, you will be able to design effective and efficient practices and will understand how to deal with misbehavior. Then you will be able to teach the skills and plays necessary to be successful in football (which are outlined in chapters 7, 8, and 9).

Teaching Football Skills

Football coaches should begin teaching skills before conducting full-pad workouts and scrimmages. Bill Walsh, former head coach of the San Francisco 49ers, was adamant about never putting a player in jeopardy. As he stressed, "The techniques of football should be developed before full-go scrimmages are conducted" (August 2003, coaches clinic, Canton, OH).

Many people believe that the only qualification needed to teach a skill is to have performed it. Although it's helpful to have performed it, teaching it successfully requires much more than that. And even if you haven't performed the skill before, you can learn to teach successfully with the useful acronym IDEA:

I Introduce the skill.

D Demonstrate the skill.

E Explain the skill.

A Attend to players practicing the skill.

Introduce the Skill

Players, especially those who are young and inexperienced, need to know which skill they are learning and why they are learning it. You should therefore follow these three steps every time you introduce a skill to your players:

1. Get your players' attention.
2. Name the skill.
3. Explain the importance of the skill.

Get Your Players' Attention

Because youngsters are easily distracted, you should do something to get their attention. Some coaches use interesting news items or stories. Others use jokes. And still others simply project enthusiasm to get their players to listen. Whatever method you use, speak slightly above your normal volume and look your players in the eyes when you speak.

Also, position players so that they can see and hear you. Arrange the players in two or three evenly spaced rows, facing you. (Make sure they aren't looking into the sun or at a distracting activity.) Then ask all of them if they can see you before you begin to speak.

Name the Skill

More than one common name may exist for the skill you are introducing, but you should decide as a staff before the start of the season which one you'll use—and then stick with it. This will help prevent confusion and enhance communication among your players. Key words that describe a mental picture are best. The term *swim technique* is an example of using a key word to describe a skill. In this technique, the player tries to get his defender to overcommit; then, he puts his outside arm on the defender's shoulder and "swims" his other arm over his defender, ending by pushing off the arm (much like a swimmer following through on his stroke).

COACHING TIP You may find it helpful to write out in detail each skill that you will teach. This clarifies what you will say and how you will demonstrate and teach each skill to your players.

Explain the Importance of the Skill

As Rainer Martens, the founder of the American Sport Education Program (ASEP), has said, "The most difficult aspect of coaching is this: Coaches must learn to let athletes learn. Sport skills should be taught so they have meaning to the child, not just meaning to the coach." Although the importance of a skill may be apparent to you, your players may be less able to see how the skill will help them become better football players. Offer them a reason for learning the skill, and describe how the skill relates to more advanced skills.

Demonstrate the Skill

The demonstration step is the most important part of teaching sport skills to players who may never have done anything closely resembling the skill. They need a picture, not just words. They need to see how the skill is performed. If you are unable to perform the skill correctly, ask an assistant coach, one of your players, or someone more skilled to perform the demonstration.

These tips will help make your demonstrations more effective:

- Use correct form.
- Demonstrate the skill several times.
- Slow the action, if possible, during one or two performances so players can see every movement involved in the skill.
- Perform the skill at different angles so your players can get a full perspective of it.
- Demonstrate the skill with both the right and left arms or legs.

Explain the Skill

Players learn more effectively when they're given a brief explanation of the skill along with the demonstration. You should use simple terms and, if possible, relate the skill to previously learned skills. Ask your players whether they understand your description. A good technique is to ask the team to repeat your explanation. Ask questions such as "What are you going to do first?" and "Then what?" If players look confused or uncertain, you should repeat your explanation and demonstration. If possible, use different words so that your players get a chance to try to understand the skill from a different perspective.

Complex skills are often better understood when they are explained in more manageable parts. For instance, if you want to teach your players how to provide pass protection blocking, you might take the following steps:

1. Show your players a correct performance of the entire skill, and explain its function in football.
2. Break down the skill and point out its component parts to your players.
3. Have players perform each of the component parts you have already taught them, such as maintaining proper body position, delivering a blow to stop the defensive charge, and using proper footwork.
4. After players have demonstrated their ability to perform the separate parts of the skill in sequence, reexplain the entire skill.
5. Have players practice the skill in gamelike conditions.

Young players have short attention spans. A long demonstration or explanation of a skill may cause them to lose focus. Therefore, you should spend no more than a few minutes altogether on the introduction, demonstration, and explanation phases. Then involve the players in drills or games that call on them to perform the skill.

Attend to Players Practicing the Skill

If the skill you selected was within your players' capabilities and you have done an effective job of introducing, demonstrating, and explaining it, your players should be ready to attempt the skill. Some players may need to be physically guided through the movements during their first few attempts. Walking unsure players through the skill this way will help them gain the confidence to perform the skill on their own.

Look at the entire technique, and then break it down into components. For example, when teaching a defensive back to cover man-to-man, your drill sequence could consist of the following:

1. Stance
2. Start
3. Backpedal

How to Properly Run Your Drills

Before running a drill that teaches technique, you should do the following:

- Name the drill.
- Explain the skill or skills to be taught.
- Position the players correctly.
- Explain what the drill will accomplish.
- Identify the command that will start the drill, such as a snap count or "Hut."
- Identify the command that will end the drill, such as a whistle.

Once the drill has been introduced and repeated a few times in this manner, you will find that merely calling out the name of the drill is sufficient; your players will automatically line up in the proper position to run the drill and practice the skill.

4. Angle backpedal
5. Leaving the backpedal
6. Pattern recognition and pattern reaction

Each segment of the drill should take only a minute or two once the players master the skill, and this sequence will provide players with the needed tools to play man-to-man coverage.

Your teaching duties, though, don't end when all your players have demonstrated that they understand how to perform a skill. In fact, your teaching role is just beginning as you help your players improve their skills. A significant part of your teaching consists of closely observing the hit-and-miss trial performances of your players. You will shape players' skills by detecting errors and correcting them using positive feedback. Keep in mind that your positive feedback will have a great influence on your players' motivation to practice and improve their performances.

Remember, too, that players may need individual instruction. So set aside a time before, during, or after practice to give individual help.

Helping Players Improve Skills

After you have successfully taught your players the fundamentals of a skill, your focus will be on helping them improve the skill. Players learn skills and improve on them at different rates, so don't get frustrated if progress seems slow. Instead, help players improve by shaping their skills and detecting and correcting errors.

Shaping Players' Skills

One of your principal teaching duties is to reward positive effort or behavior—in terms of successful skill execution—when you see it. A defensive lineman neutralizes, defeats, and sheds a blocker and moves to get in on the tackle, and you immediately say, "That's the way to do it! Great effort and pursuit!" This, plus a smile and a thumbs-up gesture, go a long way toward reinforcing that technique in that player. However, sometimes you may have a long dry spell before you see correct techniques to reinforce. It's difficult to reward players when they don't execute skills correctly. How can you shape their skills if this is the case?

Shaping skills takes practice on your players' part and patience on yours. Expect your players to make errors. Telling the player who made the tackle that he did a good job doesn't ensure that he'll have the same success next time. Seeing inconsistency in your players' technique can be frustrating. It's even more challenging to stay positive when your players repeatedly perform a skill incorrectly or when they lack enthusiasm for learning. It can certainly be frustrating to see players who seemingly don't heed your advice and continue to make the same mistakes. And when the players don't seem to care, you may wonder why you should.

Although it is normal to get frustrated sometimes when teaching skills, part of successful coaching is controlling this frustration. Instead of getting upset, use these six guidelines for shaping skills:

1. **Think small initially.**

Reward the first signs of behavior that approximate what you want. Then reward closer and closer approximations of the desired behavior. In short, use your reward power to shape the behavior you seek.

2. **Break skills into small steps.**

For instance, in learning to execute a pass protect block, one of your players does well in the initial move and setup but stands up too straight and doesn't get into good hitting position—thus making it easier for defenders to move around him. Reinforce the correct technique in the initial move and setup, and then teach the player how to get into the correct hitting position by keeping his eyes up and his rear end down. Once he masters this, you can shift the focus to getting him to keep his feet shoulder-width apart.

3. **Develop one component of a skill at a time.**

Don't try to shape two components of a skill at once. For example, in dropping back to throw a pass, quarterbacks must first secure the snap from the center and then use one of the drop steps—the crossover, the backpedal, or the rollout. Players should focus first on one aspect (receiving the snap from the center, using good hand positioning and presenting a good target for the center), then on the other (dropping back and using one of the techniques just mentioned).

Players who have problems mastering a skill often do so because they're trying to improve two or more components at once. You should help these players isolate a single component.

4. As players become more proficient at a skill, reinforce them only occasionally and only for the best examples of the skill.

By focusing only on the best examples of a skill, you will help players continue to improve once they've mastered the basics.

5. When players are trying to master a new skill, temporarily relax your standards for how you reward them.

As players focus on the new skill or attempt to integrate it with other skills, their old, well-learned skills may temporarily degenerate.

6. Go back to the basics.

If, however, a well-learned skill degenerates for a while, you may need to restore it by going back to the basics.

Coaches often have more-skilled players provide feedback to teammates as they practice skills. This can be effective, but proceed with caution: You must tell the skilled players exactly what to look for when their teammates are performing the skills. You must also tell them the corrections for the common errors for that skill.

Detecting and Correcting Errors

Good coaches recognize that players make two types of errors: learning errors and performance errors. Learning errors are those that occur because players don't know how to perform a skill; that is, they have not yet developed the correct motor pattern in the brain to perform a particular skill. Performance errors are made not because players don't know how to execute the skill, but because they have made a mistake in executing what they do know. There is no easy way to know whether a player is making learning or performance errors; part of the art of coaching is being able to sort out which type of error each mistake is.

The process of helping your players correct errors begins with you observing and evaluating their performances to determine if the mistakes are learning or performance errors. You should carefully watch your players to see if they routinely make the errors in both practice and game settings, or if the errors tend to occur only in game settings. If the latter is the case, then your players are making performance errors. For performance errors, you need to look for the reasons your players are not performing as well as they know how; perhaps they are nervous, or maybe they get distracted by the game setting. Find out the reasons for the decline in performance and help the players tackle those issues.

If the mistakes are learning errors, then you need to help the players learn the skills, which is the focus of this section.

When correcting learning errors, there is no substitute for knowledge of the skills. The better you understand a skill—not only how it is performed correctly but also what causes learning errors—the more helpful you will be in correcting your players' mistakes.

One of the most common coaching mistakes is to provide inaccurate feedback and advice on how to correct errors. Don't rush into error correction; wrong feedback or poor advice will hurt the learning process more than no feedback or advice at all. If you are uncertain about the cause of the problem or how to correct it, you should continue to observe and analyze until you are more sure. As a rule, you should see the error repeated several times before attempting to correct it.

Correct One Error at a Time

Suppose Danny, one of your wide receivers, is having trouble catching deep passes over his shoulder. He's getting open, but you notice that he's not reaching back with both hands so that he sees both the ball and his hands at the moment of the catch. You also notice that his hands are not positioned correctly when he catches the ball. What do you do?

First, decide which error to correct first, because players learn more effectively when they attempt to correct one error at a time. Determine whether one error is causing the other; if so, have the player correct that error first, because it may eliminate the other error. In Danny's case, however, neither error is causing the other, but they are related. In such cases, players should correct the error that is the easiest to correct and will bring the greatest improvement when remedied. For Danny, this probably means placing his little fingers together to receive the ball and then working on reaching back with both hands to make the catch. Improvement in his hand position will likely motivate him to correct the error of not reaching back with both hands so he can see the ball at the moment of the catch.

Use Positive Feedback to Correct Errors

The positive approach to correcting errors includes emphasizing what to do instead of what not to do. Use compliments, praise, rewards, and encouragement to correct errors. Use video clips of the player executing the skills properly to create mental images of proper technique. Acknowledge correct performance as well as efforts to improve. By using positive feedback, you can help your players feel good about themselves and promote a strong desire to achieve.

COACHING TIP   Avoid starting your feedback to players with the word *don't*. By telling players what you want them to do instead of what not to do, you will create success rather than failure.

When you're working with one player at a time, the positive approach to correcting errors includes four steps:

1. Praise effort and correct performance.

Praise your player for trying to perform a skill correctly and for performing any parts of it correctly. Praise the player immediately after he performs the skill, if possible. Keep the praise simple: "Good try," "Way to hustle," "Good form," or "That's the way to follow through." You can also use nonverbal feedback, such as smiling, clapping your hands, or any facial or body expression that shows approval.

Make sure you're sincere with your praise. Don't indicate that a player's effort was good when it wasn't. Usually a player knows when he has made a sincere effort to perform the skill correctly and perceives undeserved praise for what it is—untruthful feedback to make him feel good. Likewise, don't indicate that a player's performance was correct when it wasn't.

2. Give simple and precise feedback to correct errors.

Don't burden a player with a long or detailed explanation of how to correct an error. Give just enough feedback so that the player can correct one error at a time. Before giving feedback, recognize that some players readily accept it immediately after the error; others will respond better if you slightly delay the correction.

For errors that are complicated to explain and difficult to correct, you should try the following:

- Explain and demonstrate what the player should have done. Do not demonstrate what the player did wrong.
- Explain the cause or causes of the error, if this isn't obvious.
- Explain why you are recommending the correction you have selected, if it's not obvious.

3. Make sure the player understands your feedback.

If the player doesn't understand your feedback, he won't be able to correct the error. Ask the player to repeat the feedback and to explain and demonstrate how it will be used. If the player can't do this, you should be patient and present your feedback again. Then ask the player to repeat the feedback after you're finished.

4. Provide an environment that motivates the player to improve.

Your players won't always be able to correct their errors immediately, even if they do understand your feedback. Encourage them to "hang tough" and stick with it when corrections are difficult or when they seem discouraged. For more difficult corrections, you should remind players that it will take time, and that the improvement will happen only if they work at it.

Encourage players who have little self-confidence. Saying something like, "You were catching the football much better today; with practice, you'll be able to watch the ball into your hands and catch all of them," can motivate a player to continue to refine his receiving skills.

Other players may be very self-motivated and need little help from you in this area; with them you can practically ignore step 4 when correcting an error. Although motivation comes from within, you should try to provide an environment of positive instruction and encouragement to help your players improve.

> **COACHING TIP** Good coaching is saying it once and letting the player do it a thousand times. Repetition of proper technique is the secret.

A final note on correcting errors: Team sports such as football provide unique challenges in this endeavor. How do you provide individual feedback in a group setting using a positive approach? Instead of yelling across the field to correct an error (and embarrass the player), you can substitute for the player who erred, and then make the correction on the sidelines. Focus your message in a positive way—you are not punishing the player by taking him out; rather, you are using the time as an instructional moment where you can clarify tasks and encourage better performance. Coaches who pull kids out and leave them on the sideline after an error do the kids a disservice. These coaches fail to help teach the players how to perform better. Likewise, they create an atmosphere where mistakes are punished rather than an atmosphere where mistakes are accepted as an opportunity to improve skills. Providing individual feedback on the sidelines has three advantages:

- The player will be more receptive to the one-on-one feedback.
- The other players are still active and still practicing skills, and they are unable to hear your discussion.
- Because the rest of the team is still playing, you'll feel compelled to make your comments simple and concise—which is more helpful to the player.

This doesn't mean you can't use the team setting to give specific, positive feedback. You can do so to emphasize correct group and individual performances. Use this team feedback approach only for positive statements, though. Keep negative feedback for individual discussions.

> **COACHING TIP** Recognize that the introduction of competition and contact may initially adversely affect a player's focus on learning proper skills; however, with practice this can be overcome. Start your teaching at half speed. Then, as the players master the skill and become comfortable executing the skill, you can increase the level of contact and competition.

Dealing With Misbehavior

Players will misbehave at times; it's only natural. You can respond to misbehavior in two ways: extinction or discipline.

Extinction

Ignoring a misbehavior—neither rewarding nor disciplining it—is called extinction. This can be effective in certain circumstances. In some situations, disciplining young people's misbehavior only encourages them to act up further because of the recognition they get. Ignoring misbehavior teaches youngsters that it is not worth your attention.

Sometimes, though, you cannot wait for a behavior to fizzle out. When players cause danger to themselves or others, or when they disrupt the activities of others, you need to take immediate action. Tell the offending player that the behavior must stop and that discipline will follow if it doesn't. If the player doesn't stop misbehaving after the warning, you should use discipline. For example, you may need to pull the player from the remaining drills. You should then explain how the player is negatively affecting the overall production of the team, and you should let the player know that continuing down this path may lead to a possible suspension.

COACHING TIP Be clear from the beginning about what your expectations are for your players, and be consistent in your dealings with them.

Extinction also doesn't work well when a misbehavior is self-rewarding. For example, you may be able to keep from grimacing if a youngster kicks you in the shin, but even so, that youngster still knows you were hurt. Therein lies the reward. In these circumstances, it is also necessary to discipline the player for the undesirable behavior.

Extinction works best in situations where players are seeking recognition through mischievous behaviors, clowning, or grandstanding. Usually, if you are patient, their failure to get your attention will cause the behavior to disappear.

However, make sure that you don't extinguish desirable behavior. When youngsters do something well, they expect to be positively reinforced. Not rewarding them will likely cause them to discontinue the desired behavior. The challenge is to make playing football a fun and memorable experience.

Discipline

Some educators say we should never discipline young people, but should only reinforce their positive behaviors. They argue that discipline does not work, that it creates hostility, and that it sometimes develops avoidance behaviors that may be more unwholesome than the original problem behavior. It is true that discipline does not always work and that it can create problems when used ineffectively. But when used appropriately, discipline is effective in eliminating undesirable behaviors without creating other undesirable consequences. You must use discipline effectively, because it is impossible to guide players through positive reinforcement and extinction alone. Discipline is part of the positive approach when these guidelines are followed:

- Discipline players in a corrective way to help them improve now and in the future. Don't discipline to retaliate or to make yourself feel better.

- Impose discipline in an impersonal way when players break team rules or otherwise misbehave. Shouting at or scolding players indicates that your attitude is one of revenge.

- Once a rule has been agreed on, ensure that players who violate it experience the unpleasant consequences of their misbehavior. Don't wave discipline threateningly over their heads. Just do it, but warn a player once before disciplining.

- Be consistent in administering discipline.

- Don't discipline using consequences that may cause you guilt. If you can't think of an appropriate consequence right away, tell the player you will talk with him after you think about it. You might consider involving the player in designing a consequence.

- Once the discipline is completed, don't make players feel that they are "in the doghouse." Always make them feel that they're valued members of the team.

- Make sure that what you think is discipline isn't perceived by the player as a positive reinforcement; for instance, keeping a player out of a certain drill or portion of the practice may be just what the player wanted.

- Never discipline players for making errors when they are playing.

- Never use physical activity—running laps or doing push-ups—as discipline. To do so only causes players to resent physical activity, something we want them to learn to enjoy throughout their lives.

- Use discipline sparingly. Constant discipline and criticism cause players to turn their interests elsewhere and to resent you as well.

OFFENSE

This chapter focuses on the offensive techniques and tactics that players need to learn in order to perform effectively in youth football games. Remember to use the IDEA approach to teaching skills: introduce, demonstrate, and explain the skill, and attend to players as they practice the skill (see page 76 in chapter 6). This chapter also ties directly into the season plans in chapter 11, describing the technical skills that you'll teach at the practices outlined there. If you aren't familiar with football skills, you may want to rent or purchase a video so you can see the skills performed correctly. Also, the *Coaching Youth Football* online courses offered by the American Sport Education Program (ASEP) and American Youth Football (AYF) can help you further understand these skills. (Refer to page viii for more information.)

The information in this book is limited to football basics. As your players advance in their skills, you will need to advance your knowledge as a coach. You can do this by learning from your experiences, watching and talking with more experienced coaches, and studying resources on advanced skills.

Offensive Technical Skills

The offensive technical skills you will teach your players include assuming a proper stance, blocking, running the ball, playing quarterback, receiving, and centering the ball. Mastering these techniques will allow your offensive players to better execute your offensive tactics—or plays—during the game. These basic skills serve as the foundation for playing football well at all levels. As Vince Lombardi said, "I don't care about the fancy formations and trick plays; the team that blocks and tackles better will win the football game." Football players must practice proper techniques at every practice from youth football to the pros. A good way to remember football basics is to use these popular street commands: Ready, set, go. "Ready," or "break down," represents bending at the knees, "set" is the athletic alignment at each particular position, and "go" is the snap count (usually a number or hut call).

COACHING TIP Your offensive philosophy must be an integrated segment of your overall philosophy of the game. Outscoring the opponent is everyone's objective in the great game of football. But how you outscore your opponents may be as varied as the offenses of today. On any given Sunday, you can witness NFL teams running offenses ranging from variations of the century-old single wing offense to the modern spread offenses with empty backfields. Find out what works best for your team.

Stance

The stance is the proper alignment of a player's body at the start of each play. Following is a description of the stances you should teach players at each offensive position. The basic stance in football is taken on a command of "break down."

From this basic, balanced stance, all position-specific stances evolve. A player must first break down, then "set" his body to the proper alignment and angle. The final stage is the "hut" on offense or the "hit" on defense.

Offensive Line

When teaching your offensive linemen their stance, start with a four-point stance (as shown in figure 7.1), then move to a three-point stance as needed. To assume a four-point stance, linemen should do the following:

FIGURE 7.1 Proper four-point stance for offensive linemen.

- Place the feet shoulder-width apart, keeping the knees bent, the weight balanced evenly on both feet, and the toes aligned.
- Drop both knees to the ground.
- Reach straight out with both hands slightly in front of the shoulders, and pick up the knees.
- Keep the back straight with the rear end over the feet, the eyes up, and the shoulders even.

COACHING TIP   Beginners may feel uncomfortable in this stance and may adjust their feet so that one foot is way behind the other. If you see this, ask the player to bring the back foot forward so that it is no more offset than toe to instep. A more even foot alignment allows the player to step easily with either foot.

This stance is used for straight-ahead blocking or blocking to one side or the other. It forms a good foundation for evolving to a three-point stance.

Once offensive linemen are comfortable with a four-point stance, instruct them to lift one hand and to adjust the position of the feet slightly to move into a three-point stance (see figure 7.2). Use the following points to teach the offensive linemen to assume a three-point stance.

FIGURE 7.2 Proper three-point stance for offensive linemen.

- Place the feet shoulder-width apart, in a heel–instep relationship, with the inside foot back.

- Put very little weight on the down hand that forms a tripod with the feet. This will allow for quick forward, backward, and lateral movement.

- Place the left arm loosely across the left thigh.

- Keep the back straight, with the eyes up to see defenders across the line of scrimmage. (Do not strain your neck to see higher than your field of vision; look up through your eyebrows.) This position is the strongest and safest for the back and neck.

Check to see that the player's shoulders and back are level. If the shoulders are not level, the down hand is usually in the center of the blocker's body and needs to be moved more to the outside, under the blocker's shoulder. When the back is tilted, the blocker needs to bring his rear end up and keep the power angle in his knees.

Receivers

Receivers use two basic types of stances. The first stance used by wide receivers is a two-point, or upright, stance (see figure 7.3). The advantages of this stance are that receivers can get off the line of scrimmage without being held up and that they are in immediate position to receive quick passes. To assume a two-point stance, receivers should do the following:

- Place the feet shoulder-width apart, in a heel–toe relationship, with the foot closest to the football back more than the other.

- Bend the knees in a comfortable position.

- Keep weight on the balls of the feet with a majority of the weight on the front foot.

- Keep the back straight, leaning forward slightly.

- Square the shoulders to the line of scrimmage.

FIGURE 7.3 Proper two-point stance for receivers.

- Hold the arms in a comfortable position, ready to swim over or rip under a defender.

- Turn the head in toward the offensive center to check alignment and see the ball when it is snapped.

COACHING TIP Check to make sure that receivers move forward on the snap and don't step back to start. They should roll over the front foot and step across the line of scrimmage with the back foot.

The second stance is a three-point stance. In this stance, receivers distribute their weight evenly; the shoulders are up, and the eyes are focused either directly downfield or on the football (see figure 7.4). The feet are staggered, which allows for good explosion from the line of scrimmage. This stance is typically used on short-yardage situations where in-line blocking is required of receivers. To assume the three-point stance, receivers should do the following:

FIGURE 7.4 Proper three-point stance for receivers.

- Place the feet shoulder-width apart, in a heel–toe relationship, with the foot closest to the football staggered in a comfortable sprinter's position.
- Point the knees and toes straight ahead.
- Keep the back straight, parallel to the ground, and the eyes up.

Make sure that receivers in a three-point stance drive out and forward—rather than rise up—as they come out of their stance to release from the line; check to see that the majority of their weight is on the down hand and front foot.

Center

To help young players get in the proper position to make the snap to the quarterback, have centers assume a four-point stance and then lift up their snapping hand to place the ball on the ground where they can easily grasp it (see figure 7.5). Later, if they are in the correct position, they can progress to a three-point stance with the nonsnapping hand. To assume a four-point stance, centers should do the following:

- Position the feet shoulder-width apart; the toe of the foot on the side of the snapping hand should be even with the instep of the other foot.

FIGURE 7.5 Proper four-point stance for centers.

- Drop both knees to the ground.
- Reach straight out with both hands so that they are on the ground slightly in front of the shoulder pads, and pick up the knees. Be sure that the rear end is over the feet and that a power angle exists in the knees.
- Lift the snapping hand and place the ball in position. The ball should be placed with the laces to the outside and rotated slightly toward the ground.
- Grasp the front half of the ball with the fingers over the laces, and prepare to lift and turn the ball sideways so that the quarterback can take the snap.

Make certain that centers have their back straight and shoulders even before the snap. They should keep the ball even with the shoulder pad on the side of the snapping hand. At the snap, the ball should hit the top hand of the quarterback with a loud "pop" as his backstop hand closes on it.

Quarterback

A quarterback's stance must be poised and relaxed, reflecting confidence. The quarterback's feet should be comfortably spread, approximately shoulder-width apart, and should be as close to the center's feet as possible. Quarterbacks should bend their knees slightly and drop their hips while remaining as tall over the center as possible. It is the quarterback's responsibility to adjust the height of his stance to fit each center. The quarterback's shoulders should be parallel to the line of scrimmage, and his eyes should be up to check the position of the defense. See figure 7.6 for an example of a proper quarterback's stance.

FIGURE 7.6 Proper stance for quarterbacks.

COACHING TIP Beginning quarterbacks often bend at the waist and position their feet too far from the center's feet. If you see this, move the quarterback closer to the center, and instruct the quarterback to bend the knees so that he can reach under the center to take the snap.

Running Backs

The most common stance for halfbacks and fullbacks is a two-point stance (see figure 7.7). In this position, running backs are in an upright stance with the eyes up, which allows them to see the quarterback and the offensive line. Players at these positions must accelerate quickly from their backfield spot. Before the ball is snapped, running backs should do the following:

- Stand with the feet about shoulder-width apart and with the weight on the balls of the feet.
- Keep the feet nearly parallel to allow a quick burst in any direction.
- Bend the knees slightly and place the hands on the knees.
- Keep the shoulders up and the eyes looking ahead.

FIGURE 7.7 Proper two-point stance for running backs.

If your running backs use the four- or three-point stance, teach them the same technique for getting into their stance that you teach the offensive line players.

COACHING TIP　Be sure that running backs move either forward or laterally on the snap, based on the play called in the huddle. If they step back to get started, they may need to adjust their weight on the down hand so that they can move easily in any direction. Stepping back usually occurs when running backs do not anticipate where they should move on the snap. Moving the hand back a few inches creates a balanced stance with the weight on the balls of both feet.

Blocking

Blocking is the cornerstone of all successful offensive teams. Teams use blocking to move a defensive player out of the area where they want to run the football and to keep defensive line players from tackling the quarterback.

An offensive lineman, for example, should visualize himself uncoiling on the snap count like a snake striking its prey. Defensive players can use their hands, so an offensive player must use the snap count to his advantage. At the snap, the player rolls his up knee toward the ground while keeping a straight back. The player's second step is a short one. At contact, the player should focus on striking under the opponent's pads with both hands in a lifting motion. You can refer to this technique as having the player "fire out." Keep in mind that the player should employ short steps initially. Then, once he has gained the advantage of driving the opponent backward, he can elongate his steps. This sequence is shown in figure 7.8.

FIGURE 7.8　Offensive block: *(a)* approach, *(b)* contact, and *(c)* follow-through.

COACHING TIP　Have your offensive linemen imagine being a bulldozer, driving their opponents back off the ball to open lanes for their running back.

Offensive line players block in some manner on every play. Running backs block when they are not carrying the football, and wide receivers block when they are not catching the football. You can start by teaching your players basic blocks; these are the blocks that are critical for a successful youth football program. Then, as your team becomes more experienced, you may want to add more advanced blocks.

Basic Blocks

Basic blocks allow a team to implement a diverse offensive attack. These blocks are the easiest for you to teach and the easiest for your players to learn. All teams need to master the basic blocks used in youth football. The basic blocks include the drive block, the hook block, the cutoff block, and the cross block.

Drive Block   The drive block is a one-on-one block used most often when a defensive line player lined up directly over an offensive player must be moved for the play to succeed (see figure 7.9). When teaching your players the drive block, emphasize these points:

- Explode from the stance with the foot closest to the opponent and drive the hips forward on the third and fourth steps through the block.

- Start with short, choppy, and explosive steps; then lengthen to power steps as momentum is gained.

- Step with the foot on the side of the shoulder used in blocking.

FIGURE 7.9   Drive block.

- Deliver the block from a wide base, and keep the eyes up and the shoulders square.

- Anticipate the forward movement of the defensive player.

- Keep the head on the side of the opponent, between the opponent and the ballcarrier.

- Come off low and get under the pads of the defensive player.

- Punch the hands into the opponent to establish momentum, and deliver the blow on impact with the hands or forearms. Keep the feet moving when climbing up the defender, and strive to get chest to chest with him.

COACHING TIP   Emphasize to players to use short, choppy steps and to continue chest-to-chest contact when they are blocking. The defender will attempt to shed the block by creating space between himself and the blocker so he can throw the blocker off. The blocker's short, choppy steps will help him to maintain contact, eliminating the defender's ability to throw him off.

If blockers are pushed to one side and fall off their block, this may indicate that they are not maintaining a wide base (i.e., they are narrowing the split between their feet) as they make contact with the defensive player.

COACHING TIP Offensive line blockers should stab the palm of the inside hand directly into the defensive player's chest as they take their second step. This will stop the forward movement of the defensive player and allow the offensive blocker to position the body to the outside.

For additional drive-blocking practice, see the drill on page 124 at the end of this chapter.

Hook Block The hook block is used when an offensive player is blocking a defensive player located on the blocker's outside shoulder and the offense is running the ball to the outside of the block. The blocker seals off the opposing end so that the running back can run around the end to the outside. The blocker takes a short lateral step with the outside foot, makes contact on the second step, and swings around to contain the rusher (see figure 7.10). The blocker hits the defender at or slightly above waist level and keeps the point of contact to the side on which the sweep is being run. When teaching your players the hook block, emphasize these points:

FIGURE 7.10 Hook block.

- Remain low.
- Step laterally with the foot opposite the side of the shoulder used to block. The first lateral step should be short and quick.
- Fire out, using the power angles of your legs in each short step, and get under the pads of the defensive player.
- Take the second step directly toward the center of the defensive player's chest, driving the palm of the hand directly into the chest of the defensive player. The other hand should drive up and under the shoulder pad of the defensive player.
- Position the body so the defensive player cannot move to the outside.

For additional hook-blocking practice, see the drill on page 125 at the end of this chapter.

Cutoff Block   The cutoff block is used to block a defensive player located on the blocker's inside shoulder, in the inside gap, or in front of the offensive lineman to the inside. The blocker takes a short directional step to the inside and in front of where the defensive player is lined up. When teaching players the cutoff block, emphasize these points:

- Anticipate the defensive player's forward movement.
- Explode off the outside foot (see figure 7.11a), and make contact with the outside shoulder pad into the side of the defensive player (see figure 7.11b).
- Keep the shoulders in front of the defensive player, cutting off penetration.
- Drive the defensive player down the line.

If blockers fail to get the frame of their shoulders in front of the defensive player's body, you should tell them to adjust the angle of the first step so that it is in front of the defensive player's alignment. This adjustment puts blockers in the proper position to stop the defensive player's movement across the line of scrimmage.

For additional cutoff-blocking practice, see the drill on page 124 at the end of this chapter.

FIGURE 7.11   Cutoff block.

Cross Block   The cross block can be used to create an element of surprise, to adjust for a mismatch at the line of scrimmage, or to block against a defensive alignment that is difficult to block straight on. In this block, two adjacent players work together to block two defensive players. When both defensive players are on the line of scrimmage, the outside blocker will usually go first using a cutoff block. When one defensive player is on the line and the other is lined up off the line (in a linebacker position), the player blocking the defensive player on the line will go first. The second player on the cross block needs to take a short drop step with the foot on the side of the block; this player allows the first blocker to move, and then, while staying low, drives into the assigned defensive player (see figure 7.12). Blocking form and execution are the same except for the timing between the blockers. Cross blocks can be performed by teammates who line up next to each other—a center and a guard, a guard and a tackle, or a tackle and a tight end. This is a bang-bang play; timing and explosive power are key.

FIGURE 7.12   Cross block.

> **COACHING TIP**   Have players practice blocking against air, handheld shields, or lightweight standup blocking bags to see just how fast they can execute the cross block. Speed in executing the block gives the offensive linemen the opportunity to move into their block before the defensive player has a chance to react.

If the timing between the two blockers is off, make sure that the second blocker is not waiting for the first blocker to get all the way into his block before starting to move to his defensive player. The second blocker should step back and then drive to his block at the same time that the other player moves into his block.

For additional cross-blocking practice, see the drill on page 125 at the end of this chapter.

Advanced Blocks

Once your team has mastered the basic blocks, you can begin to teach them more advanced blocking skills. Advanced blocks require a great deal of coordination, and the offensive blockers must work as one unit. This coordination takes time to practice and should be introduced after the basic blocks have been mastered. The advanced blocks include the double-team block, the zone block, the down-field block, and the pass protection block.

Double-Team Block   The double-team block should be used when you need to have two adjacent blockers working together on one defensive player. When the blockers execute this block correctly, it becomes one of the offense's most powerful blocks. The blockers move simultaneously—the inside blocker using a drive block and the outside blocker using a cutoff block.

The blockers should drive the defensive player down and off the line of scrimmage. The inside blocker should step with the outside foot directly at the midsection of the defensive player and should hit with the outside shoulder pad. The outside blocker should step down with the inside foot. Then, on the second step, this blocker should drive the outside shoulder pad into the side of the defensive player.

When contact is made, both blockers should bring their hips together (inside blocker's outside hip to outside blocker's inside hip) to provide a combined wall against the defensive player. By keeping a tightly aligned hip-to-hip position, the blockers will not allow the defender to split them to fill the gap. Tell the blockers to think the following: *Plow the defender back off the line of scrimmage.* See figure 7.13 for an example of the double-team block.

COACHING TIP   If the defensive player is able to split the two blockers, this may indicate that the blockers are not bringing their hips together as they work to drive the defensive player off the line.

For additional practice of double-team blocking, see the drill on page 127 at the end of this chapter.

FIGURE 7.13   Double-team block.

Zone Block   The zone block is a combination block using two offensive players against two defensive players. It is most often used against a defensive lineman and a linebacker who may or may not be blitzing. The zone block is very difficult to teach and should be added to your team's blocking scheme only after the previous blocks have been mastered. This blocking scheme requires that the two blockers read the defense's movement together. The zone block is usually used against a defense where the outside blocker has a defensive lineman lined up in front of him and the adjacent inside blocker has a linebacker lined up in front of him.

With the ball being run to the outside, both blockers move together on the snap. Both players should step laterally with the outside foot. The outside player should use a hook block technique and should stop the charge of the defensive player with the second step. The inside player should see the linebacker and determine if he is moving to the outside behind the defensive lineman or charging straight ahead (see figure 7.14).

FIGURE 7.14   Zone block.

COACHING TIP   If the defensive lineman penetrates across the line, go back and make certain that the two blockers are giving first priority to blocking this player before either one moves off to pick up the linebacker.

If the linebacker is moving to the outside, the inside blocker should continue into the defensive lineman and use a hook block technique. In this case, the outside blocker should continue to the outside and chip off or scrape off the lineman as the blocker continues upfield to block the linebacker with a drive block. When the linebacker charges straight ahead, the inside blocker should adjust his path to be in position to execute a drive block on the linebacker using the inside shoulder. The outside blocker continues to perform a hook block on the defensive lineman. Reading the defender who comes into your zone as your responsibility is a technique that can also be applied to pass blocking against a stunting defense.

For additional zone-blocking practice, see the drill on page 128 at the end of this chapter.

Downfield Block Although most blocks occur near the line of scrimmage, blocking is also needed in other situations. Receivers often need to block for their teammates in order to create space for them to run or to help them avoid a tackle. The downfield block is used in these situations. When using the downfield block, players must make sure that the block is made above the defender's waist to avoid injury.

To perform a downfield block when the ballcarrier is directly behind the blockers, the blockers should use a run block technique. This is a block made past the line of scrimmage on a defender who is trying to reach the ballcarrier. In this situation, the players block the defender at full or three-quarter speed by attacking aggressively with the forearms and shoulders (see figure 7.15). When blocking a defensive player who is backing up, blockers should run straight through the block. Doing so creates space for the ballcarrier, allowing him to pass the defender. If the defensive player is attacking up the field, blockers should block the player away from the ballcarrier's path, or they may block the defender in the direction the defender wants to go, letting the ballcarrier cut off the block. Blockers should shorten their stride and widen their base as they near the defensive player. The downfield blocker must know the projected path of the ballcarrier in order to anticipate the defender's angle to the ball. A good ballcarrier will set up his blockers by not choosing a side until the blocker is in front of him.

FIGURE 7.15 Downfield block.

COACHING TIP Blockers should focus on and aim for a point 5 yards past the defensive player so that they learn to run through the block.

If blockers have difficulty executing the downfield block, and the defensive player is avoiding the block, make sure that the blockers are running under control with a shortened stride and are not leaning forward at the waist. Controlled body position and movement allow downfield blockers to adjust their path at the last moment and make contact with the defensive player.

For additional downfield-blocking practice, see the drill on page 131 at the end of this chapter.

Pass Protection Block The pass protection block keeps the defender from getting to the quarterback before the quarterback can throw the football. The initial move and setup by an offensive lineman are extremely important in pass blocking. The offensive line player must set up quickly, stepping to the inside with the inside foot first, and must push up into a two-point stance with the down hand. This movement projects the offensive line player into a set position with the shoulders up, the eyes open wide, the back straight, the rear end down, and the hands and arms up. The player should position the feet shoulder-width apart with the knees bent so that the body weight is maintained over the feet (see figure 7.16). This allows backward or lateral movement in a split second. The elbows should be positioned into the sides, and the forearms and hands should be brought up with the palms open in front of the body. The faster your players can set their position, the better pass blockers they will be.

FIGURE 7.16 Proper pass protection–blocking position.

COACHING TIP When facing defenses that allow a wide upfield rush by the defensive player, offensive tackles must learn that they may have to turn toward the sideline and force an outside rusher up the field past the quarterback's position.

The depth at which the pass blocker sets up off the line of scrimmage varies with the pass action called and the opponent's defensive front alignment and charge. Offensive linemen who are pass blocking must position themselves between the quarterback and the defensive pass rusher. They can do this by backing off the line of scrimmage quickly after the snap. Tell your offensive line players that they should never be beaten to the inside. Offensive running backs who are pass blocking must also position themselves between the quarterback and the defensive rusher, although they will be setting up a few yards deep in the backfield before the snap.

For additional practice of pass protection blocking, see the drills on pages 126 and 128 at the end of this chapter.

Running the Ball

Running the ball involves many skills, including getting the handoff, carrying the ball, using blockers, and being the blocker. If much of your offense consists of running rather than passing plays, then developing the ability of your running backs to gain yardage is an important ingredient for your offensive team.

Getting the Handoff

Most running plays are designed for one of the running backs, rather than the quarterback, to carry the ball. Once quarterbacks take the ball from the center,

Pass Protection Tips

Pass protection blocking is different from other blocks. Pass protection is different because the offensive player must sit and wait for the defensive player rather than fire out aggressively on the snap of the ball. Following are a few helpful tips that coaches can use when teaching this block.

Punch

Delivering a blow to stop the charge of the defensive line player takes good timing. The blocker must learn to shadow the defender and stay set. He should let the defensive line player get as close as 6 inches (15 cm) away from him and then deliver the blow to stop the charge. The blocker must deliver the punch with open hands, keeping the elbows close to the rib cage. When delivering the punch, the blocker should also roll the wrists to achieve power. The blocker's hands and arms must stay within the planes of the shoulders. After delivering the blow, the blocker should recoil, stepping back from the defensive line player.

When a blocker lunges at the defensive player, the blocker must keep his back straight. Blockers must avoid bending forward at the waist and putting their head and shoulders in front of their hips. The forward lean makes it easier for the defensive player to move around the offensive blocker to reach the quarterback.

Patience

Patience may be the most difficult thing to teach offensive line players. Offensive line players must learn to be protectors, not aggressors. They must keep their legs under them and must always remain in a good blocking position even after delivering the punch. Instruct offensive line players to keep their rear ends down and their knees bent at all times.

Offensive line players are required to execute some of the most unnatural skills in all of sport. Keeping an opponent from making a play without using your hands requires discipline. Line players must have an unselfish team attitude, must have a solid work ethic, and must be smart enough to avoid penalties.

Footwork

The most important skill for offensive line players is the ability to move their feet. The correct foot movement is a shuffle, with the player keeping one foot in contact with the ground at all times. Offensive linemen should never cross their feet and should always keep their body between the defensive player and the quarterback. They should always keep their back to the quarterback. A familiar mistake is for the blocker to move his feet up and down. The blocker should move his feet only when he is sure of the defender's charge.

their next job is to move into position so that they can hand off the ball to the running back. When running backs get the handoff from the quarterback, both palms of the hands should be open to the quarterback with the thumbs out and elbows in; the fingers should be spread in position to secure the ball. The quarterback is responsible for placing the ball firmly into the pocket formed by the running back's hands at the midsection, and the running back is responsible for securing the ball. When the ball is placed in the belly, the running back will bring one hand over the ball, clamping it with his elbow. Running backs should keep both hands on the ball until they get beyond the traffic at the line of scrimmage. If both players do their jobs, the handoff should be successful. Figure 7.17 shows a running back in proper handoff position.

FIGURE 7.17 Proper handoff position.

COACHING TIP If fumbles occur on the exchange, you should check the path of both players to the handoff point, the placement of the football by the quarterback, and the arm placement of the running back.

On some running plays, the running back may not receive a direct handoff from the quarterback. Instead, the ball is pitched or tossed so that the running back can quickly get to the outside of the formation. The running back must watch the ball into both hands and must not run with the ball until it is caught. In preparing to catch the ball, the running back's hands should be wide open with the little fingers together and palms up for a ball at waist level (see figure 7.18a on page 104) or with the thumbs together for a toss chest high (see figure 7.18b). On making the catch, the running back should secure the ball and should be prepared to make a cut and head up the field.

Carrying the Football

After receiving the ball, the running back must protect it at all costs. Teach ballcarriers to immediately tuck the end of the ball under the arm and to cover the front point of the ball with the hand (see figure 7.19 on page 104). The running back's free hand should secure the "baby in the cradle" when the ballcarrier is being tackled. Teach your players to carry the ball in the arm away from the defense. When ballcarriers run to the right, the ball should be in the right arm, and when they run to the left, the ball should be in the left arm. Ballcarriers should never switch the ball when in traffic; they should wait until they are well beyond the line of scrimmage. Because ballcarriers may cut back across the defense, the best strategy is to keep the ball secure until they are up the sideline.

FIGURE 7.18 Proper hand position when catching the pitch.

FIGURE 7.19 Proper carrying position.

COACHING TIP When players fumble the ball, check to make sure that *(a)* they never get in the habit of bringing the ball up away from the body as they run, *(b)* the ball is in the proper hand, and *(c)* the hand is placed firmly over the point of the ball.

Using Blockers

Coach your running backs to run toward the hole that has been called unless they see that it is closed. They should then head upfield to gain what yardage they can. Teach them to run with a forward lean. This helps them stay low and have a good forward drive.

Instruct the running backs to make their cut at the last moment. They should approach the line of scrimmage with their shoulders square to the line. To prevent the defender from getting a solid read, a good running back will fake the defender by taking a step away from him and then cutting back close as if the ballcarrier were cutting right through the defender. Coach running backs to set up each of their blockers by running on the blocker's outside hip, and then, at the last moment, cutting inside as the blocker blocks the defender. When in the open, a good back will judge the deep defender's route toward him. If the ball-carrier weaves out and then in, the defender is at the ballcarrier's mercy. Once the defender gets his feet crossed, the ballcarrier should make his move.

At times a running back will be his own blocker. The running back must lower his shoulders and keep his legs churning for every yard. Games are won and lost by the difference in yardage made after being contacted.

Being the Blocker

In addition to running with the ball, the running backs must also block for their teammates. On running plays, when the running backs are not running with the ball, they become blockers. As they near the defender, the blockers should widen their base, shorten their stride, and bend at the knees. When running backs are blockers on running plays, they should explode off the foot on the side of the shoulder that they're using to make the block. They should also keep their shoulders between the defender and the running back carrying the ball. Following are additional techniques for blocking:

- When a running back is not carrying the ball but is blocking on running plays, the running back uses a running drive block.

- When lead blocking through the line, the blocker should head straight at the defensive player and try to run through the player with the block (using the shoulder away from the desired path of the ballcarrier).

- When blocking the end player on the line, the running back is required to make contact using his outside shoulder pad on the defender's inside hip for inside running plays. For any running play going wide, the running back makes contact using his inside shoulder pad on the outside hip of the defender.

In addition to blocking on running plays, running backs also need to block on passing plays. Pass protection blocking for a running back is different than for an offensive lineman because the defender takes time to reach the blocker. Running backs usually block linebackers who may rush from the outside or inside of the formation. In both situations, the first step for the running back should be a quick step to the inside with the inside foot.

COACHING TIP If backs are sliding off their blocks, this may indicate that they are not maintaining a wide base or that they are turning their head away from the defender as they make contact.

When blocking an outside rusher, the running back will bring the outside foot around so that he is facing the sidelines and is in position to use the rusher's momentum to block the rusher up the field, past the quarterback. Blocking an inside rusher requires the running back to bring the outside foot even with the

inside foot and to be square to the line. From this position, the running back can stop the rusher's charge and redirect the rusher to the outside or inside away from the quarterback's position. In both cases, the running back should remember to do the following:

- Keep the feet shoulder-width apart.
- Keep the knees bent.
- Keep the back straight and the shoulders up.
- Keep the elbows in at the sides and keep both hands in front of the jersey's numbers with the palms facing forward.

When the rusher is about to make contact, the running back hits out hard with both hands, recoils, and then sets to hit out again.

When running backs miss a block, it is often because they are leaning at the waist and lunging at the defensive pass rusher rather than setting and hitting out from a balanced position.

The running back–blocking drill on page 135 can help your running backs practice good blocking technique.

Playing Quarterback

Quarterbacks must be able to call the plays in the huddle and call out the cadence to start the play once the offense is positioned at the line of scrimmage. In addition, they must be able to execute the needed physical skills that the position demands. Quarterbacks also need to be mentally prepared to lead the offense. They should be taught the assignments of the entire offensive team once they have mastered this position. Quarterbacks must have a knowledge of the terminology used in calling plays and must act as a positive motivating force for the offense when it is on the field. Coaches must spend extra time with quarterbacks to make certain that they are prepared both physically and mentally. Teach your quarterbacks how to take snaps, play out of the shotgun formation, hand off, throw pitches and laterals, and throw passes.

Taking the Snap

Offensive plays begin with the center handing or snapping the ball to the quarterback. For an offensive play to be successful, the exchange of the ball from the center to the quarterback must be executed in a smooth motion.

In a tight formation, quarterbacks should place their throwing hand, or pressure hand, so that it pushes up on the center's rear end. This pressure tells the center where to snap the football. Quarterbacks should position the bottom hand, or catch hand, so that the thumbs are together (some coaches like the quarterback to hook the bottom thumb over the top thumb so that the bottom hand does not drift open) and the fingers are extended, giving the center a good target for the ball (see figure 7.20*a*). Quarterbacks should bend their elbows slightly to allow for the center's firing out on the snap. Quarterbacks must adjust their stance to the height of the center.

Figure 7.20*b* illustrates a quarterback receiving the snap. Quarterbacks look downfield as the snap is being made; after receiving the snap, they immediately turn their head to see where to hand off the ball. When quarterbacks locate their target, they should keep their eyes on that player. On passing plays, they bring the football into the chest and then raise it up and back to the ear in a ready-to-throw position. Quarterbacks should not swing the football away from the body when moving to make a handoff or dropping back to pass.

FIGURE 7.20   Quarterback receiving the snap.

COACHING TIP   If quarterbacks are fumbling the ball, check to make sure that they are getting the snap correctly, that the ball is being brought up to their hands by the center, and that they are securing the ball into the body with both hands.

Coordination between the center and the quarterback is essential. Inconsistent snaps may be caused by the quarterback moving in the opposite direction of the center, who is moving to make a block while snapping the ball. The quarterback must know where the center is moving and must follow the center's movement until the ball is secure. The center's blocking movement should be practiced during your regular practices.

Ball skills require many repetitions. Players should do 1,000 snaps—followed by handoffs, passes, pitches, and catches—and then do them again.

Shotgun Formation

When quarterbacks start in the shotgun formation, they line up about 5 to 7 yards behind the center, depending on the particular play or their arm strength. They should look at the defense and scan the field for particular defensive formations. This enables them to see who might be open or alerts them to call an audible if the defensive set indicates that a change of play is needed. When using a shotgun formation, an important key is having a center who can accurately snap the ball to the quarterback the necessary 5 to 7 yards.

Handoffs

On all offensive plays where the running back will carry the ball, the quarterback must get the ball to the running back after taking the snap from the center. Quarterbacks are completely responsible for the success or failure of the handoff. They must adjust to the running back's path and speed and must get him the football. Quarterbacks should keep both hands on the ball as long as possible and place or press the ball firmly into the ballcarrier's abdomen, allowing the give hand to ride the ball into place until the running back takes it. If the quarterback is faking a handoff, he should allow the empty hand to ride the ballcarrier's abdomen for several steps.

COACHING TIP   Failure to complete the handoff is often caused when the quarterback is too close or too far away from the running back when attempting to make the handoff. Review the footwork needed by both players for proper positioning on each play.

Pitches and Laterals

Quarterbacks should use a two-hand push pass or an underhand toss on all pitch plays. Quarterbacks need this skill for running plays when there is no time to hand the ball to the running back. This will usually be an offensive running play where the running back starts immediately to the sidelines and catches the ball while running to the outside of the formation. The quarterback must learn to pitch or toss the ball in front of the running back—at the level of the running back's hip—so that the runner is not forced to slow down to make the catch. Quarterbacks should take a little off the ball on pitchouts and laterals. They should not attempt a spiral—tell them to think of basketball passes.

A pitch play or a toss play is a lateral, not a forward pass. The ball is thrown either to the side or back—in relation to the line of scrimmage—rather than forward. A dropped lateral is not an incomplete pass. It is a fumble, and either the offense or the defense can recover and gain possession of the ball.

Throwing the Football

To successfully throw the ball, the quarterback must master four skills: grip, throwing position, release, and follow-through. Even if the other 10 offensive players do their jobs correctly, if the quarterback cannot accurately throw the ball to the intended receiver, the passing segment of the offense will not be successful.

Grip Quarterbacks should spread their fingers over the laces of the ball and hold the ball slightly behind the center position on the ball (using a secure grip). Some quarterbacks even put their index finger on the back tip of the ball. This enables quarterbacks to get a feel for the ball. It helps them to put the ball in a position that works best for them. Quarterbacks keep the ball in ready position close to their armpit before raising it straight up to throw. Figure 7.21 shows the proper grip with the ball in ready position.

FIGURE 7.21 Proper grip for the quarter-back with the ball in ready position.

Throwing Position Have the quarterback practice picking up the ball with one hand and bringing it to his chest. The quarterback should then use both hands to bring the ball to the throwing position just behind the ear (see figure 7.22a). Next, the quarterback should move the nonpassing hand away from and in front of the ball (see figure 7.22b). The upper part of the passing arm should be about parallel to the ground, and the nonpassing shoulder (left shoulder for a right-handed passer) should be pointing to the intended receiver. The feet should be about shoulder-width apart with the weight partially on the back foot. The quarterback will plant the back foot to break the momentum of dropping back. The body will resemble a tent peg (leaning away from the line) before the throwing motion begins.

FIGURE 7.22 Proper throwing position for a quarterback.

Release Quarterbacks should start the throwing motion with their legs by stepping directly at the target with the front foot, then bringing the hips and shoulders in line with the direction of the front foot. Good passers use their legs as much as their arm to throw. They step at the target and rotate the body so that the hips and chest face the target as the arm comes through. The ball should be thrown from behind the ear (see figure 7.23)—it should be released high with a strong wrist snap and with the palm turned down toward the ground (imagine pulling it down from up high). As the ball is released, the fingers should drag across it to cause it to spiral. The index finger is the last to leave the ball and should be pointed directly toward the target. The quarterback's entire body should move directly toward the

FIGURE 7.23 Proper release positioning for a quarterback.

receiver as the ball is released. For a good drill, string a rope (clothesline) about head high and have the quarterback throw over the line. For other quarterback-specific drills, see pages 132 and 133.

COACHING TIP Errors in accuracy can be a result of quarterbacks not moving the entire body toward the target as they throw passes. Make certain that quarterbacks push off the back foot and step at the receiver rather than simply setting up and using arm action to deliver the ball.

Follow-Through Quarterbacks should not lower the passing arm down across the body too quickly after releasing the ball. Instead, they should try to make the hand "follow the ball" to the target, and they should rotate the passing hand so that the palm points to the ground (see figure 7.24). Have the quarterback exaggerate the index finger pointing at the target.

FIGURE 7.24 Proper follow-through for a quarterback.

> **COACHING TIP** If a quarterback's passes are being blocked or the quarterback is throwing low, make sure that the quarterback brings the ball over the shoulder rather than throwing it in a sidearm motion out to the side of the shoulder pad.

Drop-Back Passes

Next, quarterbacks must learn how to apply proper throwing technique to a game or gamelike situation. When quarterbacks take the snap from the center and drop back to pass, they vary their steps based on the distance of the receivers' pass routes down the field. Short passes require a three-step drop and medium to deep pass routes require a five-step drop before throwing the ball (see the quarterback three- and five-step drop-back drill on page 132). A quarterback's last step should stop his movement away from the center and allow him to set up to step and throw.

Receiving

Receiving involves running disciplined pass patterns—pass routes—and catching the football when the quarterback throws it. Wide receivers are an important part of your offensive attack. They need to understand that they can make big contributions to helping the offense move down the field and score.

Running Patterns or Routes

When the quarterback calls a play in the huddle, the receiver learns what pass route to run. For offensive plays, pass routes can be selected from many options on what is called a pass tree. Because a receiver runs a variety of pass routes at different depths from the line of scrimmage, offensive coaches have designed these routes to resemble a tree with each route representing a branch. The pass tree is discussed in more detail in the "Passing Game" section on pages 119 to 121.

The most important thing to teach receivers about running pass routes is to explode off the line of scrimmage. This allows receivers to immediately drive down the field, and it forces the defensive back—who is trying to keep the receiver from catching the ball—to start running away from the line of scrimmage. When running routes, receivers should run to the outside shoulder of the defensive back, forcing the defender to turn his shoulders parallel to the line of scrimmage to cover the receiver. Once a defender turns his body, it is easy for the receiver to run a pass route in the opposite direction or to stop and quickly turn back to the quarterback to make the catch. A good technique for the receiver is to weave from the outside hip of the defender to the inside hip. Receivers should not tip off the defender if they are going deep; they should release from the line of scrimmage with the same body lean for each pass route, whether it's a short out or a go pattern.

COACHING TIP   Teach receivers the exact distance they should run up the field before they reach the breaking point. Also teach them the distance they will usually travel before the ball reaches them at the receiving point. Practicing these routes over and over helps receivers instinctively know how far to run and where the ball should be when they catch it during a game.

Receivers must also come under control at the breaking point (the point a certain distance off the line of scrimmage where they stop running straight up the field) and adjust their path to move in the direction of the pass route called in the huddle. At this point in the pass route, receivers should lean their upper body in the direction they want to go next. They should roll over the foot on the side of the body in the direction they are headed, turn the head and shoulders, and react to the football. They should anticipate catching the ball after they have adjusted their pass route. The point where receivers make the catch is referred to as the receiving point. The distance that receivers run to reach the receiving point varies depending on the pass route they are running and the timing of the pass from the quarterback. To practice this skill, refer to the breaking- and receiving-points drill on page 129.

COACHING TIP   When players are slow coming out of their break, it is usually because they have planted a foot, which stops their momentum so that they have to start moving all over again. Coach players to lean with the upper body in the direction that they want to go and to roll over the foot on that side. This maneuver allows them to keep their momentum through the entire pass route.

Catching the Football

Properly catching the football is a matter of concentration and dedication. First and foremost, receivers should always watch the football into their hands. If the football is thrown high, receivers should catch it with their thumbs together and with their wrists cocked slightly back (see figure 7.25a); if it is thrown low, receivers should catch it with their little fingers together and their palms up (see figure 7.25b). Receivers should catch the football in their hands without trapping it against their body. They should work on reaching out with both hands toward the ball when making a catch so that they can see both hands and the ball at the moment of the reception (see figure 7.26). Receivers should then tuck the ball under the arm and protect it after making the catch.

COACHING TIP   To help receivers with their sense of touch and their concept of good hands, you can teach them to use a visual image. Have them imagine shaking the bones out of their hands until their bones dissolve and their hands just become flesh.

FIGURE 7.25   Receiver catching *(a)* a high ball and *(b)* a low ball.

FIGURE 7.26   Receiver preparing to catch the ball with the hands away from the body.

Give receivers ample opportunities in practice to catch the types of passes they will see in games. As a coach, you cannot expect players to perform skills in a game that they have not worked on in practice. Success in practice will help the receivers gain confidence, and first downs and touchdowns will reinforce that catching the ball is fun.

COACHING TIP   Dropped passes usually occur when receivers don't have their hands together, when they don't reach for the ball, or when they take their eyes off the ball at the moment of the catch. If receivers drop passes, check these three areas and explain the importance of each part of the receiving motion in making the catch.

Centering the Ball

Players at the center position must learn how to bring the ball up from the ground to the quarterback's hands—called centering the ball—in both a tight formation and in a shotgun formation.

In the tight formation, the quarterback lines up directly behind the center; the quarterback's hands are open and ready to receive the ball directly from the center. At one point in the ball exchange, both the center's hands and the quarterback's hands will be touching the ball (see figure 7.20b on page 107). The snap should be hard and direct, going through the center's legs and into the quarterback's waiting hands. For beginning centers, it is often easier to start in a four-point offensive line stance (as shown in figure 7.1 on page 89) and then place the ball under the player's snapping hand. This places the ball slightly in front of and just to the inside of the center's shoulder pad.

In the shotgun formation, the center snaps the ball through the legs to the quarterback, who is 5 to 7 yards behind the line of scrimmage. The snap should be crisp, but not so fast that it is difficult to handle. The ball should reach the quarterback in the area from the belt line to the middle of the chest—and with a nice spiral—so that it is easy to grab. The center should look between the legs to locate the quarterback and then bring the eyes up before the snap.

Centers should first practice snapping the ball to the quarterback slowly, making sure they are placing it properly with the laces at or near the fingers of the quarterback's throwing hand. Early in the season, a coach should lie on the ground and look up at the snap to determine if it is filling the quarterback's hand properly. The players should then practice at full speed. They should perform 1,000 center–quarterback exchanges each day. Once the snap is secure, have centers move straight ahead, move to the right or left, or set to pass-block while making the exchange as they would in a game.

COACHING TIP   If centers have trouble blocking a player directly in front of them or to the side of their snapping hand, tell them to take a short lateral step with the foot on the side of the snapping hand. This moves a portion of the body in front of the defender and allows the center to have time to get both hands into position to block.

Offensive Tactics

Once your team understands and can properly execute the individual offensive technical skills, they can begin putting them together into offensive schemes, or tactics. The plays you teach your offense will make up your offensive tactics, or your game plan. When designing offensive tactics, start with plays—either running or passing plays—that use the skills your team has mastered. (When working with beginners, running the ball is usually easier to teach because handing off is a simpler skill than the throwing and catching required for the passing game.) Remember that the key to tactical success is using plays that optimize your players' strengths. For example, if your quarterback can pass accurately and your receivers can catch the ball, you should feature offensive tactics that highlight passing. Conversely, if blocking and running the ball are your team's strengths, your game plan should feature running plays.

The objectives you set for your team's offensive tactics must be realistic and important—not just to you, but also to your players.

Scoring is the most obvious objective when a team is on offense, but scoring is merely an outcome produced by the team's ability to achieve three goals. The following are the three most important goals an offensive team can strive to accomplish:

1. Execute consistently.

To execute consistently, you must run the same plays throughout the season and work on them continually. Select a simple offense (one that has some deception) and teach it well. A few well-executed plays can give even the best opponents all they can handle. If your offense uses too many plays, chances are your team members, not your opponents, will be confused. A confused player is not an effective player.

Consistent execution stems from your players understanding the plays and practicing them repeatedly. Every player must know what is expected of him for each play. Teaching assignments is not enough. Equal time must be spent teaching every player the techniques he needs to carry out his assignment. And, as I will repeat many times, a player must see a clear, vivid picture in his mind of what you want him to do.

Practicing these plays against the defense that you expect opponents to play will help your players visualize the way they should run each play. If your players know that a team goal is consistent execution, they'll be more eager to perform the plays as often as necessary to make them work in a game. Teach your receivers the proper patterns to run, and teach your quarterback the proper depth to drop when throwing the football. Your players need to practice running a pattern many times before they'll feel confident that it will work. Develop a game plan early in the week and then simplify it so that on game day you have only a handful of plays. By using a limited number of plays each week and giving the players enough repetitions to eliminate mistakes, you'll help your team execute consistently.

2. Move the football.

The object on offense is to move down the field and score by using a good mix of running and passing plays. Running basic plays against the defense you anticipate seeing is the best way to prepare your team to move the football in a game. The offensive players must believe that they can march the football down the field regardless of the team they're playing or the defense they're facing. Select plays that use the strengths of your offense and that expose the defense's weakness.

3. **Maintain possession.**

Obviously, when the offense controls the football, the opponent cannot score. To keep control, the offense must consistently produce first downs and eliminate turnovers by protecting the football. An offensive game plan with effective running plays combined with short, quick passes is difficult to stop. Using a good mix of plays keeps the chains moving steadily toward the opponent's goal line. Maintaining possession is especially important when your team has a narrow lead at the end of a game. The other team can't score if it doesn't have the ball.

Evaluating Talent

The most important key to success is to match your player talent with a workable offensive philosophy. You should take an inventory of your team's individual skills and character (coachability). The factors you evaluate for your player inventory are similar to those considered by a general manager in the NFL.

COACHING TIP   Be sure to design your offense based on players' skills, while also considering the team talent. For example, a good passing quarterback needs receivers to support him, and a running back needs a strong offensive line to help create holes for him to charge through. Football is truly a team sport.

Following are some of the questions you should ask yourself when taking inventory:

- Do I have an offensive leader at quarterback (a player who is smart, passes well, can read keys on options, and understands the game)? One of your strongest leaders should be the quarterback. However, you won't necessarily have a passing offense just because you have a strong quarterback. Without good receivers, a passing offense will not be very effective. Keep in mind that strong quarterbacks may also be known for their running skills.

- Do I have a game breaker (a player who is fast, is elusive, has good hands, and is football savvy)? If so, make sure this player is part of the game plan.

- Do I have a power runner (a player who is strong, has good judgment, and can make short-yardage gains)? If so, and if you have a strong offensive line to support him, you can place more of an emphasis on your running game.

Once you have completed a talent inventory, you must experiment with the pieces of the puzzle until you discover the combinations that work best. That is what makes football a great sport. The total team is greater than the sum of its parts.

COACHING TIP   Be sure to be selective with your coaches, too. You will want to select a detail-oriented offensive line coach, because the offensive line block is one of the most unique skills in all sports.

Running Game

Most teams can develop a successful running attack through the dedicated practice of basic fundamentals. Keep in mind that field position may dictate the use of specific plays. For example, running from a power formation on third and long (as opposed to using a spread formation and running a draw) will diminish your chances of gaining a first down. If you're having trouble blocking up front, you may not want to run counter plays that require a lot of time to execute. Many games are won as a result of covering short yardage and converting goal-line plays into scores, and many games are lost when a team simply gets stopped on a fourth down and one or a fourth down and goal. If you are a passing coach, you may dread the thought of having to convert a first down to ensure a win. But if you are a running coach, these short-yardage situations are probably what you hope for. The running coach relies on ball control. Each down and distance is different, as is the ball position on the field. A good coach has a game plan that details plays for each situation, and those plays are practiced during the week.

COACHING TIP Winning football games requires respect for and detailed attention to field position. You must be aware of your real estate situation when calling plays. Two keys to winning are being able to score in the red zone and avoiding turnovers on your own side of the 50-yard line.

When developing an effective running game, the most important step is to design plays in which the blocking and backfield action work together and cause indecision and confusion for the defense. The backfield action on any play must be designed to put the running back at the point of attack just as the hole is opening. Three types of blocks can help accomplish this: fast or quick blocking on straight-ahead plays (see figure 7.27), fold blocking on slower-hitting plays (see figure 7.28, page 118), and power blocking on sweeps (see figure 7.29, page 118).

FIGURE 7.27 Fast or quick block for straight-ahead plays.

FIGURE 7.28 Fold block for slower-hitting plays.

FIGURE 7.29 Power block for sweeps.

You should also set up the running game so that it is effective and easy to communicate. The simplest way to communicate running plays is to number each hole (the natural gaps between the offensive blockers) and each running back. Figure 7.30 shows an example of how to do this. The running back runs the ball into the hole that is called. For example, play 32 means that the number 3 running back runs the ball through the number 2 hole. Calling out "32" is much easier and quicker than specifying that the running back runs through the gap between the guard and center.

FIGURE 7.30 Numbering holes and running backs.

In developing a running game, consider the different series of plays that can be successful. All series should include built-in dimension—that part of a given series that provides variation for backfield movement. Dimension will make it difficult for the defense to determine the point of attack when the ball is snapped, which forces the defense to respect your entire attack. An example of a series is a dive 30 and a trap 30. These both involve the number 3 running back running through the hole right in the center of the line, but the running back gets there using different actions and the blocking is different.

The running game should give you the opportunity to run the football in every offensive hole. By incorporating a series of plays, you'll be able to run to the various holes in more than one way. The game plan, however, should include only four or five running plays chosen from the total series of plays. These are the plays you will perfect for a given opponent.

Successful football teams use runs that are effective against the opponent they are playing. For example, if the defense is coming across the line of scrimmage very hard, you would use the trap series. Against a hard-charging defense, it is easier for offensive line players to get an angle if a trap is called. Sometimes defenders take themselves out of (overrun) the play; other times they can be blocked from the side. Against a reading defense, the dive and sweep would be effective. If the defense stacks the line of scrimmage (and the defense has more defensive people on the line than you have blockers), you may be better off throwing the ball.

Running backs are an integral part of a good running offense. Coach them to gain yardage on every play. They should be competitive and have the desire to be successful. Running backs who are difficult to tackle and who keep their feet driving will create more touchdowns.

COACHING TIP The game of football is about the players. Do not overcoach formations and employ too many plays. Bombarding players with too much instruction will make them confused and hesitant. A mentally hesitant player is not effective. Keep it simple!

Passing Game

If you have a highly skilled player who can throw the ball, you are a fortunate coach. However, you need to understand that long passes have a lower percentage of completion. Prominent NFL coach Bill Walsh was the master of passing strategy. Walsh believed that one completion out of four attempts was a good percentage on long passes over 30 yards. He knew that the distance that passes travel is proportional to the percentage of completions. Therefore, the 5-yard handoff will have a higher percentage of completions. If short passes are completed more often, receivers and running backs (who have become an integral part of the receiving corps) should work hard for more yards after the catch. Hooks, curls, and crossing patterns can be very productive. You must pay careful attention to details such as protection and passing routes, so extra planning is required. However, the short passing game can be developed with patience and good drills.

Keep the passing attack simple so that the quarterbacks and receivers know what to do. Timing is important to the success of a passing attack, so you must allow time in practice for players to perform many repetitions of the basic patterns. Also, with young quarterbacks, you must not ask them to throw pass routes that they do not have the ability to throw. When your team has trouble completing passes, make sure that the pass is timed properly based on the route the receiver is running and the distance the quarterback drops when setting up to throw.

The passing game starts with a pass tree (see figure 7.31). These are patterns that the receivers run to get open to catch the football. The passing game takes time to develop, and you must be patient in bringing the separate parts of this offense together. Here are the pass patterns (as shown in figure 7.31) that you can teach your players:

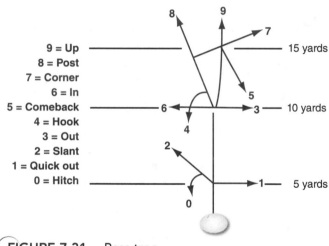

FIGURE 7.31   Pass tree.

- Hitch—The hitch pattern is run at 5 yards. The receiver should run straight down the field and then quickly turn back to the inside to make the catch.

- Quick out—The quick-out pattern is very successful when the defensive player is playing off the receiver and to the inside. The receiver runs downfield 5 yards and then cuts sharply to the sideline, catching the ball just before stepping out of bounds.

- Slant—The slant pattern is a quick pattern where the receiver runs straight down the field for 5 yards and then angles in at a 45-degree angle to the center of the field. The quarterback takes three steps and throws.

- Out—The out pattern is run in the 10- to 12-yard area; the receiver runs straight down the field and then breaks sharply to the sideline.

- Hook—When the defensive player retreats too fast or is playing off the receiver and to the outside, the hook pattern can be used. The receiver drives deep for 10 to 12 yards and then curls back to the football.

- Comeback—The comeback is a pattern that is run off the up pattern. The receiver bends to the outside at 10 yards, starts straight up the field for 5 yards, and then breaks sharply to the outside, coming back toward the line of scrimmage to make the reception.

- In—The in pattern is also run at 10 to 12 yards and is the opposite of the out pattern. The receiver runs straight down the field and then breaks sharply to the center of the field. The receiver should keep running across the field.

- Corner—The corner is similar to a post, except the receiver starts into the post for four steps and then breaks to the outside at an angle, toward a corner of the field.

- Post—The post is similar to the up pattern in that it is a deep pattern. At 10 yards the receiver breaks deep to the inside at an angle toward the center of the field.

- Up—The up pattern is a good option if the defensive back is playing tight on a receiver with speed. The receiver runs up the field 10 yards, bends to the outside, and then sprints straight up the field on the outside of the defensive back.

Throwing on the Run

A quarterback must always have the ability to throw on the run. Quarterbacks may need to throw on the run as part of a designed play or when they are forced to scramble out of the pocket because of the pass rush. Throwing while moving is a skill that requires practice. See the throwing on the run drill on page 132 for more practice.

Hurry-Up Offense

The two-minute, or hurry-up, offense is a specialty within the passing offense. With two minutes left in the half or in the game, teams often don't huddle; the quarterback calls out an audible to call the plays. Players should be aware of the clock and should go out of bounds to stop the clock when they have the ball. Players need to remember to hustle up to the line quickly to ensure that they are efficiently using the time remaining. Defenses that have held their opponent all game will sometimes appear helpless in the last minutes of the contest. The passing coach only wants to have the ball last with a chance to come from behind. A few late pass completions can shift the momentum and change the results of a hard-fought game.

Option Game

An option offense is traditionally a high-scoring fast-break attack. A good option quarterback will read the defense to determine whether he should

- keep the ball and turn upfield,
- lateral the ball to the trailing back, or
- pass the ball to a receiver down the field.

Football players who also play basketball adapt to this brand of offense quickly. The advantage of option football is that it reduces the coverage of each player to a one-on-one situation. Because of the nature of the option execution, many teams get a taste of the option while practicing the rugby kickoff return (see the drill on page 187 of chapter 9). The rugby concept of having someone to lateral to at your side as you run down the field is a close cousin to the actual option offenses of today. Defenders must respect the ballcarrier's ability to lateral the ball; therefore, they may not be as aggressive in their tackling. If properly executed, the option offense can score quickly and often.

Because the ball is pitched in close proximity to the defense, there is a greater risk of turnovers. However, option teams are not as concerned about field position or turnovers, because the potential for long runs and big plays balances the risk factors for turnovers. For the option game to work, the quarterback and running backs need to practice the reads and pitches until they become habits. Proper drilling of quarterback reads and running back pitchouts will be the key to your success with option football.

COACHING TIP Players enjoy closing practice with sneak attack plays. These plays shouldn't distract you from your offensive design, but they are nice to have in your back pocket. For example, the "wait a minute" play is used when you are playing a team that is undisciplined in getting in and out of their huddle. In this play, your quarterback will yell, "Wait a minute!" and then turn to the side while the ball is snapped to the fullback.

Limiting Mistakes

The game of football is said to be a game of perfection, but in reality, the team that makes the least mistakes will win. Accepting imperfection may be the most perfect way to prepare. A football game is like a two-act play. Many teams dominate in the first half (act one), only to fall behind before the gun goes off (act two). As a coach, you are the director of this play. Here are the mistakes that most often change the outcome of a game:

- Fumbles
- Bad punt snaps

- Interceptions
- Penalties

However, as a coach, you can help prevent these mistakes. Be sure to insist on proper execution of skills. Step in when you spot an error. Pull the player aside and provide guidance and support for correcting the error. Keep your instruction clear, simple, and positive. Then, have the player go back in and continue to monitor her progress. If you are actively engaged in practice—ready to step in and provide guidance—this should help your team avoid these mistakes.

Offensive Drills

The need for active instruction when running through drills with your players cannot be emphasized enough. Proper execution of skills, combined with repetition after repetition, will help ensure that your players have the tools they need to succeed. This will make the skills become automatic or instinctual for your players. An instinctive player is more effective than a thinking player.

➤ DRIVE BLOCKING

Offensive linemen line up directly in front of defensive linemen as shown in the diagram. Place a 12-inch (30 cm) wooden board between each offensive lineman and defensive lineman. This board will force players to keep a wide base, which helps them to maintain their power angle. The coach tells the offensive linemen which shoulder to use for the block. Every offensive lineman takes a fit position under the defensive lineman's shoulder pads. On "hut," each offensive lineman drives his defensive lineman straight back off the line using his legs, arms, and hands; the offensive lineman should maintain a straight back the entire time. If the offensive lineman does not keep a wide base, he will step on the board. The offensive lineman drives the defensive lineman behind the line for three or four steps until the whistle is blown.

Next, repeat the drill, but ask the offensive linemen to start from the one-step approach, uncoiling on "hut" and driving the defensive linemen off the ball. Repeat with the offensive linemen starting from a three-point stance; on the snap count, the offensive linemen should fire out (as described on page 93) and drive the defensive linemen (first with short, choppy steps, then switching to longer power steps) until the coach blows the whistle.

Each of these variations should be performed twice, using each shoulder to block.

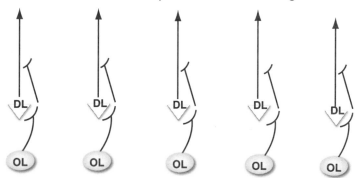

➤ CUTOFF BLOCKING

Offensive linemen act as blockers and line up in front of defensive linemen as shown in the diagram. The coach tells the offensive linemen which shoulder to use for the block. The offensive linemen keep the defensive linemen from penetrating down the line by driving them back and blocking with the shoulder until the whistle is blown. The offensive linemen should try to get their shoulders in front of the defensive linemen. Repeat the drill using the opposite shoulder.

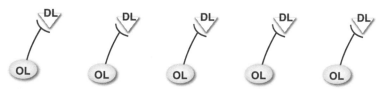

➤ HOOK BLOCKING

Offensive linemen act as blockers and line up on the inside shoulder of the defensive linemen as shown in the diagram. The coach tells the offensive linemen which shoulder to use for the block. The offensive linemen keep the defensive linemen from working to the outside by driving them back with their far shoulders, arms, and hands until the whistle is blown. Repeat the drill using the opposite shoulder.

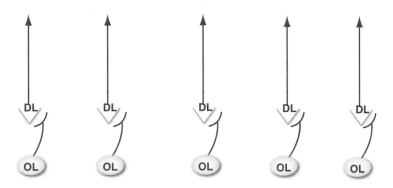

➤ CROSS BLOCKING

Players divide into groups of four with two offensive linemen who act as blockers and two defensive linemen as shown in the diagram. The coach tells the offensive linemen which shoulder to use for the block. The outside offensive lineman in each group blocks first, and as he is blocking, the second offensive lineman steps back with his first step to provide room for the first blocker to clear. The two offensive linemen should separate the two defensive linemen by opening a running lane. Both offensive linemen should use their shoulders to block and should get their shoulders in front of the defensive players. The offensive linemen will drive until the whistle is blown. Repeat the drill using the opposite shoulder.

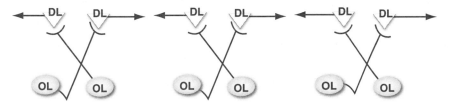

➤ PASS PROTECTION BLOCKING

Offensive linemen act as blockers and line up directly in front of the defensive linemen as shown in the diagram. A cone or flag denoting the quarterback is positioned behind the offensive linemen. The coach moves down the line, calling out the snap count to each group. On the snap count from the coach, each defensive lineman rushes straight at an offensive lineman at half speed and does not take a side. Each offensive lineman moves off the line and punches out with the arms and hands to block the approaching defensive lineman. Each offensive lineman attempts to get into a position between his defensive lineman and the quarterback. The offensive linemen drive until the whistle is blown. Repeat the drill by resetting to hit out again.

In a variation of this drill, the drill is performed the same as described, but the two outside offensive linemen face toward the sideline and push the defensive linemen up the field, wide of the quarterback. The three inside offensive linemen stay to the inside and in front of the defensive linemen, slow the charge, and force them wide of the quarterback.

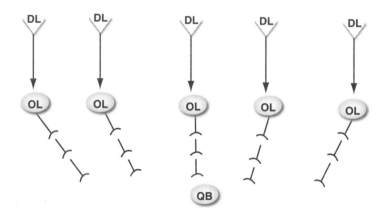

➤ SANDWICH DRILL

An offensive lineman lines up over a defensive lineman or linebacker. A running back (or the next offensive blocker in line) lines up 5 yards behind the offensive lineman. The space for the running back is limited by two blocking dummies positioned 2 yards on each side of the lineman. The line coach, who is behind the defense, gives the starting count and calls the signal, and the running back advances forward. The offensive lineman blocks the defender back or to either side and sustains his block until the whistle blows. To change things up and regulate the degree of difficulty, you can move the running back closer to the offensive lineman, which allows the back to clear the hole faster, or you can move the running back farther back to make the blocker sustain longer. This drill teaches offensive linemen to sustain their block until the back gets past the first level of defense and into the defensive secondary.

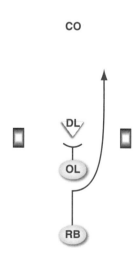

➤ THREE-SECOND DRILL

To start the drill, the offensive line and defensive line set up normally. The quarterback starts at a center position and drops back five to seven steps (either to the right or the left). A defensive lineman or linebacker aligns over the outside shoulder of each offensive lineman. The defense is told to take a wide run around on the pass rush, forcing the offensive lineman to reach step to front up the rusher. If the blocker keeps the defender off the quarterback for three seconds, the blocker wins. Have your offensive linemen imagine that they are a camera on a tripod, always keeping square to the defensive lineman's rush.

To change things up, have the defender spin off the reach block to the inside; the offensive lineman must then recover from the reach step to punch and shuffle back to the inside to front up the defender. Or, to increase the level of difficulty, have the offensive blocker place his inside hand behind his back. The blocker then has only one arm to stab the charge of the defender. This variation is commonly referred to as the Zorro drill, because the blocker looks a bit like Zorro fencing against an enemy. When the blocker is using only one hand, footwork becomes more important.

This drill teaches the importance of a hand punch to control the defender and foot quickness to front up the defender. Blockers also learn the importance of always forcing a defender to go around them, which is the long way to the quarterback. Ultimately, the drill teaches the offensive line to continue pass protecting for more than three seconds.

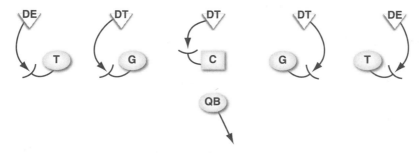

➤ DOUBLE-TEAM BLOCKING

Players divide into groups of three with two offensive linemen who act as blockers and one defensive lineman as shown in the diagram. The inside offensive lineman uses the outside shoulder, and the outside offensive lineman uses the inside shoulder to make the block. This enables the two players to come together and generate as much power as possible against the defensive lineman. The offensive linemen drive until the whistle is blown. Repeat the drill using the opposite shoulders.

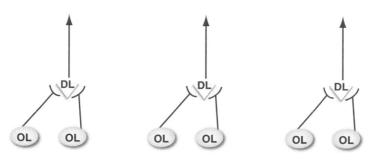

➤ FREE-MAN DROPOUT

Three defenders line up over three offensive linemen, and another defender is positioned outside the blind side of the quarterback—the offense's left if the quarterback is a right hander, or the offense's right if the quarterback is a left hander. The coach will instruct one of the three lined-up defenders to drop back off the line of scrimmage. The offensive lineman who does not have his defender rushing will slide out to the free pass rusher on the blind side. If another defender breaks free while the blocker is on his way to the blind-side rusher, the blocker must block the defender who breaks free. Blockers should never let a rusher cross their face, giving the rusher a short route to the quarterback. If blockers cannot contain the rusher, they should make sure that the rusher has to take the long way around them.

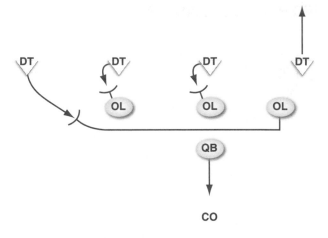

This drill teaches teamwork among the offensive linemen. They also learn to shuffle quickly to the blind side in order to ensure added protection of the quarterback.

➤ ZONE BLOCKING

Players divide into groups of four with two offensive linemen, one defensive lineman, and one linebacker as shown in the diagram. The two offensive linemen block the defensive lineman. To start the block, the offensive lineman who is directly in front of the defensive lineman uses the inside shoulder, arm, and hand; and the second blocker uses the shoulder, arm, and hand nearest the defensive lineman. Based on the linebacker's and defensive lineman's movement, one offensive lineman comes off the defensive lineman's block to ensure that both the linebacker and the defensive lineman are blocked effectively.

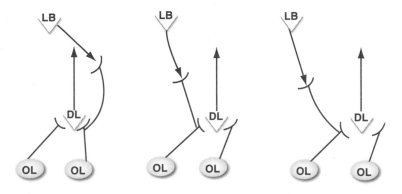

➤ BREAKING AND RECEIVING POINTS

Two wide receivers line up on a designated yard line as shown in the diagram. The coach determines the type of pass route to be used and instructs the wide receivers to run specified routes one at a time. A ball is not used in this drill. For short routes (5-yard routes with a three-step drop by the quarterback) and medium routes (10- to 12-yard routes with a five-step drop by the quarterback) coming to the center of the field, the wide receiver runs 6 yards after the break before reaching the receiving point. For short and medium routes to the outside, the wide receiver runs 8 to 10 yards after the break. On deep patterns or play action (routes of more than 12 yards with a seven-step drop by the quarterback), the wide receiver's receiving point should be extended by 3 to 4 yards. The coach should stress the need to keep the breaking point constant for every route and to keep running to reach the receiving point. The wide receivers return to the original starting positions after running the route. Repeat the drill.

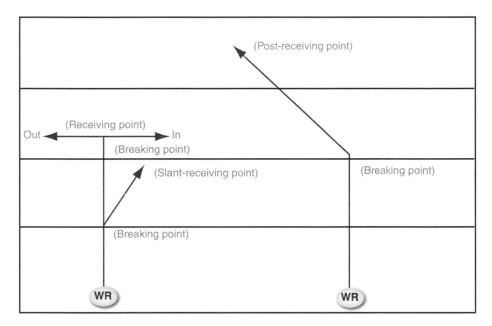

➤ BALL CALL AND TURN

A receiver and passer (either a coach or quarterback) begin 10 yards apart. The receiver has her back to the passer. The passer calls "ball" as the pass leaves her hand. The receiver turns and adjusts to the path of the throw to make a catch. For more difficulty, move the receiver closer or delay the call.

➤ ROUND THE CLOCK

A passer throws the ball to a receiver in a variety of positions—these positions correspond to the face of a clock. For example, a pass to 3 o'clock would be shoulder high to the receiver's left, and a pass to 7 o'clock would be below his waist to his right. The receiver should catch all passes with his eyes on the ball so that his head bobs down on low balls and his head bobs up on high throws.

➤ SIDELINE TAP DANCE

A receiver is lined up 1 yard from the sideline. A passer throws the ball down the sideline; the receiver must make the catch without stepping out of bounds by tapping his back foot inside the sideline.

➤ TAP AND GO

This is one of the best drills for helping both the quarterback and the receivers develop their skills on the long pass. The quarterback lines up on a hash mark, and the receiver lines up on the hash mark to the quarterback's right (both the quarterback and the receiver will change sides after several attempts). The quarterback pats the ball, and the receiver runs a go route. The quarterback will throw the ball with air under it in a high arch. This lets the receiver time his run for the catch. The receiver should not raise his arms until the ball is above him.

➤ DISTRACTION CATCH

This drill includes a quarterback, a receiver, and two defenders. The defenders serve as distractions. They are set up 10 yards away from the quarterback and are in motion. A receiver runs a 12-yard out or hook pattern as the two defenders cross in front of him with their arms up. The defenders let the ball go between them so the receiver can make the catch if he is concentrating on the ball. To change things up, ask the defenders to tip the ball up so the receiver can practice catching the rebound.

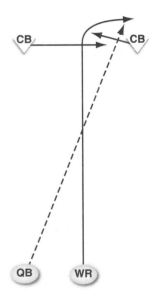

➤ BAD BALL DRILL

A passer throws the ball low (on occasion, actually skipping it on the ground) or throws the ball in an end-over-end flight path high in the air or to one side or the other to the first receiver in a line. This drill helps the receiver work on maintaining a set position, ready to adjust to the ball's flight path.

➤ DOWNFIELD BLOCKING

Players divide into groups of three with one wide receiver, who acts as a blocker, one running back, and one defensive back as shown in the diagram. The wide receiver blocks the defensive back to allow the running back to run past the defensive back. The wide receiver and defensive back start 5 yards apart. On the whistle, the wide receiver charges toward the defensive back and aggressively blocks the defensive back with his forearms and shoulders; the defensive back tries to get through the block and tackle the running back.

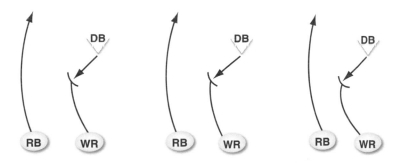

➤ THROWING ON THE RUN

Begin with at least six players all serving as quarterbacks in this drill. Have the quarterbacks form a circle 12 yards in diameter. Give the ball to one of the quarterbacks. The quarterbacks will then run clockwise in the circle (later, they will run counterclockwise). While running, the quarterback with the ball throws to one of the quarterbacks across from him. While continuing to run, that quarterback throws back across the circle to another quarterback across from him, and so on. The emphasis should be placed on opening the shoulder toward the intended target, especially when throwing across the body. Having a right-handed quarterback run left, for example, will help to emphasize to him the importance of properly aligning his shoulders during the throw.

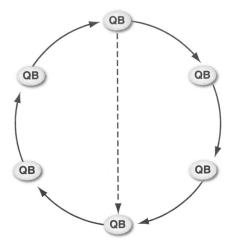

➤ QUARTERBACK THREE- AND FIVE-STEP DROP BACK

A quarterback lines up behind a center as he would in a game. The center has the ball and, on the coach's command, hands the ball to the quarterback to start the drill. If a center is not available, the coach can hand the ball to the quarterback. Once the ball is handed to the quarterback, the quarterback executes a three- or five-step drop with the ball in both hands (held number high) as he starts the drop. On a three-step drop, the quarterback stops the drop with the third step and is prepared to step and throw. On a five-step drop, the quarterback stops the drop with an elongated fifth step, comes under control, and is prepared to step and throw. For the five-step drop, if field conditions are bad, the quarterback should shorten the final step and keep his feet under his hips.

➤ PASSING FORM

Quarterbacks are lined up facing each other 10 yards apart. They use this as a warm-up drill to review their form. The quarterback with the ball should start the drill as if receiving a snap from the center, bringing the ball into his chest. He should keep the ball high (near his ear), get set with the front of the ball pointing backward, and bring his hips, shoulders, and elbow toward the target. As he brings the ball forward, the quarterback ends with an aggressive wrist snap, causing the spiral motion of the ball. The quarterback should follow through with the index finger pointing to his partner (the target) as he steps through. Some quarterbacks will be natural passers; others will need to have specific drills designed to correct their form.

Following are some other ways a quarterback can practice his passing form:

- **Passing from the knees.** The quarterback is down on both knees. He picks up the ball in front of him and throws. This position forces the quarterback to use a shoulder turn and wrist snap to execute the pass.

- **Passing with the wrong knee up.** The quarterback is resting on the knee opposite his throwing arm. He picks up the ball from the ground and throws, using his shoulder, wrist, and a partial hip turn. A variation can be to have the quarterback follow through by touching the ground in front of him with his index finger.

- **Passing over the rope.** The quarterback drops back and throws the ball high enough to clear a rope strung head high across the goalpost. This ensures a high delivery. Emphasize that the quarterback should hold the ball with both hands chest high as he drops back and should hold it shoulder high for the delivery motion.

> ## GAUNTLET

Seven players are actively involved in this drill. Set up additional stations as necessary to ensure that you are keeping all of your players engaged. Defensive players line up three to a side, parallel to one another, for a total of six defensive players (two lines of three facing each other). The defensive players should be a yard apart and a yard across from one another. The running back starts a yard or two in front of the first set of defensive players. The ball is handed off to the running back, and the running back runs through the double lineup of defensive players, who are trying to pull the ball out of the running back's hands.

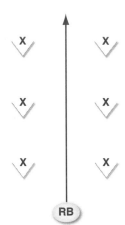

This drill teaches players how to secure the football and develop practical running skills while preventing a fumble. Players should cradle the ball like a baby, with four points of the body securing the ball: the elbow, the hand that has the ball, the ribs, and the hand opposite the ball. The player should keep the shoulders round and the legs digging.

You can change the gauntlet drill to a short-yardage situation by having the defense set up shoulder to shoulder. The offensive player runs through the defenders' shoulders while the defenders try to punch the ball out from the bottom or pull it out from the top. This can add some intensity to the drill for older, more experienced players.

A number of variations exist with this drill. You can ask the running back to do any of the following:

- **Touch the line.** After clearing the gauntlet, the running back leans forward and touches the ground twice—the second time, he may need to push himself back up.

- **Cut back.** After clearing the gauntlet, the running back cuts at a sharp angle to the right and then to the left. On the next repeat, the running back should cut to the outside, first right and then left.

- **Spin off a tackler.** After clearing the gauntlet, the running back spins off a tackler to his right, then spins off a tackler to his left.

- **Achieve short yardage.** Gaining that needed yard has more to do with mindset than technique. Have the running back drive through the tacklers, who are now shoulder to shoulder. The running back should come out the other end of the gauntlet with legs driving.

- **Perform a Heisman Trophy run.** The running back takes a handoff or pitchout and puts all the previous skills together on one run for a touchdown. Remind players of some great runs they may have witnessed in the pros or college—Steve Young and Marcus Allen made these kinds of runs for touchdowns.

➤ RUNNING-BACK BLOCKING

Two running backs act as blockers, and each lines up to the inside of two outside linebackers as shown in the diagram. A cone or flag denoting the quarterback is positioned behind and to the inside of the running backs. The running backs block one at a time, and the coach indicates which running back blocks first. The running back blocks the linebacker to the outside and attempts to direct him away from the quarterback. The block should be made off the outside foot; the blocker should make contact with his outside shoulder on the linebacker's inside hip. Run the drill at half speed. Players return to their original starting positions after the run. Repeat the drill.

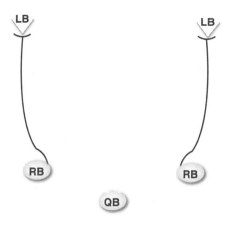

A variation of this drill requires the running back to block an inside linebacker to the outside and inside. The block should be made off the outside foot, and the blocker should make contact with his outside shoulder on the linebacker's inside hip.

➤ **TWO-MINUTE DRILL**

Set up at the goal line or a simulated goal line. Use your 11-person offense, and set up a scenario where you are down in the last two minutes of a half or a game. Have players work through plays with an emphasis on preserving time. Emphasize hustling to the line, getting out of bounds when a player has the ball (to stop the clock), spiking the ball when necessary to stop the clock, and so on. This will help your players become familiar with situations where the clock is ticking away. With no time-outs, the pressure is on to get the ball down the field and score.

You should have a series of plays that your team can run automatically without a huddle. Using your best play to the right and best play to the left is a good strategy in this situation. The audible (calling the play at the line) can also be used successfully if the players are prepared. Keep in mind that the field-goal setup will require a heads-up for substituting the kicker and holder and the extra time to set the tee.

 ➤ **VICTORY FORMATION**

Have your team line up in a tight offensive formation. The team will practice snapping the ball and taking the knee. This may be the most fun of all drills, because it implies that your team has the lead with little time to go. Emphasize in this drill that the line must close down their splits by staying tightly together. The backs line up next to the quarterback. The fastest player lines up directly behind the quarterback, 15 yards deep; this player serves as a safety in case of a dropped ball. When the quarterback takes a knee, the whistle blows, and the referee (the coach in this case) signals for the clock to start. Have your team practice the countdown and celebrate the victory when the game ends. This is a good time to remind your team to practice respect for the game and good sporting behavior with a traditional handshake.

DEFENSE

There are more ways to score on defense than there are on offense. Interceptions, fumble recoveries, safeties, blocked field goals, blocked punts, and punt returns are all opportunities for the defense to score points. However, the primary job for the defense is to stop the offense—either by forcing a punt, intercepting the ball, or recovering a fumble.

Defensive football skills and strategies are said to require more natural instincts than offensive football does. A solid defense is essential to winning. The saying "Offense sells tickets, and defense wins championships" is a long-held football creed. In fact, Woody Hayes always allowed his defensive coaches to draft all the other players for the squad after he chose his quarterbacks.

Because defense is natural and reactive, some coaches think that there is not as much to teach on the defensive side of the ball. This is untrue. If the strategy you employ on defense is sound, you will be rewarded with aggressive play. If the defense is complicated, the players may hesitate. A confused player is a slower player. Avoid giving one player two responsibilities within your defensive strategies. Even on the professional level, the assignment of two jobs is seldom successful. Thus, providing multiple responsibilities to a youth player is not recommended. Keep it simple. A good coach will set his defense and insist on the players executing the call, hustling to the ball, and hitting hard (contact is an equalizer to great speed and skill).

The test of a good defense is as follows:

- Does it define the **force** responsibility (gap responsibility)?
- Does it define the **contain** responsibility?
- Does it define the **pursuit** responsibility?
- Does it define the pass **coverage** responsibility?

Who forces, contains, pursues, and covers on every call? If your players have a clear mental picture of their responsibility, this will be their ultimate goal.

Defensive Technical Skills

The three units on defense—linemen, linebackers, and defensive backs—must all be fundamentally sound in their techniques.

These basic skills are an integral part of all defensive football, serving as the foundation your players will build on to play well at all levels. The basics that your defensive players must master include assuming the defensive stance, defeating blockers, tackling, rushing the passer, and covering receivers.

Defense Must Be Fun

Defensive football players are the aggressive kids who love to run and make contact. If you encourage emotion in defensive players, they will become excited when they make a tackle, recover a fumble, or intercept a pass. This excitement adds to team unity, and the players will perform at a higher level. Encourage team tackling, with everyone pursuing the ball until the whistle blows. Defensive squads usually adopt a visual nickname such as "Swarming Bees" or "Purple People Eaters." This motivates defensive players to swarm the ballcarrier and adds to team spirit.

Defensive football is played better when the assignments are simple and do not cause hesitation from a player thinking about which technique or responsibility he must choose on each call. "Move on movement, deliver a blow, fight against pressure, pursue, and tackle" is the creed for the defensive line. The linebackers' creed is "Read and react." And the defensive backs' creed is "Line up deep as the deepest and wide as the widest, and read pass keys first." All units should understand their role. A good defensive play will see all defenders at the ball when the play ends. Football broadcasters often marvel at the number of defenders in on a tackle. The gang tackle mentality is "All of us are better than just one skilled opponent." Success on defense will soon create a freewheeling atmosphere of fun and love of the game.

DEFENSE

Stance

For the defensive player, the proper initial alignment of the body is key to reacting instantly and being able to effectively play defense. Teach the defensive line players, linebackers, and defensive backs the proper stances for their respective positions. Be sure to emphasize to defensive players that they must move out of their stance immediately when the ball is snapped. This will counter the advantage that the offense has of knowing where the ball is going and when the play will begin.

Defensive Line

The typical stance for defensive line players is similar to the offensive line player's three-point stance (see figure 7.2 on page 89). However, some defensive line players are more comfortable with the outside hand on the ground, creating a four-point stance as shown in figure 8.1 on page 140.

When in either stance, players should place more weight on their hands so that they can move forward; they should also use a stance that is a little wider than the offensive stance so that they have better balance when they're being blocked. Players should keep their outside hand (the hand away from the blocker) free to try pass rush techniques and to keep from getting hooked. The player's body must be low to the ground and must control the line of scrimmage from under the opponent's shoulder

FIGURE 8.1   Four-point stance for defensive linemen.

pads. Most coaches put their larger players on the front line. These players need to be able to stop the run and rush the passer. A good lineman will control his run gap and beat the blocker on pass attempts.

COACHING TIP   Many defensive linemen—in an elongated stance with their feet behind their hips—rise up rather than uncoil forward on the snap of the ball. This makes them easier to block. If you see defensive linemen standing straight up, ask them to move into their stance, and watch to see if they move their feet back as they place their hands on the ground. Correct them immediately and have them place their hands on the ground without adjusting foot position.

Linebackers

Linebackers should have a good balanced stance, which means that their feet are shoulder-width apart and staggered (see figure 8.2). The knees should be bent slightly to ensure a low body position with the hands near the upper thighs. Their eyes are focused on the player whom they will get the cue from. One foot is slightly forward; linebackers step with this foot first as they react to the key and find the football.

If linebackers are being engulfed by the blocker and can't disengage by shedding (throwing off the blocker), this may be because they have their shoulders in front of their hips and

FIGURE 8.2   Proper stance for linebackers.

feet, which forces them to lean into the blocker. Teach linebackers to stand in a more upright stance with their shoulders only slightly in front of their hips. They should bend at the knees (not at the waist) so that they have an uncoil to their hitting. Linebackers should unload their punch by using a short extension of the knees and hips. "Jack him up" is a common phrase used to describe hitting a player on the rise; linebackers also refer to this action as a "kiss."

Defensive Backs

Defensive backs should line up with a slightly staggered stance in a relaxed position (see figure 8.3). Before the play starts, the defensive backs should position their head so that they can look to the ball and see the start of the play. Good defensive backs look through the receivers to the quarterback. Their shoulders should be in front of their hips, and their arms and hands can hang down in a relaxed position.

Corners keep their feet slightly staggered, with the inside foot back. They should bring their outside foot to the center of the body so that it is on the ground in line under the chin; the foot should be turned so that the player can push off the side of the foot and not just the toes. Corners should push off their front foot and take a step back at the start of each play.

Free safeties line up with a square stance, and strong safeties line up with a slightly staggered stance similar to corners. The toes are pointed straight ahead, and the players

FIGURE 8.3 Proper stance for defensive backs.

should assume a slightly crouched position with the knees slightly bent. The eyes are focused on the player whom the safety will "key" from. Safeties can take a short read step on the snap and then react to the play.

Defeating Blockers

Every defensive player needs to understand the importance of defeating an offensive blocker before locating the offensive player with the ball and moving to be part of the tackle. A defensive lineman's or linebacker's first indication that the offense will run the ball is when the offensive linemen aggressively attack across the line of scrimmage the moment the ball is snapped. In that instant, defensive players must determine who the blocker will be—this is crucial to their ability to defeat the block.

For the defensive linemen, the blocker will be close, directly in front of them or to one side or the other. A good defensive lineman can feel the pressure of the block and either stuff the blocker into the hole or "rag-doll toss" the blocker. Linebackers who are lined up off the line will have more time to determine who is going to block them. Defensive backs, who are lined up the farthest off the line of scrimmage, will easily see who is assigned to block them on each play.

COACHING TIP If a defensive back steps forward on the first step rather than back, the receiver often reaches the defensive back too quickly. Emphasize to defensive backs that they should push off their front foot and take a first step (a read step) back with their back foot, stepping so that they start their momentum away from the receiver they want to cover.

Once a defensive player has determined the offensive player assigned to block him, he needs to attack by stepping into the blocker, keeping his shoulder pads below the blocker's pads. In the case of a defensive lineman, as he steps to meet the blocker, he needs to bring up his forearm or hand into the blocker's body as his shoulder pad makes contact. Once the blocker's momentum has been stopped, the defensive player needs to push the offensive player away and off the block with his other hand (i.e., shed the blocker), locate the player running with the ball, and move in that direction to make the tackle. A linebacker may have the chance to use the same forearm or hand shiver technique to defeat the blocker if the blocker rises up as he comes off the line of scrimmage. A linebacker or defensive back may find that the blocker is lower than he is in his stance; when this occurs, he will need to defeat the blocker by extending both arms and stopping the blocker by hitting out with the palms of both hands into the shoulder pads of the blocker. Whenever possible, a defender should keep his outside arm and shoulder free—the other tacklers will help make the stop if the defender keeps the ballcarrier to the inside.

COACHING TIP If a defensive player is continually getting blocked, the player may be looking into the backfield and trying to find out who has the ball rather than locating and defeating the blocker first. A good defender will learn to feel pressure and beat the blocker.

Tackling

If you want to have a good defensive team, you must teach your defensive players how to tackle. As the players grow and progress in their learning of the game, you must be sure to teach them the proper tackling techniques. When first introducing your players to tackling, have them start at half speed until they master the correct technique and feel comfortable with the contact associated with making a tackle.

Tacklers should always be in the proper hitting position with their shoulders up, back straight, knees bent, and feet shoulder-width apart. They should also focus on a target when making the tackle—generally the area near the runner's belt buckle. If tacklers always focus on this target, their opponents will not be able to fake them out with a fancy shoulder move, head fake, or spin maneuver.

All tackles should be made with the shoulder pad and never with the helmet. Tackling with the helmet will not only cost your team a penalty, but can also cause serious injury. You must stress to your players that they should always keep their shoulders up and eyes open and that they should position their body so that they tackle with one shoulder pad or the other—and never with their head.

The three basic tackles that your players will use are the front-on tackle, the angle tackle, and the open-field tackle. Following are coaching points for each type.

Front-On Tackle

Defensive players use the front-on tackle when they line up straight across from the offensive runner coming toward them. Tacklers should first make sure that they are in a good hitting position and are ready to make the tackle.

Tacklers must maintain a wide, balanced stance while keeping the feet moving with choppy steps. The back is arched, and the knees are slightly bent. The head and arms should extend in front of the body, and the shoulders should be up. A front-on tackle means that the ballcarrier is coming straight toward the tackler—it does not mean that the tackler leads with the head! Be sure that tacklers slide their head to the outside before making contact.

When executing the front-on tackle, tacklers explode off the foot on the same side as the shoulder that they will make the tackle with. They drive their shoulder into the runner's abdomen as they thrust their hips through (see figure 8.4). With their arms, they grasp behind the legs of the ballcarrier, lifting and pulling the ballcarrier toward them as they take him off his feet. Tacklers should remain under control so that they don't overrun the ballcarrier or dive and miss the tackle.

If players are missing tackles, make sure that they have widened their feet and shortened their stride and that they are bending their knees and not leaning forward at the waist. For additional practice of front-on tackling, see the drill on page 159.

FIGURE 8.4 Proper front-on tackling technique.

Angle Tackle

The angle tackle is necessary when the ballcarrier runs a wide play or gets close to the sideline. Tacklers must first make sure that they are in a good hitting position, and they must maintain a good balanced stance when preparing for this tackle.

When executing the angle tackle, tacklers must drive the shoulder in front of the ballcarrier's number, across the line of his run, and upward on the runner at about waist level (see figure 8.5). When players are making an angle tackle with the ballcarrier breaking to their right, for example, they use the left shoulder pad to make the tackle, and they explode off the left foot. The back should be arched to lift and drive through the ballcarrier. With the arms, tacklers should grasp the runner behind the legs and lift him off the ground, keeping their feet moving with short, choppy steps as they finish the tackle. Tacklers should remain under control and ready to move in any direction.

FIGURE 8.5 Angle tackle.

> **COACHING TIP** If players have trouble getting their shoulder in front of the ballcarrier, check to see that they are taking off with the correct foot. Players should use the shoulder pad and foot on the same side when making the tackle. By cutting off the angle, the defender has gained the leverage upfield.

For additional practice of angle tackling, see the drill on page 161.

Open-Field Tackle

After the runner has cleared the line of scrimmage or when a receiver has caught the football and has just one player to beat, defensive players must make an open-field tackle. Tacklers should learn that the most important thing to do in the open field is to get hold of the opponent and pull him to the ground (see figure 8.6). In the stance, tacklers must remain under control with their legs bent, shoulders up, and back straight; they must be prepared to move in any direction.

When executing the open-field tackle, tacklers should remember that their number one priority is to grasp the runner. They should use the sideline to their advantage, penning in or getting an angle on the runner. Once a tackler has a hold on the runner, help should soon arrive. But, if possible, the tackler should try to drive the ballcarrier out of bounds or pull him to the turf. Tacklers shouldn't worry about driving through the player or delivering a hard blow. The sole responsibility is to get hold of the player and prevent the score.

Players who must tackle a ballcarrier in the open field often lunge at and miss the ballcarrier. Remind them to be patient and to make certain where the ballcarrier is going. Then they should commit by opening up and stepping with the foot on the side of the direction that the ballcarrier is moving.

Tackling the Passer

Tackling a good quarterback is as difficult as tackling in the open field. Quarterbacks often have a unique ability to avoid the pass rush. If a pass rusher jumps to block the pass, a good quarterback will duck under the rusher and scramble to buy time. The more time

FIGURE 8.6 Open-field tackle.

your defense gives a quarterback, the more difficult it will be for your coverage to stay in their zones or stay on their receiver. Many big gains are a result of the quarterback and the receivers having time to beat the defenders. The key to tackling the passer is to read his drop and react to his intentions. If the drop is three steps, he wants to pass short. If it is five steps or seven steps, he is looking deeper. Pass rushers should not raise their hands until the quarterback's guide hand comes off the ball. They should tackle from the top down. Tacklers should try to strip the ball from the quarterback's passing hand with a chopping motion.

COACHING TIP Don't overlook a tall player who can bat the ball down on a pass attempt. Keep statistics on the number of bat-downs your players get. Align that tall player on the side of the quarterback's throwing arm. Getting in the quarterback's field of vision will disrupt even the best passers.

Rushing the Passer

When the offense runs the ball, they use aggressive blocking when the play begins. And when the offense is going to pass the ball, the offensive blockers sit back rather than fire out. Defensive linemen must recognize this change and immediately think about charging across the line to put pressure on—or rush—the quarterback. At this time, defensive players must determine which offensive blocker will block them. On the pass, the defensive player must defeat that block before looking for the quarterback.

To improve the pass rush of the defensive line players, teach them to know where the quarterback will set up, and encourage them to plan their pass rush technique before the play begins. If defensive players have an idea of which pass rush technique they will use as they charge from their stance, this will increase their chance of defeating the pass protection block and reaching the quarterback.

When teaching pass rush techniques to young players, teach only a few techniques that your players can perfect. Defensive players can rush the quarterback in three ways: the bull rush technique, the rip or swim technique, and the spin technique.

COACHING TIP Have each of your players get into the habit of calling out "Ball!" once the ball is in the air. On this call, all defenders should break to the ball for an interception or tip possibility. On an interception, the alarm called out by players is "Fire!"

Bull Rush Technique

In a bull rush, the defensive player controls the offensive blocker by locking both arms into the offensive blocker's armpits. Then, with the leverage provided by locking the elbows, the defensive player lifts the offensive line player up, forcing the blocker back into the quarterback (see figure 8.7). This type of rush requires good arm and hand strength.

FIGURE 8.7 Bull rush.

COACHING TIP If players using a bull rush are blocked right at the line of scrimmage, make sure they drive their feet with short, choppy steps; have good forward lean; and have a wide base. This continued forward charge will ensure that they move across the line of scrimmage and force the blocker back into the area where the quarterback is setting up to throw.

Rip or Swim Technique

In the rip or swim pass rush technique, the defensive player moves around the offensive blocker and then attacks the quarterback. The rip and the swim movements are similar; the arm farthest from the blocker repositions the blocker, while the arm closest to the blocker creates the movement for the defensive player to move past the blocker.

In the rip technique, the defender moves the forearm up and under the blocker's arm (see figure 8.8a) in an attempt to knock the blocker off balance and allow the defender to move around the blocker. If the defensive player is going to his right, he uses the left arm to rip. The right arm should push the blocker's left arm up and back. As the defender rips with the left arm, he steps by the blocker with the left leg.

In the swim technique, the defender extends the arm and "swims" over the top of the blocker (see figure 8.8b). If the defensive player is going to his right, he uses the left arm to swim. The right arm should push the blocker's left arm down and in. As the defender swims with the left arm, he steps by the blocker with the left leg. Once the arm is over the blocker, the defender pushes off and moves toward the quarterback. The swim motion and the push-off should be one continuous movement.

Players who have trouble executing either the rip or the swim technique often start the move too far away from the blocker or use the wrong technique for the opponent. The rip technique is often more effective for a shorter defensive player. A taller player often has more success using the swim technique. Try to match the physical stature of your players with the pass rush technique that will work best for them. To further practice these techniques, see the pass rush drill on page 159.

FIGURE 8.8 *(a)* Rip and *(b)* swim technique.

Spin Technique

In the spin technique, rushers use their hands and arms to spin around the blocker and get into the offensive backfield. The defender spins a full 360 degrees in getting around the blocker. The defender should start the spin by moving in close to the blocker, hitting the blocker in the chest with the forearm on the side of his spin. The defender then throws the opposite leg and arm around as the forearm pushes off the blocker.

A blocker can adjust his position to make a block if the player doesn't make solid contact with the blocker or if he tries to spin from too far a distance. Defensive players using this technique to rush the passer should make certain that they are close enough to the blocker to make good contact with their forearm as they start the spin.

Covering Receivers

On any offensive pass play, you will have a group of defensive players rushing the quarterback as he sets up to throw, and the remaining defensive players will be trying to prevent the ball from being caught if it is thrown by the quarterback. These remaining players are involved in what is called the pass coverage. These players usually include the defensive backs and the linebackers. The primary objective in covering receivers is to stop them from catching the pass, and if they do, to make certain that they are tackled immediately. The defense must be able to cover the receivers to stop the offense from moving the ball through the air.

Proper Alignment

In a proper alignment, the defensive corners should line up 5 to 7 yards off the wide receivers. The safeties should line up 8 to 12 yards deep off the tight end or slot receiver. If you are playing only one safety, she should line up deep in the middle of the field. From this position, the corners and safeties are in position to make plays if the offense runs or passes the ball.

Backpedal

When an offensive play begins, the defensive backs need to start moving away from the line of scrimmage until they determine whether it is a running or passing play. Running backward—backpedaling—is the initial movement your defensive backs will make at the start of every play. The backpedal should start with a step backward with the back foot and a push off the front foot. As players backpedal, they should bend forward at the waist, reach back with each step, and pull the body over their feet. Their arms should move in a normal, relaxed running fashion. They should keep their shoulders in front of their hips. Players should remain under control so that when receivers make their break to their final pattern to catch the ball, the defenders are ready to drive on them.

If players have trouble maintaining a smooth back-pedal, make sure that they are not leaning back and that their hips and shoulders are not behind their feet. They should keep the arm action the same as when they run forward.

Pass Coverage

You will consider two basic types of pass coverage as part of your defensive tactics. In man-to-man coverage, one defender is assigned to and stays with one receiver all over the field for the entire offensive play. In zone coverage, the defensive players drop—move into—a designated area of the field and are responsible for defending any pass thrown into that area.

Man-to-Man Pass Coverage   In a man-to-man defense, each player on the defense covers a specific offensive player (see figure 8.9). This defense works best when you have athletic players with speed who have the ability to run backward and react to the offensive player's pass pattern. Playing man-to-man pass defense requires mental toughness and a willingness to accept the challenge of staying with a receiver for the entire play. You must also consider the team you are playing against. If your defenders can match your opponent in speed and athletic ability, you may want to feature a man-to-man pass defense to provide tight coverage on your opponent's pass receivers.

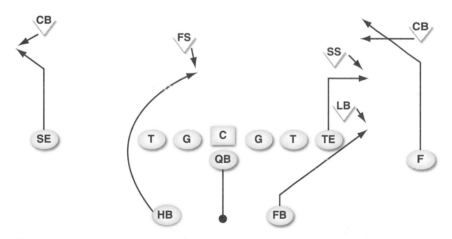

FIGURE 8.9   Man-to-man pass coverage (5-2 cover 1).

When using the man-to-man pass coverage, defensive players must keep their eyes focused on the belt region of the receiver they are responsible for. They should maintain a 3- to 4-yard cushion between themselves and the receiver. If the defender is losing ground to the receiver, he should execute a speed turn (pivot turn and run). Defensive players should learn to let the receiver take them to the ball by recognizing and reacting to the receiver's pattern. Players should look for the ball only when they are running with the receiver and can physically reach out and touch the receiver.

Zone Pass Coverage   In a zone defense, each defensive player covers a certain area of the field (see figure 8.10). Zone coverage is different from man-to-man coverage; the defensive players are assigned an area of the field to cover, and they focus their eyes on the quarterback, not on a particular receiver as they do in man-to-man pass coverage. Zone pass coverage can help guard against big offensive plays because help from another defensive player is never too far away. Mistakes made in zone defenses are often not as costly as those made in man-to-man defenses. This is a good type of pass defense to use when your opponent has superior speed. A disadvantage of the zone defense is that the opponent can overload a zone by putting more offensive receivers into the zone than there are defensive players. In this case, the defender in that zone should cover the deepest offensive player in the zone until the ball is thrown to an offensive receiver in front of him.

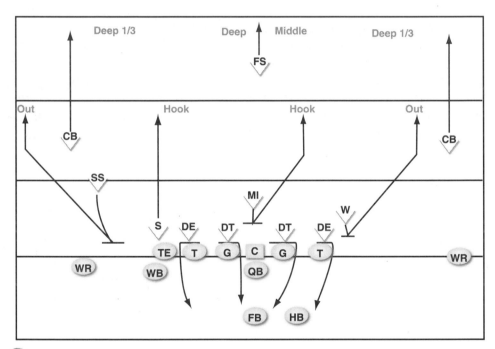

FIGURE 8.10   Zone pass coverage alignment (4-3 cover 3).

COACHING TIP   Breaking up the pass—either by deflecting the ball away from the receiver or by jarring the ball loose just as it is being caught—is a great defensive play and is equal to tackling the ballcarrier on a running play before the ballcarrier gains yardage. Even defensive linemen can bat the ball away if they read that the throw is coming when the quarterback drops his guide hand to throw.

When using zone coverage, players line up in their respective positions, and on the snap, players drop into their assigned areas (zones) on the field. Each player should focus on the quarterback and the ball and should watch for the ball to leave the quarterback's hand. When the quarterback is set and ready to throw, the underneath defensive players (the defensive players not assigned to cover a deep area of the field) should stop backpedaling, settle, and take short, choppy steps. The players assigned to a deep zone should continue backpedaling in their deep zone until the quarterback releases the ball. As the quarterback starts moving forward to throw, all the defensive players should break in that direction and allow the ball to take them to the intended receiver.

When drilling players on zone pass defense, do not always use receivers. Instead, use a cone or a shirt to designate the location of the wide receivers and tight end. In addition, have one player act as a quarterback; this player should drop back a full five steps, set up, step, and pass. This type of drill teaches the defensive players to focus on the quarterback and the ball and to break in the direction of the pass the minute the ball leaves the passer's hand. Once receivers are reintroduced into the drill, you may see that a defensive player is not reacting the instant the quarterback throws the ball. If this occurs, you should immediately check to see where the defender is looking. Is he looking at the receiver running in his zone instead of looking at the quarterback?

COACHING TIP In a game, if the quarterback is completing passes over the heads of the defensive players in the underneath zones, make sure that these players are not stopping their drop or coming up in reaction to an offensive receiver crossing the field in front of them. The defenders should continue to drop back as long as the quarterback is dropping back.

For more practice using zone coverage, see the drills on the top of page 163 and on page 166.

Defensive Tactics

Just as offensive coaches have to take an inventory, so do defensive coaches. Here are some of the attributes you should look for when evaluating your defensive players:

- The ability to make the play. First look for players who have a nose for the football. Much of football is difficult to put into words, but players who can "smell the ball" (i.e., players who seem to have an innate sense for where the ball is going) will be there to make the play. These players may not be the biggest, strongest, or fastest players. Therefore, you should look hard for this ability in your players.

- Agility, speed, and toughness. Defensive players need to be agile and fast, as well as hard-nosed. For example, linebackers must be tough enough to fill their run gap and fast enough to get to their starting point on passes.

- The knowledge to play according to down and distance. This is another huge asset. The timing of a play on short yardage is faster than on long-yardage attempts. Defenders must always be aware of the situation at hand.

Once you have evaluated your defensive players, it is time to develop the defense. Every defensive scheme has a purpose. A scheme can be designed to blitz (rush the passer), penetrate, pursue, contain, or perform in various ways to disrupt or stop the offense when they run the ball. You can align the 11 players that make up the defensive team in a variety of ways. This alignment indicates the number of players from each defensive group (defensive line, linebackers, and defensive backs) that you have on the field for any play. Your defensive alignment must capitalize on the team's strengths and compensate for its weaknesses.

You should choose your defense based on how many linemen you have compared to how many linebackers you have. If you have a somewhat big, slow team, you may be more successful using four linemen and three linebackers. This is called the 4-3, or even, defense; in this defense, the offensive center is uncovered. Such a defense is helpful in trying to control and contain the offense. If most of your players are smaller and more active, you may want to use three linemen and four linebackers. This is called a 3-4, or odd, defense; in this defense, there is a defensive player over the offensive center. With the 3-4, you can do more blitzing and take advantage of your team's quickness.

Once you have determined your style of defense, stay with it.

Setting Goals

Following are the three most important goals that a defensive team can strive to accomplish:

1. **Prevent the easy touchdown.**

Although the obvious objective on defense is to keep the opposition from scoring, a more functional objective of defensive play is to prevent the opposition from scoring the easy touchdown with a long pass or a long run. If you have a defense that challenges every yard, your opponents will have to earn every point they score. Emphasize to your defense that stopping a team on third down is vital. You should praise your defensive players for preventing third-down conversions and forcing the opponent to punt the ball, giving your offense more opportunities to produce.

2. **Get possession of the ball.**

The defensive team may gain possession of the ball by preventing the opponent from getting a first down on four downs, forcing a punt, recovering a fumble, or intercepting a pass. Players, especially defensive backs, should be cautioned never to gamble on an interception if missing the ball can result in a touchdown. Even if a team goes for a fourth-down try on a long bomb (some coaches think this is as good as a punt), tell your players not to try for an interception unless they have an open field. Knocking the ball down can give you better field position than an interception on fourth down.

3. **Score.**

The defense can score by returning a punt, a fumble, or an intercepted pass. The defense can also score by downing the ballcarrier in the offensive team's own end zone for a safety.

In addition to these three important goals, you must also be flexible; understand the differences between man-to-man and zone coverages; teach your players attacking, contain, and pressure defenses; and keep your defense fun. Finally, as your players advance, you will teach them how to read the offensive plays.

Flexibility

Team defense involves a group of players performing their individual techniques for the good of the team. Get the right players at the point of attack at the right time, and your team will be successful.

The offense's position on the field, the score, the time left in the game, and the type of offense your team is facing are all factors that influence the defense that you should run. You must prepare the defense to cover various formations and series of plays. For example, if the offense lines up with a wingback and is running the ball successfully to that side, you could slant your entire defensive line into the gaps in that direction. If the offensive team is employing a spread formation using three or four wide receivers, you may want to use a four-deep coverage and substitute an extra defensive back into the game for a linebacker or lineman. This is called a nickel defense. Substituting two defensive backs is called a dime defense.

By knowing the mechanics of football and learning as much as you can about the strengths and weaknesses of your defense, you will be able to make the proper adjustments during the game. You should also consider limiting the defense according to the skill level of your team. It is more effective to run a few defenses well than to run many defenses poorly. Remember, a player who is too busy thinking of what his assignment should be will not be as aggressive, and a confused player will hurt the defensive team concept.

Defensive Alignments

Let's take a closer look at the different types of defensive alignments to see how your choice of coverage can affect the game.

Man-to-Man Defense

In man-to-man defense, each player on the defense is assigned a specific offensive player to cover. This defense works best when you have athletic players with speed. Inexperienced or slower players tend to get beat more often in one-on-one situations, leading to big gains or scores for the other team.

Think in terms of the team you are playing. If they have fast, athletic receivers, you may want to play a zone defense to reduce the risk of getting beat for a big play. Consider how your opponents are performing—as well as the abilities of your own players—when deciding whether or not to use man-to-man coverage.

Most offenses will set a player in motion to get a presnap read on the defense, so opponents will have an easy time reading man-to-man coverage. Some defenses will cover man-to-man with the inside–outside responsibility changing as a receiver crosses the face of the opposite defender; however, crossing patterns may require the defense to switch to zone coverage.

Zone Defense

In a zone defense, each defensive player is assigned a certain area of the field to cover. A zone can help guard against big plays, because defensive help is never too far away. Mistakes made in zone defenses are often not as costly as those made in man-to-man defenses. A disadvantage of using a zone is that the opponent can overload a zone; in this case, the defender in that zone should cover the deepest offensive player in the zone until the ball is thrown to a different player.

When using the zone defense, your players should remember to line up as wide as the widest and to cover as deep as the deepest. A player can travel one-third the distance that the ball travels if he keeps his eyes on the passer.

By carefully analyzing the abilities of your opponent and your own team, you will be better prepared to make a proper decision on whether to use man-to-man or zone coverage. In addition to knowing how and when to use those coverages, you must know the basics of attacking defense, pressure defense, and contain defense.

Attacking Defense

Use the attacking defense when the offense moves the ball well or if your defense is particularly strong. When using the attacking defense, you should adjust your basic alignment based on what your opponent is doing. For example, if the other team is running the ball up the middle at your linebackers, switch to a defense that puts a defensive line player in the middle who can move across the line of scrimmage through the gaps between the offensive blockers. This forcing style will disrupt the blocking of the offensive play, and your team may gain the advantage.

COACHING TIP You should incorporate the best physical skills of your defensive players into your defense and then work to perfect these strengths. This is more effective than trying to teach every type of defense to your players.

Pressure Defense

A pressure defense uses eight players within 5 yards of the line of scrimmage who can rush or be in position to play the run (see figure 8.11). One or more linebackers are assigned to blitz—charge across the line of scrimmage—through predetermined gaps the instant the ball is snapped. The pressure defense forces the offensive team to make mistakes. An example of this type of pressure is when the defense forces the quarterback to throw the football before he is ready by rushing the linebackers in addition to the defensive linemen. The pressure defense also changes the tempo of the game, preventing the opponent from retaining possession of the football and driving down the field.

Use the pressure defense when you are confident in your players' abilities and techniques. This is important because in this defense your defensive backs are isolated one on one with their receivers and may not get help from the safety.

The pressure defense provides a good change-up (as opposed to being the defense you use on every down). Have it ready to use in all down-and-distance situations where you need added pressure across the line to stop the offensive team. You may not want your defensive backs playing man-to-man pass coverage for the entire game, but you can use the pressure defense when you think

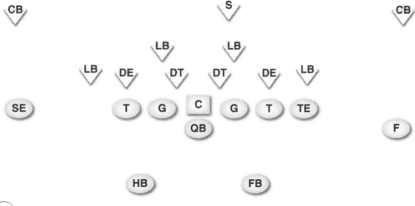

FIGURE 8.11 Pressure defense alignment (4-4 defense).

that they can execute the pass coverage for a few plays without being beaten on a deep pass route. If you find a blitz that gives the offense trouble or that they cannot pick up, keep using it until they make the proper adjustment.

When using pressure defense, teach your defensive players the following points:

- Faking the blitz occasionally will prevent the offense from gaining a presnap read.

- A pressure defense uses man-to-man pass coverage, and the defenders try to bump the receivers as the receivers start to run their pass routes.

- Designated linebackers attack the line of scrimmage on the snap, trying to disrupt the offensive players' blocking schemes.

- Defensive players can jump up into the line of scrimmage and then retreat. They can loop on their pass rush. The defense can overpower an offense by rushing more defensive players on one side of the ball than there are offensive players to block.

Contain Defense

The contain defense plays a little softer than the attacking or pressure defense. In a contain defense, the goal is to keep the offense from getting outside or deep. This type of defense requires disciplined players who fully carry out their assignments. It is effective in normal and long-yardage situations just before the half and at the end of the game to ensure a victory. Effective tactical coaching is very important to the success of a contain defense. The defensive players must be able to recognize formations, types of running plays, and types of passes—and they must adjust in order to stop the play.

In a contain defense, the end player on the line of scrimmage—which could be a defensive end, a linebacker, or a defensive back—is responsible for contain (for turning the ballcarrier back to the middle of the field). This player must be aligned and in position to be able to react to any ballcarrier who tries to run outside of him. After defensive players read their keys, they first control the gaps or areas of the field that they are responsible for and then react to the football. The defensive backs may use zone coverage on passes to ensure that the receivers do not get behind them. Figure 8.12 shows a sample alignment for a contain defense.

COACHING TIP If you find that defensive players are late in moving to their assigned gaps, make sure that they are lining up so that they can see the center snap the ball and can move with the movement of the ball.

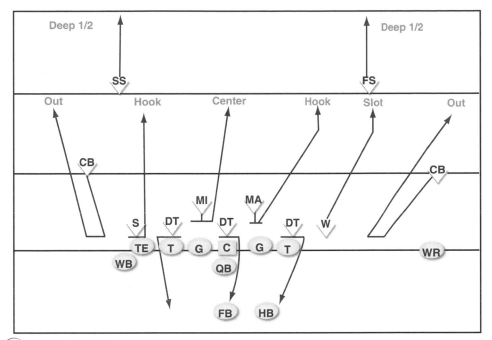

FIGURE 8.12 Contain defense alignment (3-4 cover 2).

Reading the Play

You should try to ensure that your defensive players have fun, and one way to increase their enjoyment is to teach them how to read offensive plays. This is a more advanced skill, so you should stick to just a few reads and be sure to keep things as simple as possible.

The most basic read is made by keying in on an opponent's formation, tendencies in play selection, or individual player cues. For example, the first key for defensive linemen or linebackers is the player directly in front of them, then the offensive player to their right or left. The movement of the player directly in front of the defensive player should alert the defensive player to a run or pass play. If the offensive line player or blocking back sets up to pass protect, the defensive players can assume that it's a pass play, and they should focus on covering their receiver. If the defensive players see the offensive line player or blocking back perform a drive block, they can anticipate a running play and move into position to stop the ballcarrier. If the quarterback drops behind the running back, the draw play is not possible, so your defenders can drop deeper into their zones.

> **COACHING TIP** Everyone should hold to a standard of ethics that reflects the spirit of the game. However, some coaches will employ trick plays, and you need to keep your defense alert to this possibility. When your opponents spend an inordinate amount of time in the huddle, expect a trick play.

In addition to paying attention to what the offense is doing, defensive players also need to understand their team's defense for the play, because the type of coverage will affect the decisions they make. For example, with both zone and man-to-man pass coverage, defensive backs can look in at the quarterback at the start of the play to try to pick up cues that the quarterback is sending. In man-to-man coverage, however, after two steps, the defensive back must refocus on the wide receiver. This defender will learn to read the receiver's body position. For example, if the receiver is running tall, he is not likely moving into a deep pass pattern.

Reading what the offense will do next is an important skill for every football player to have. Learning this skill will not only present a challenge for your young players, but will also bring a new level of energy and excitement to your practice.

Defensive Drills

Defense involves more natural instincts than the skills needed for offense. In most cases, defensive players who react rather than think are best. Following are drills based on the four pillars of defense—force, contain, pursuit, and coverage—what defensive players need to know in order to be successful.

➤ FRONT-ON TACKLING

Players are divided into two groups and are positioned as shown in the diagram: one group of ballcarriers and one group of tacklers. On the coach's command, the first ballcarrier in line and the first tackle in line start toward each other at half speed. At 5 yards, the tackle explodes off the left foot and makes contact with the left shoulder pad to make the tackle. The tackle must remember to keep the eyes up and not tackle with the helmet. Players switch lines after each player has had a turn.

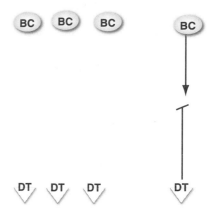

➤ PASS RUSH

Players divide into two groups of five defensive line players and five offensive line players positioned directly across from each other as shown in the diagram. Another player acts as the quarterback and is positioned as shown in the diagram. The coach indicates a pass rush technique and indicates which defensive line player and offensive line player go first. The coach signals the snap count to the offensive player and calls out a cadence to start the drill. On the coach's command, the defensive player rushes the quarterback until the whistle is blown. The defensive linemen and offensive linemen start at half speed until they have mastered the pass rush techniques. Players rush one at a time to avoid injury, and the coach should work on one technique at a time. Players switch positions after the rush is completed, and the drill is repeated.

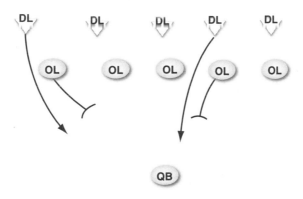

➤ SHORT-YARDAGE AND GOAL-LINE TECHNIQUE

Line up five defensive linemen against five offensive linemen on the goal line with a ballcarrier 7 yards deep in the backfield. The defensive linemen are trying to beat the offensive linemen across the line of scrimmage and prevent the ballcarrier from scoring a touchdown. The defensive linemen win the drill if they prevent the offense from scoring a touchdown. The offensive linemen win if the ballcarrier crosses the goal line.

Defenders must focus on keeping their shoulders low and elbows bent, creating a tail-up stance for a scoop charge. Using the lineman technique, they fire out low, under the pads, and lift upward.

To take this drill to the next level, introduce a middle linebacker, who exchanges gap assignments with the down linemen. This will help your defensive players with gap assignments. Although the offense knows the starting count and will have a jump start, they do not know where defensive gap responsibilities are.

➤ CONTAIN DRILL

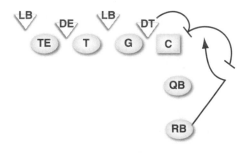

This drill uses six offensive players as follows: a center, guard, tackle, tight end, running back, and quarterback. (If you have enough players, include a backside guard.) This offensive alignment is referred to as a half line. The defense consists of a defensive tackle, a defensive end, and one or two linebackers depending on the front you are practicing. Players will rotate from quarterback to running back to blocker to a defensive position. The coach will set up the alignment. Any defender assigned to contain must first deliver a blow to the blocker he is lined up over (usually the tight end), keeping his outside arm and shoulder free. Emphasize to players that they should not let anyone outside of them. Most big plays occur when a quarterback or a ballcarrier breaks contain and gets outside. Initiated by the coach, various plays can evolve from here. The running back may attempt to kick the defender out or execute a hook block on the defender. On a running back kick-out block, the defender must squeeze down the running lane of the ballcarrier. If the defender is hooked, he must deliver a blow with his inside shoulder or forearm, keeping the play away from his outside and forcing it to his inside. Once your players have run this drill a few times, feel free to incorporate the following variations:

- Ask the quarterback to fake to the running back and then attempt to get outside of the defender.

- Ask the fullback to hook-block the defender as the quarterback attempts to sprint outside of the defender.

- Ask the quarterback to use an option run against the defender and pitch the ball outside to the running back, who attempts to get outside of the defender.

➤ ANGLE TACKLING

Players are divided into two groups and are positioned as shown in the diagram: one group of ballcarriers and one group of tacklers. On the coach's command, the first ballcarrier in line and the first tackle in line start toward each other at half speed. At 5 yards, the ballcarrier breaks at an angle to his right. The tackle breaks to his left at the same time. The tackle explodes off the right foot and makes contact with the right shoulder pad to make the tackle. Players switch lines after each player has had a turn.

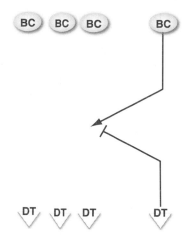

➤ CUTBACK RUNNER TECHNIQUE

Many running backs make big plays by baiting the linebacker to overrun the ball. Linebackers, along with three offensive linemen and one running back, are involved in this drill. The coach stands behind the first linebacker in line and points in the direction that he wants the running back to run. The coach then uses a starting count or yells "Go!" to initiate the drill. The linebacker shuffles toward the hole with his shoulders square to the goal line 1 yard behind the ballcarrier; when the ballcarrier cuts up toward the line of scrimmage, the line-

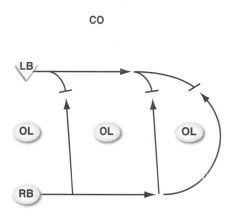

backer is in position to fill from the inside to a front-up position for the tackle, thus eliminating the most dangerous running play—the cutback.

Remind the linebacker to trail the ballcarrier a little so that once the ballcarrier declares which way he is going, the linebacker can front him up. Defenders should always keep their shoulders up, using the widest part of their body to tackle, rather than trying to just tackle with their arms. If the linebacker is unable to stop the running back, you should stop the play to provide direction as needed and then start the drill over again. Be sure to remind players that this is one of the most important defensive drills, because bigger plays normally occur when running backs see openings and cut back.

➤ FEET-FREE DRILL

This drill requires three offensive blockers, a running back, and a linebacker. The offensive blockers come out on the line on their hands and knees, across from the linebacker. The coach stands behind the linebacker and signals for one or multiple blockers to scramble on his call. Once the play is initiated, the blocker or blockers who were told to scramble do so while the running back makes his move. This drill teaches the linebacker to keep his hands in front of him and to protect his feet and legs. The goal for the linebacker is to use his free arms and hands to tackle the running back. He must keep his feet and legs free of the blockers (who are still on their hands and knees) as he shuffles down the line to meet and tackle the ballcarrier, who is attempting to turn up before reaching the sideline. The purpose of this drill is to help the defender improve his footwork and provide him with an opportunity to fine-tune gamelike reactions.

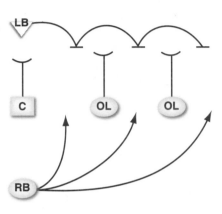

➤ THREE-DEEP ZONE DROP

Defensive backs position themselves as shown in the diagram. The coach designates which defensive back drops first. This defensive back assumes a proper stance, and on the coach's command, drops into the proper zone using the backpedal technique. As the defensive back drops, his focus should be on the coach and the ball. You may practice the strong safety's drop by having the defensive back sprint to get width, swing the inside leg around, and then move into the backpedal. After the defensive back has dropped 7 or 8 yards, the coach can raise the ball, point in the direction of a pass, and then throw the ball. The defensive back should roll over his foot in that direction and break to the area of the pass. Players drop one at a time and repeat the drill as an entire group. A change-up to this drill is to have the defensive back execute a speed turn and recover to look over his shoulder to the quarterback. This drill can also be adapted for a two-deep zone by designating two defensive backs to act as safeties and aligning them properly.

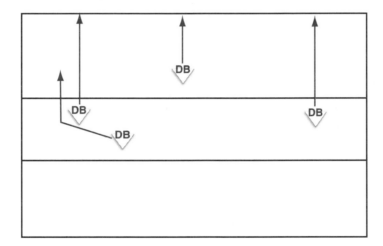

➤ TIP DRILL

Defenders form a line facing the coach, who acts as a quarterback. The coach throws to the first player in the line, who tips the ball into the air. The second defender in line must adjust to the tipped ball. This player can do either of the following:

- Catch the ball, yell "Fire!" and sprint up the nearest sideline for a touchdown.
- Tip the ball to the third defender behind him.

Repeat the drill until all defenders have executed the drill.

➤ MAN-TO-MAN COVERAGE

A defender and a receiver line up across from one another. The receiver attempts to beat the defender by baiting him with a cue that is opposite what the pass route will be. Deep passes should look like short breaks, and in cuts should look like out cuts. The defender needs to read the receiver while keeping a distance cushion until he can close on the route.

A good defender never crosses his feet or opens his hips until he knows the receiver's intent. Telling the defender to look through the receiver to the quarterback should also help; the defender can read the intent of the quarterback by his drop and passing action.

Timing is important in this drill. A receiver has only about two seconds to fool the defender. The defender needs to be able to read the situation without overcommitting. Remind defenders to remain in their backpedal. To modify the man-to-man coverage drill, indicate a fourth-quarter scenario where your team is trailing. This can help increase the intensity of the drill.

➤ FOOTWORK DRILL

Four pass defenders line up facing the coach, who acts as a quarterback. When the coach drops back, the defensive backs drive to their starting point (12 to 15 yards deep in the middle of their zone). The defenders keep their hips open and their shoulders over their feet and square to the line of scrimmage while they are reading the coach. The coach's action will give the defenders a read so they can react on the play. At this point, the coach can do one of three things:

1. Put the ball in a running back's hands (another defensive player who serves as a running back for this drill) for a draw play to the running back (see figure a); the coach can simply lower the ball as in a handoff.

2. Plant his back foot and run forward (as in a quarterback draw; see figure b). If it is a draw play, the defenders will plant and drive forward without taking a false step.

3. Continue to drop back for a pass play (to another defensive player serving as a receiver in this drill; see figure c). When the coach's guide hand (e.g., left hand for right-handed coaches) comes off the ball, the defenders should level up and break to the ball. Good defenders have the ability to travel one-third the distance of the passing yardage of the ball.

If a defender gains possession of the ball, the defender should call out "Fire!" and sprint up the nearest sideline for a touchdown.

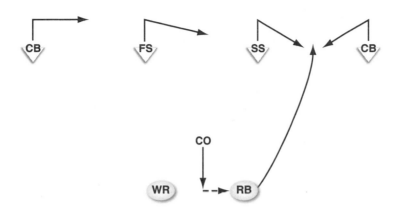

a

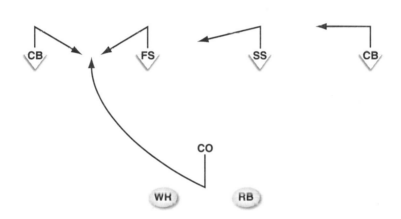

b

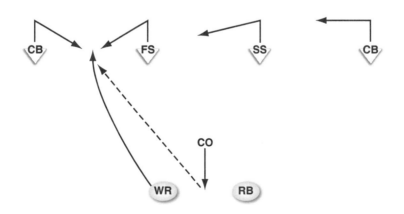

c

➤ ZONE COVERAGE

The fundamental principle of zone coverage is that a defender who breaks when the passer releases the ball can travel one-third the distance that the ball is thrown. To execute zone coverage, a defender must be aware of the quarterback, must keep his shoulders over his feet in a balanced shuffle, and must get to the middle of his zone. The defender must break step to the ball as the ball is released, drive to the ball and not the receiver, and intercept the ball at its highest point. The defender should imagine that all passes are thrown to him.

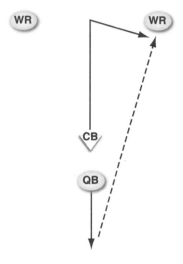

Have two receivers line up 15 yards apart from each other and facing the quarterback. One defender is lined up over the quarterback. When the quarterback drops back, the defender drops to the middle zone between the two receivers. Once the defender is at the same depth as the receivers, he levels his hips and breaks in the direction of the ball, which can be thrown to either receiver. The defender should be able to intercept the ball if he has executed the proper cover technique.

➤ FILLING YOUR GAP RESPONSIBILITY

Use either players or blocking shields to show and align the gaps. The drill calls for a four- or five-player front (a 4-3 or 3-4). Ideally, all seven defensive front players, including linebackers, should be on the field. One offensive back lines up against the defense. The coach stands behind the defense, indicating to the offensive back to run straight ahead, to the left, or to the right. The coach calls out defensive plays (alignments and stunt responsibilities), and each defender fills his gap or pass rush lane according to the call.

This is a good review of defensive fronts. The defense reviews the situation and reacts. The drill helps to ensure that defenders know their gap responsibilities in a gamelike situation (setting up the defense and then reacting to the direction of the play). Ideally, you will be able to review all of your defensive fronts with this drill, which is normally set up in 10-minute segments. For example, you could do eight fronts in 10 minutes.

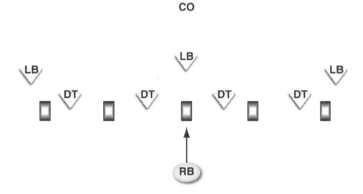

➤ FIVE YARDS OUTSIDE YOUR OWN COLORS

The primary reason for defenders to stay 5 yards outside their own colors (i.e., 5 yards outside of a defensive teammate pursuing a ballcarrier) is to maintain a proper pursuit angle toward the ballcarrier if the closest defender misses the tackle or if the ballcarrier cuts back across the field. The second reason is that one blocker cannot block more than one defender if the defenders are spread apart as they converge on the ball.

In this drill, your full defensive unit works together, using their pursuit angles. The drill begins when the ball is pitched out to the running back. As the running back turns upfield, the defenders break out in pursuit. The first play-side defender pursues the ballcarrier with an aiming point 5 yards in front of the ball; the second defender is 5 yards back at a 5-yard angle to the defender in front of him; the third defender is 5 yards behind the second defender, again at a 5-yard angle to him; and so on.

No offensive blockers are used in this drill. The defenders simply work on their alignment against air.

SPECIAL TEAMS

A mistake in the kicking game—also called special teams—can cost your team major field position and even the victory. When two evenly matched teams compete, the special-teams units are often involved in the play that ultimately determines the winner. George Allen, hall of fame coach most known for his time with the Los Angeles Rams, was a proponent of spending one-third of the team's practice time working on special teams—in other words, the amount of time spent on special teams was equal to the amount of time spent preparing the offense and defense.

Special teams is an integral part of a successful football team. As the coach, you must remind all players that their contributions on special teams are just as important as their contributions on offense and defense. To maximize the contributions of players, you should keep assignments simple.

Kicking, coverage, and protection are equally important in special teams. With tryouts, you will discover natural kickers and punters. The better your kickoff and punt returns, the better your starting field position. On kick coverage, most successful teams consistently keep their opponents in their own territory. One of the biggest challenges in special teams is protecting the punter and then shifting into coverage mode to make the downfield tackle. In coverage, how effective your players play in the open field (in space) is more important than size. Practice will show those players who have a sense for coverage on kickoffs and punts. Choose good players who match up with their opponents. A good general rule is speed on speed and big players on big players. At the same time, you must also assign suitable players to protect your kicker or punter.

Rules of the Kicking Game

The following are rules that apply only to special teams. You should teach these rules to players as you coach the different phases of the kicking game.

- A player signals a fair catch by extending an arm above the head and waving it from side to side. The receiving player cannot hit or be hit after a fair catch, and the ball cannot be advanced after the catch.
- On a punt, the kicking team may down the football after the ball has hit the ground.
- No one on either team may block below the waist.
- No player on the receiving team may touch the punter or kicker unless the receiving team has blocked the kick or the kicker runs with the ball.
- A field goal is a scrimmage kick and uses the same rules as the punt.
- On a kickoff, after the ball has traveled 10 yards, it is a free ball and either team can gain possession of it.

SPECIAL TEA

In this chapter, we first discuss the technical skills you will teach your team. Then, we focus on the special-teams tactics you will use.

Special-Teams Technical Skills

The phases of the kicking game can be broken down into two general areas. The first area is when your team kicks the ball during a kickoff, punt, point after touchdown (PAT), or field goal. The second area is when your team receives a kick during a kickoff or punt return and when your team tries to block a PAT or field goal.

The kicking game may make up about one-third to one-fourth of a football game. A critical component at this time is having the correct players on the field. Coaches need to drill on this daily by calling out "Punt team" or "Return team" at any given time during practice to test the attention of the special-teams players. A player who participates on special teams must have his mind in the game at all times. Being absent mentally may cost the team a penalty or an opponent's score. As my high school principal said, "Be where you're supposed to be when you're supposed to be there."

Your players need to understand the basic technical skills involved with special teams, including the skills used on the punt team, the kickoff team, the placekicking team, the kickoff and punt return teams, and the PAT and field-goal block teams.

COACHING TIP Set up a specific time during practice for the entire team to concentrate on a phase of special teams. During this time, the team should work on corresponding phases of the kicking game. For example, in practice 1, focus on the punt and punt return team by practicing the fake punt (pass or run) and punt blocks if used. In practice 2, focus on the kickoff and kickoff return teams by practicing onside kicks and onside prevent team. And in practice 3, focus on the PAT and field-goal team and the field-goal block team by practicing fake field goals (run or pass) and the defense against the fake.

Punt Team

The punt team is the special-teams segment used most often during a game because teams almost always punt on fourth down. One challenge for the punt team is to mentally switch from an offensive protection mode to a defensive coverage mode as soon as the ball is kicked.

Two players are the most critical components of the punt team. The center, known as the long snapper, snaps the ball back between the legs to the punter, who can be lined up 10 to 15 yards away depending on the ability of the center. The punter catches the snap from the center and executes the punt. The remaining

players block the opposing players until the punter kicks the ball. After the punt, they run down the field prepared to tackle the opposing player who is attempting to run the punt back up the field.

Punt coverage involves organizing your punt team so that they can cover the punt and down the ballcarrier before he can advance the ball upfield. The punter should kick the ball for distance and keep it in the air long enough to give the coverage team time to get downfield and make the play.

"Bust momentum" describes the action of forcing a defender to straighten up on his attempt to rush the punter. Without body lean, the rusher will have difficulty blocking a punt. Blockers also need to get free of the defender so they can move down the field and tackle the returner. By using a palm shiver (striking the opponent with the palm of the hand, usually in an upward motion, to slow his charge and momentum) followed by a rip or swim pass rush technique, the blocker will be ready to cover more effectively. Ideally, your blockers should eventually form a half-circle cup around the returner, stopping him on all sides in order to prevent the run.

You should make sure that the players know that they must block first—until the ball is kicked—before they make their way down the field; otherwise, the punter will not have time to get the ball off.

Long Snapper

Long snapper may be one of the most important positions on a football team. Not only must a punt snap be accurate, but it must also have some speed. Sure, successful punt snaps go unnoticed, but a bad snap can cause lost yards, and an opponent can even score off a blocked punt. I know of a high school coach who had his son practice punt snaps all winter by taking a position at the back door in their kitchen and snapping down the hallway to the front door (15 yards). Bo Schembechler, eminent college football coach at the University of Michigan, was known for timing opponents' punt snaps during pregame warm-ups. Some players are an integral part of the team simply because they can snap a punt.

When centering to the punter, long snappers start with the feet even and then reach out to grip the ball as though throwing a forward pass with the snapping hand. The other hand rests lightly on top of the ball and guides the ball during the snap. In the stance, the shoulders are even and the back is level so that the shoulders and rear end are at the same height. When long snappers see that the punter is ready, they snap the ball with both hands back between their legs to the punter with as much force as possible, aiming for the punter's belt. As they snap the ball, they allow the hands to rotate to the outside. The long snapper's most important job is getting the ball to the punter.

If the long snapper throws the ball over the punter's head, this may indicate that the long snapper's back is not level. If the snapper's rear end is higher than her shoulders, the snap will be too high. Keeping the back level will lower the snap.

Punter

Teams punt on fourth down to turn the ball over to the opponent. The punting team's objective is to give the opponent a less favorable field position. Coach your kickers to follow these guidelines for punting successfully:

- Line up 10 yards behind the center.

- Stand slightly bent at the knees and waist, with feet shoulder-width apart and palms facing up ready to receive the ball. Once the ball is received (see figure 9.1*a*), take a short step forward with the kicking foot and extend the ball forward. Then, take a normal second step with the nonkicking foot and allow the hand opposite the kicking foot to come away from the ball.

- When the ball is dropped, there should be no movement at the elbows, wrists, or shoulders. The ball should drop parallel to the ground with the tip turned slightly in. Keep the distance of the drop short—imagine kicking the ball out of your hand.

- As the kick is made, the nonkicking leg should remain in contact with the ground, and the kicking leg should make proper contact on the center of the ball. The kicking leg will then extend and follow through (see figure 9.1*b*). Also remember that foot speed is not as important as making proper contact with the ball.

FIGURE 9.1 Proper kicking technique for the punter.

> **COACHING TIP**   Remind your players to keep their shoulders in front of their hips during the entire kicking motion.

The key to coaching punters is to teach correct technique and then allow them to practice and develop their rhythm. They should strive for consistency in height and distance.

Kickoff Team

The kickoff team is the team that will be on the field after you have scored and at the beginning of the game or the start of the second half. The kicker is the only player on this team who uses a special technique. The remaining 10 players on the kickoff team run down the field as the ball is kicked and try to get into position to tackle the returner, who is trying to run the ball back up the field (see figure 9.2).

Kickoff coverage is configured the same as punt coverage.

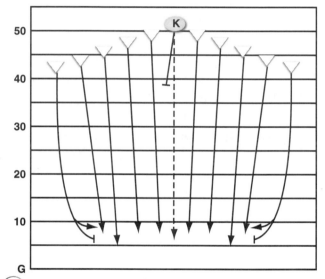

FIGURE 9.2   Kickoff team alignment.

Kicker

To kick the ball down the field as far as possible, the kicker must run at the ball to build momentum for the kick. To achieve this momentum, the kicker should do the following:

- Place the ball on the tee.
- Line up with the kicking foot directly behind the ball and the tee, and place the nonkicking foot to the side of the tee.
- Take one step back with the kicking foot.
- Turn and take approximately eight more steps straight back from the ball.
- Turn and make certain that the body is still in line with the ball.
- Turn and take five steps to the side opposite the kicking foot.
- Face the ball and take a short step forward with the kicking foot.
- Start the forward run to the ball by taking a short step forward with the kicking foot.
- Slowly build speed and momentum on the approach to the ball.

- Place the nonkicking foot 4 inches (10 cm) behind and 6 inches (15 cm) outside the ball, pointing straight down the field.

- Keep the shoulders forward, the eyes on the ball, and the kicking leg behind the body; allow the kicking leg and foot to swing in a nice arch to the ball.

- Hit the ball with the top of the arch on the kicking foot at a point 4 inches from the bottom point of the ball.

- Keep the head down throughout the kick and allow the kicking leg to follow through in a smooth motion.

- Become a safety and get in position in front of the path of the returner.

COACHING TIP If the kicker is not getting elevation on the ball, the plant foot may be too far away from the ball. This causes the kicking foot to make contact with the ball at the center of the ball or higher, resulting in a low kick.

Remainder of the Kickoff Team

The two outside players on the kickoff team should run down near the sideline and make sure that the kickoff returner cannot get to the outside of the field. Emphasize to your players that they should do the following:

- Stay in their assigned lanes relative to their teammates as they run down the field.

- Never follow a teammate's path down the field.

- Locate the ball over their inside shoulder, taking an outside–in approach.

- Avoid blockers on the same side the ball is being returned on. Use the hands to keep the feet free.

- Maintain control by shortening their stride as they near the ballcarrier so that they are in position to make the tackle.

COACHING TIP Players must sprint down the field, avoid blockers, then come under control (with the shoulders up and the knees bent so that the player is ready to react in any direction) as the kickoff returner makes his move. If players are missing tackles, remind them to shorten their stride, widen their base, and be prepared to go to the left or right as they near the ballcarrier.

Placekicking Team

Placekicking is the phase of the kicking game that you'll use when your team attempts to score points by kicking a point after touchdown (PAT) or kicking a field goal; your team will attempt a field goal if the drive has been stopped and the team is close enough to the opponent's goal line. During this phase of the kicking game, three players use special techniques: the kicker (who makes the kick), the holder (who catches the ball from the center and places it on the tee), and the center, also known as the short snapper (who centers the ball back to the holder). The remaining eight players block the opposing players so that the kick can be made. Players must not forget to cover the kick in the event of a missed goal.

Kicker

The two basic types of placekicks are the straight-ahead style and the soccer style. Both are equally effective. Kickers should follow these steps, regardless of the kicking style they use:

- Stand three steps behind where the ball will be placed (one and a half to two steps to the side for soccer style). The kicking foot should be slightly behind the nonkicking foot, and the eyes should be on the spot where the ball will be placed.

- Take a short step with the nonkicking leg and then a slightly longer-than-normal step with the kicking leg (see figure 9.3a).

- Plant the nonkicking foot about a shoe's length away from the ball, to the side of the ball. This foot should be pointed at the middle of the goalposts. At the same time, bend the kicking leg behind the body and use a smooth swing (see figure 9.3b).

- Point the toe to create a smooth, hard surface. Contact the ball on the large bone on top of the foot. The point of contact should be about 4 inches (10 cm) above the lower end of the ball.

- Use a full follow-through. Finish with the leg in line with the opposite shoulder (see figure 9.3c).

FIGURE 9.3 Placekicking steps.

COACHING TIP If the kicker misses either to the right or the left of the goalposts, make sure that the kicker's nonkicking foot is pointed at the middle of the goalposts.

Holder

The holder should be able to catch the ball with ease and have the dexterity to place the ball on the tee correctly. Once the kicking tee is placed on the ground 7 yards from the line of scrimmage, the holder should assume the position to receive the snap from the short snapper. Holders should follow these steps:

- Kneel with the back knee on the ground and the front leg up with the foot pointing at the center of the goalpost.
- Reach down with the back hand to make sure the tee is within reach.
- Look to see if the kicker is ready to make the kick.
- Place both little fingers and thumbs together to form the target for the short snapper.
- Catch the snap and guide the ball to the tee with both hands.
- Place the index finger of the back hand on the top point to balance the ball.
- Use the other hand to gently spin the ball to place the laces of the ball to the front.

COACHING TIP If holders have trouble catching the snap, make sure that their hands are placed properly with the thumbs together and the palms facing forward and up. Holders should be able to see their hands and the ball as they make the catch.

Short Snapper

When centering to the holder, the short snapper uses the same stance and technique taught to the long snapper (see page 172). The difference is that the distance of the snap is shorter, and the target area—the holder's hands—is lower than the waist-high target of the punter. Once the snap is made, the short snapper should bring the forearms up, ready to help block.

Remainder of the Placekicking Team

The remaining players on the placekicking team always block to their inside gap first when the ball is snapped. Work with your players to focus on the following:

- Use a minimum split, with the feet about a foot apart.
- Step back with the inside foot to gain power; keep the outside foot anchored.
- Lean to the inside. Stay square to the line of scrimmage.
- Block whoever comes inside, stopping the momentum of the rusher. Use a lifting motion on the block, and take the defender's body lean away.

Kickoff and Punt Return Team

The return phases of the kicking game come into play when your opponent is either kicking off or punting the ball. The players who use special techniques are the players who catch the kick and return it up the field. The other players' major assignment is to block for the return after they are certain that the ball has been kicked.

Kick Return Players

The players who return kicks must be able to catch the ball and must be able to run the ball after the catch. The players should line up in position to see the kicker or punter (before the snap). For both returns, two players should be lined up to return the ball—one player on each side of the field. Based on the flight of the ball, one return player calls out to the other, "I have it! I have it!" The other player moves up to block. Once the kick is made, kick returners making the catch should do the following:

- Move so that they are in front of the flight of the ball.
- Reach up with both hands, with the little fingers together, so that they can see both the ball and their hands as the ball comes down. Kick returners should see the ball make contact with the hands.
- Bring the ball into the body. The head should bob as the returner tucks the ball in securely and starts the return to the designated area of the field.
- Run the ball as far up the field as possible before being tackled.

COACHING TIP On the kickoff, you may find that your returner is tackled immediately and cannot return the ball. If this occurs, make sure that the blockers are dropping back and positioning their bodies between the coverage players they are assigned to block and the area designated for the returner to return the kick.

Punt return players have the option of (a) catching the punt and running with the ball, (b) allowing the punt to hit the ground and roll to a stop, or (c) catching the ball after signaling for a fair catch. Return players signal for a fair catch by waving one arm back and forth high above their heads. Players signaling for a fair catch cannot run after the catch, and opposing players cannot tackle them.

Blockers

The remaining players on the kickoff and punt return team should each be assigned a player to block during the kick return. Players should be sure that the ball is kicked and should then position themselves between their assigned player and the area (left, middle, or right) where the ball is to be returned. Blocking on kick returns is a specialty, because each player needs to keep on the block until the returner is safely past him.

Players should strive to keep their head on the upfield jersey number of the defender and to maintain running contact with him. This is called a shadow technique. When players are blocking a containing defender near the returner who is catching the ball, they must be sure to get their head in front of the defender, using a basketball screen technique to protect the kick returner.

Point-After-Touchdown (PAT) and Field-Goal Block Team

Keep your defensive team on the field whenever your opponent lines up to attempt a PAT or field goal. The opponent can still run or pass the ball, so defenders must stay alert and must be sure that the ball is kicked. Players not involved in pass coverage should rush across the line on the snap and try to get their hands up to deflect the kick. Caution players to never touch or run into the kicker

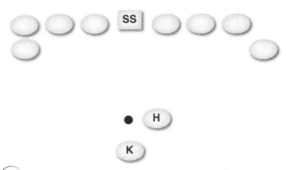

FIGURE 9.4 Specialist alignment for a PAT or field goal.

on any kick. If your players run into the kicker, this is a penalty. They can avoid this by focusing on a point 3 yards in front of the kicker and blocking the ball as it leaves the kicker's foot. See figure 9.4 for an example of the alignment for specialists on PAT or field-goal teams.

Special-Teams Tactics

Coaching special teams is a challenge in all levels of football, from the youth level to the professional ranks. The ability to play in space, or in the open field, requires a combination of skills that is unique to the sport of football.

The primary objective of special teams is to successfully execute the basic elements of the kicking game without making big mistakes. The second objective is to attack an opponent's weakness or to exploit a situation when it arises. Special teams requires thought and planning before playing games. The major areas of special teams include the following:

- *Kicking segment:* kickoff and punt, resulting in a change of possession and (you hope) poor field position for your opponent
- *Scoring segment:* PAT and field goal, resulting in the kicking team scoring points
- *Kick-returning segment:* kickoff and punt return, resulting in possession of the ball and gaining as much positive yardage as possible on the return
- *Kick-blocking segment:* PAT and field-goal blocking, resulting in stopping the opponent from scoring on a kick

Special teams requires special skills from some of your players, and also requires you to carefully plan when you will use each segment in a game. Well before the game begins, you must consider all the potential situations that could require the kicking game, paying special attention to how you might substitute on special teams in the case of injury. In this section, we first discuss the four major areas of special teams to help you better understand the tactics involved, then we focus on goals that you can implement with your special teams.

COACHING TIP Mental rehearsal of special teams can help in reviewing lineup positions, assignments, and physical execution. Coaches will often rehearse the lineup positions in meetings by calling out the squad positions. For example, the coach will shout, "Punt team, left end," and the player at the position will call out her name, "Smith!" This rehearsal will keep the players concentrating on their positions, which can be quite confusing in the heat of battle.

Kicking Segment

If you are not receiving the kick, you use your kickoff team at the start of the game or the beginning of the third quarter. You also use the kickoff team after you score a touchdown or field goal. Players on the kickoff team should be fast and should be good tacklers. One member must be able to kick the ball off a tee. On a kickoff, the ball is referred to as a "live ball," and either team can recover and gain possession after the kick travels 10 yards. The two outside contain responsibilities should be assigned to the fastest players on the kickoff team. You should also assign one player to be a safety, trailing behind the first line of coverage. If your kicker is fast, this would be a good assignment for him after he kicks the ball.

You normally use your punt team on fourth down—when your offense has failed to gain the necessary 10 yards for a first down. When punting from their own end of the field, teams typically punt from a tight formation with both outside players lined up close to the next outside player on the line of scrimmage. This helps prevent the opposing team from blocking the punt. When you are at your opponent's end of the field, you must be ready to decide what to do on fourth down. You can punt the ball, try for a field goal, or run an offensive play and try to gain the yardage needed for a first down. Anticipate what you must do so that you can make the decision without hesitation or calling a time-out. Players on your punt team should be able to first block for the punter and then tackle the opposing player returning the punt. Two players need specialized skills: The center must be able to snap the ball back to the punter, and the punter must be able to punt the ball. The members of the punting team can down the punt, stopping the return, but they cannot gain possession of the ball unless a member of the opposition touches the ball.

Scoring Segment

After scoring a touchdown, the scoring team has the opportunity to score an additional point after touchdown, or PAT, by running or passing to get across the goal line. To encourage the development of kickers, most youth football leagues will award a team two points for kicking the ball from a tee through the uprights and over the crossbar of the goalpost. Because of the difficulty in finding young players who can kick an extra point, many teams run or pass for this score. If you can develop a player with strong kicking skills, you can easily score by kicking a PAT, and you also have the potential to score three points by kicking a field goal on fourth down.

As a coach, you must know how far your kicker can kick the ball so that you can make the decision to try a field goal if the situation arises in the game. Kicking a PAT or field goal requires three players with special skills: the center (who snaps the ball to the holder), the holder (who catches the snap and places the ball on the tee), and the kicker. The remaining players on the team must be good blockers to ensure that the kicker has time to make the kick.

Kick-Returning Segment

Your kickoff return team will be on the field anytime your opponent lines up for a kickoff. Before the kickoff return team takes the field, you must tell them where you want the ball returned to—usually to the right, middle, or left side of the field. Typically, two players who can catch the kickoff and run with the ball will line up deep down the field. During pregame warm-ups, try to determine how far the opposing kicker can kick off so that you can position your returners at the proper depth. After one of the returners calls the ball, the other becomes a blocker. The remaining nine players on your kickoff return team should have good balance; they must be able to block opposing players as they run down the field. Remind all the players on the kickoff return team that a kickoff is a live ball and that they must recover and gain possession of the ball if it is kicked to them.

Your punt return team needs to be on the field anytime your opponent lines up to punt the ball. As with a kickoff return, line up two players deep down the field who have the ability to catch the punt and run with the ball. During the pregame warm-up, also try to determine the distance that the opposing punter will punt the ball so that you can position the two returners at the proper depth. The remaining nine players on the punt return team must be sure that the punter actually punts the ball; then they must block opposing players as they run down the field. Players should remember that once the ball is punted, your team has offensive possession of it, and every punt does not have to be caught or recovered. The players waiting to return the punt can (a) catch the punt and return it up the field, (b) signal and make a fair catch and take possession of the ball at the spot of the catch, or (c) let the ball hit the ground and roll until it is downed by

Goals for Special Teams

Special teams is the most critical area for gaining field position over your opponent. You can help your special teams be successful by setting goals for them and by developing a successful strategy. The location on the field where the offense starts each drive—the first play of a new series—is often governed by the execution of your special teams. This starting location—field position—is important to your team's success. The main goal of the special teams is to help the team win. Penalties must be avoided. Your special-teams players must understand that getting possession of the ball and returning the ball as far as possible up the field are important goals for all return teams. Finally, the teams kicking the ball—coverage teams—must understand that limiting return yardage gained by all kick return teams is equally important. When dealing with special teams, consider the following general rules:

- Know and adhere to the seven "dos" of special teams in order to reach team goals. These are as follows:

  1. Stay onside, and watch the ball.

  2. Avoid running into the kicker. Aim for a spot 1 yard in front of the punter's final leg swing and take the ball off his foot when blocking the punt.

  3. Focus on blocking players from the front on all returns, maintaining contact as long as possible as your ballcarrier passes you. If the number on the back of the jersey is visible, avoid the block.

  4. Keep blocks above the waist.

  5. Try to play error-free football, especially in the kicking game. Penalties can be 30 yards or more because of the distance the ball travels.

  6. Eliminate penalties that give the ball back to the offense or give them good field position.

  7. Win the battle of field position (on a kickoff, keep the opponents inside their 25-yard line). Good kicking and good coverage will accomplish this.

- Be aware of the following strategies that are important to the success of special teams:

  1. Kicking teams must make it a priority to eliminate bad snaps. Plan extra practice time for your short snapper, holder, and placekicker to work together. Also plan extra time for your long snapper and punter to work together.

2. The punt and kickoff coverage teams must make sure that the ball is kicked before they cover.

3. The return team must avoid being the victim of a fake play by always making sure that the other team has actually kicked the ball into the air. A fake punt or kick will usually occur when the opponent has good field position, close to either side of the 50-yard line. You must have all eligible receivers accounted for on every kick return in case of a fake kick that involves a pass play.

4. Coaches and players should alert their team to any big plays on special teams (e.g., onside kicks, turnovers, blocked kicks, and fake punts and field goals).

To keep your players on task, it is helpful to write down the goals for special teams. This can be done in many ways; see the progressive success chart that follows for an example.

Progressive Success Chart

Category	Goal
Kickoff coverage	Tackle opponent inside the 25-yard line (allow no long runs over 20 yards); successful onside kick
Punt coverage	Tackle opponent before he gains 7 yards (allow no long runs over 10 yards); attempt of a fake punt for a first down or more
Field-goal rush	Force the kick to be made in less than 1.5 seconds; no successful fake field goals
Kickoff return	Return the ball outside the 25-yard line (at least one run of 20 yards or more); no successful onside kicks
Punt return	Return the ball for 10 yards per attempt (at least two runs for 20 yards or more); no successful fake punts
Field-goal attempt	Solid blocking across the front and sides on each attempt; successfully attempt a fake field goal for a first down or more

an opposing player or the official blows the whistle to signal that the play has ended. Every player on the punt return team must remember that the opponent does not have to punt the ball—the opponent may try to run or pass for a first down from punt formation.

Kick-Blocking Segment

Anytime an opponent lines up to kick a PAT or field goal, you should have a group of 11 players on the field to try to block the kick (if this is allowed by your league). Players on the block team who rush the kicker must have the quickness and the desire to block the kick. These players should rush through the gaps between blockers and then raise their arms to deflect the kick. Remind every player on the PAT and field-goal block team that the opponent does not have to kick the ball; instead, the opponent may try to run or pass for a first down from the PAT and field-goal formation. Players who are not rushing the kicker should use a green dog technique (fake the rush to keep the potential receiver blocking). This assists in the coverage of eligible receivers in case the opponent tries to fake the kick and pass the ball. Caution every rush player on the block team to avoid running into the kicker. This is a penalty that usually results in the opponent getting a first down.

Special-Teams Drills

Unfortunately, practice time devoted to special teams is usually the last priority after offense and defense. Though not on the field as often as your offense or defense, special-teams units are an essential part of your football team. The prudent coach will understand the importance of giving every one of his players time to rehearse.

Following are drills designed specifically for the special-teams units. Practicing these gamelike situations will ensure fewer mistakes come game day.

➤ SNAP, PUNT, COVER, CUP, AND CATCH

Punt snapper is a critical position on the football field; a good punt snapper is considered a valuable member of the team, even in the NFL. Centering the ball for punts is a skill that must be practiced as often and as much as possible. The following is a good warm-up to use daily after prepractice stretching.

The first-string punt team lines up against air, and the center snaps the ball back to the punter. The blockers say aloud their blocking assignment and then release downfield when the ball is punted. The blockers now become tacklers (they locate the ball over their inside shoulder) as they close in on the punt returner, setting up for the tackle with eyes up and knees bent. The tacklers form a half-circle cup around the returner.

The value of this drill is in giving the center, punter, and returners a gamelike feel for those critical areas most commonly blundered—snaps, punts, and punt receiving. The blockers–tacklers also practice their open-space coverage and tackle positioning.

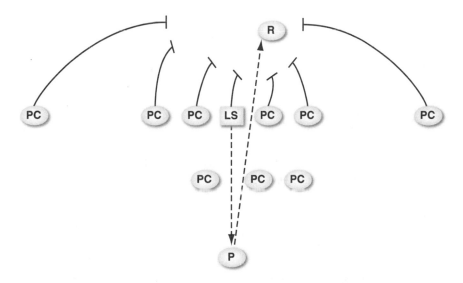

➤ POOCH PUNT

In this drill, the punter tries to set the punt within 30 to 40 yards. The emphasis is on punting the ball short so that it doesn't go into the end zone. The punter executes this by using more of his foot when kicking. The punter focuses on a high but short kick (usually inside the 10-yard line).

The punt team focuses on sprinting down the field to stop the ball. The first person down the field runs beyond the ball with his back to the goal line, serving as a backstop—his job is to ensure that the ball stays outside of the end zone. This play is for special situations when you want to keep your opponent backed up in poor field position—for example, when a field goal is too long and you are trying to preserve a lead late in the game or near the end of the first half.

➤ PUNTING DRILL

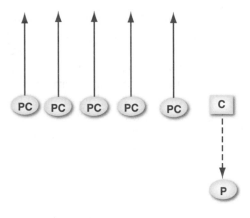

Players divide into two groups. The first group includes the center and the punter. The second group includes the punt coverage team. Both groups are positioned as shown in the diagram. The punter lines up 15 yards behind the center. When the center sees that the punter is ready, the center snaps the ball back to the punter with as much force as possible, aiming for the belt of the punter. When the punter receives the ball, the punter kicks the ball. When the ball is in the air, the punt coverage team charges downfield so that they can cover the punt. Break up the punt coverage team so that only one side goes at a time (e.g., everyone left of the center, as shown in the diagram, and then everyone right of the center). That way, you can rotate players and keep the drill going. You may also add a punt return group to enhance the drill.

➤ TWO-ON-TWO BLOCKING AND COVERING

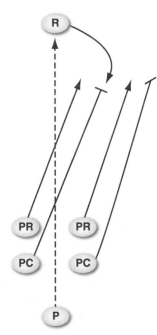

Two blockers for the punt team line up to block while two defenders line up over them. When the ball is punted (or a punt is simulated), the blockers become defenders, and the defenders aligned on them become blockers. The outside defender will attempt to keep the punt returner contained to his inside; the other defender will go directly to the point of the ballcarrier. The defenders can change responsibilities of contain and point person in order to confuse the blockers. The blockers attempt to keep the defenders away from the punt returner (keeping their shadowed position with their head on the upfield jersey number). This is a man-to-man drill, so be sure to pair up players of equal size and speed.

Tackling in the open field is not something you will want players to do every day. Getting into position to make an open-field tackle takes practice. As in all coverage drills, you should insist that the tacklers get into a good football position (shoulders up and knees bent) and cup in a semicircle at the ball. The emphasis here is gathering around the ball, breaking down, and being ready to tackle.

➤ RETURN DRILL

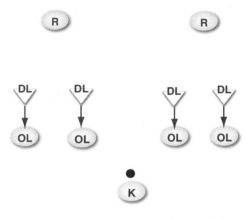

Players divide into two groups. The first group includes the kicker and the rest of the kickoff team on the line. The second group includes the kickoff returners and the rest of the kickoff return team on the line. Players position themselves as shown in the diagram. The kicker places the ball on the tee. Half of each group goes each time so that the drill can continue without breaks. The kickoff returners practice calling the ball, making the catch, and using the blocks, while the rest of the kickoff return team members practice making their assigned blocks.

➤ RUGBY KICKOFF RETURN

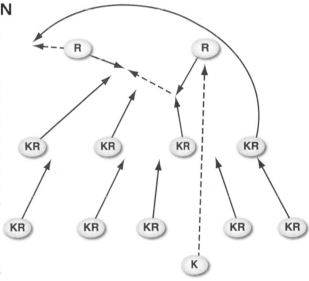

Your players will enjoy this drill more than they should, because it will be applied in games when you are behind with little time to play. Set up a scenario where it is late in the game and your team is behind, needing a touchdown to win. Kick the ball (or the coach can simulate the kick). On the kickoff return, your team trails the ballcarrier for the lateral (staying behind and outside the ballcarrier, rugby style, meaning that the players work together to lateral the ball to one another as they maneuver down the field). The goal is for your players to get as many laterals in as they can while taking the ball all the way to the goal line.

➤ KANGAROO KICK FOR THE ONSIDE ATTEMPT

The kangaroo kick is the most difficult for your opponent to catch when you are attempting an onside kick. In this drill, set up your kickoff team. The kicker aims for the top one-third of the ball, causing his kick to go end over end in a low trajectory, ideally for 7 yards. When the ball hits the ground, it jumps high over the heads of the opposing team's front line, giving the onside team a chance to beat the opponent to recover the ball. The ball must travel 10 yards before the onside team may regain possession. If the kick is executed properly, the kangaroo jump of the ball will allow your team to have an equal chance to regain possession of the ball. A good time for this drill is at the end of practice, before working on the two-minute drill, which is described on page 136.

➤ FIELD-GOAL PROTECTION AND COVERAGE

This drill helps with communication. You need a holder and kicker, and nine players serving as blockers. Set up a long field-goal situation (e.g., 5 yards farther than the distance your kicker can normally achieve). Then, have players practice the following steps:

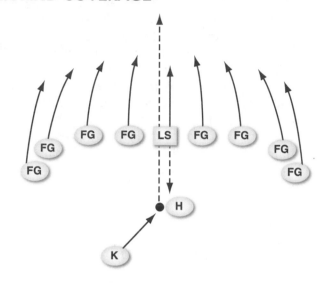

1. Huddle.

2. Break the huddle as the team leader says, "Remember to cover."

3. Kick the ball.

4. On a missed kick, the team practices covering (e.g., covering left).

➤ BLOCKING KICKS

Blocking kicks requires a special mind-set. A block occurs differently on a punt than on a field goal. On a punt, the rusher needs to aim for a spot in front of the punter's kicking foot. On a field goal, the rusher must attempt to get up high in the air, aiming 1 yard in front of the kicker (to pad for the kicker's landing) and up over top. Some players may often have a clear chance to block a kick but will never do so, while other players have a knack for it.

To practice this, line your players up so that one is the kicker and one is the defender; you can switch between punting and field goals to provide different blocking scenarios. Using a high-jump mat so blockers have a safe landing place is a good idea when you are first attempting this drill.

SPECIAL-TEAMS UNIT

➤ BALL WRESTLING

This drill can be set up in several ways. For example, you can stage a blocked punt or an onside kick. By staging an incident where the ball is available to two or more players, you can incorporate a lecture on the rule of possession. That rule states the following: If both players have possession of the ball when the whistle blows, the offense will retain possession. Therefore, it is critical for the players to cleanly wrestle the ball away from the opponent and to block him off with his back. Two or more players lined up on each side of the ball will have an equal chance at gaining possession of it when the coach calls out and simulates the ball position of a blocked punt, onside kick, fumble, or batted-away pass. Who will have the ball when the coach blows the whistle?

Coaching on Game Day

GAME DAY

Games provide the opportunity for your players to show what they've learned in practice. Just as your players' focus shifts on game days from learning and practicing to competing, your focus shifts from teaching skills to coaching players as they perform those skills in games. Of course, the game is a teaching opportunity as well, but the focus is on performing what has been learned, participating, and having fun.

In previous chapters, you learned how to teach your players techniques and tactics; in this chapter, you will learn how to coach your players as they execute those techniques and tactics in games. We provide important coaching principles that will guide you before, during, and after the game.

Before the Game

Just as you need a practice plan for what you will cover at each practice, you also need a game plan for game day. Your written game plan should consist of your best running and passing plays, as well as the plays you will call on third and 1 and on downs near the opponent's goal line. List the defenses you will use during the game, including the number of linemen, linebackers, and defensive backs you will use and the pass coverages and blitzes you have practiced. Also include your defensive call for third and 1 and your goal-line defense. Finally, the game plan should include your method of substitution—alternating players—and the plays that you plan to use during any phase of the kicking game. You may also list a trick play; players like these plays, and practicing a trick play is a good way to close practice each day. But do not fall into the mind-set that you need to trick your opponent. Good, solid plays are always more effective.

You have seen coaches refer to their game plans on the sideline. Here is a copy of a typical game plan, with adjustments for the unexpected:

Running downs	Passing plays	Special
Power 26-27	Pass 526-527	Dunk hook and ladder
Lead 34-35	Counter 356-356	Quick kick
Toss 38-39	Roll 857-957	HB pass

The game plan is important, and you cannot focus on it only on game day. Preparations should begin well before the first play of the game. Every practice should be a review of game situations and field-position play calling. Let's take a closer look at how you can prepare for game-day coaching.

Coaching Assignments

Game-day preparation should begin in the preseason when, as a staff, you decide and agree on the game-day responsibilities that each coach will assume. The staff should decide who will call the offensive and defensive plays, who will handle the special teams, who will substitute, and who will record the calls. As coaches arrive at the game, each staff member should know his or her game-day responsibilities and should prepare for the game just as the players do.

COACHING TIP Every staff member should be assigned a game-day responsibility, and the staff should work as one team during the game. While one member of the coaching staff calls all the offensive plays, another staff member can record the plays and the results, while another watches the opponent's defense to detect weaknesses that can be exploited. The same is true when the defense or special teams are on the field.

Sideline coaches and press-box coaches need to be coordinated in their assignments. Press-box coaches have the best view of the entire field. Therefore, they should be given the responsibility of checking alignments and personnel changes. Most leagues do not make sideline phones available, so these coaches' value will be in assisting with halftime adjustments.

Sideline coaches should communicate with the offensive, defensive, and special-teams units as they come off the field. The players should sit together as a unit so the coach can correct or make adjustments to their game. Sideline coaches should always note center–quarterback exchanges and center–punter snaps. A good coaching staff will continue to correct these phases of the game throughout the season.

Preparations at Practice

A day or two before a game, you should cover several things—in addition to techniques and tactics—to prepare your players for the game. First, you must decide on specific team tactics you want to use against the opponent. Second, you should discuss pregame particulars such as what to eat before the game, what to wear, and when to be at the field. It is also a good idea to walk through the steps for how the team will take the field and where the players will line up on the field for the warm-up. You should also review the group and team drills that will be used during the warm-up.

Deciding Team Tactics

Some coaches see themselves as great military strategists guiding their young warriors to victory on the battlefield. These coaches burn the midnight oil as they devise complex plans of attack. Team tactics don't need to be complex. The focus should be on consistent fundamentals and execution, moving the

ball on offense, and stopping long gains on defense. Also make sure that your team practices the sudden turnover, or the quick change from offense to defense. You should emphasize the importance of teamwork, the responsibility of every player fulfilling his role, and the importance of every player knowing his assignments on offense and defense. As you become more familiar with your team's tendencies and abilities, you can help them focus on specific tactics that will help them play better.

During the week, you should inform players of the tactics that you think will work and that you plan to use in the game. Pick out the five running plays, the three pass plays, and the four defenses that you think will have the greatest chance for success in the game. Try to practice this group of plays at every practice, and make certain that every player understands these plays and that the team can run them without error. Limiting the number of plays will allow you to repeat them during practice and instill in your players the confidence that they can execute the plays that will be called during the game. When practicing the plays, it is a good idea to chart the number of times each of your players handles the ball. Players will not be able to perform to their ability on game day if they have not had many repetitions in practice.

Depending on the experience and knowledge of your players, you may want to let them help you determine the first offensive play and the first defense that you will call in the game. It is the coach's role to help youngsters grow through experience.

COACHING TIP You may want to script the first series of plays you use in a game so that players and coaches can expect and look for the opponent's adjustments to your initial strategy.

Discussing Pregame Particulars

Players need to know what to do before a game—what they should eat on game day and when, what clothing they should wear to the game, what equipment they should bring, and what time they should arrive at the field. You should discuss these particulars with them at the last practice before a game. Here are some guidelines for discussing these issues.

Pregame Meal   In general, the goal for the pregame meal is to fuel the player for the upcoming event, to maximize carbohydrate stores, and to provide energy to the brain. Some foods digest more quickly than others, such as carbohydrate and protein, so we suggest that the player consume these rather than fat, which digests more slowly. Good carbohydrate foods include spaghetti, rice, and bran. Good protein foods include low-fat yogurt and boneless, skinless chicken. Some players might prefer to consume honey and oranges before each game for extra energy. Players should eat foods that they are familiar with and that they can digest easily. Big meals should be eaten three to four hours before the game. Of course, players who don't have time for a pregame meal can use sport beverages and replacement meals, although these are not a good replacement for the pregame meal.

Clothing and Equipment At the game, players need their team uniform, helmet, mouth guard, shoulder pads, girdle pads, thigh pads, knee pads, and shoes. They should wear their pants (with pads) and shoes and should carry their remaining equipment to the field and put it on there.

> **COACHING TIP** Having the entire team wear their game jerseys to school (if school rules permit) will help promote team unity and get the players focused on the upcoming game.

Time of Arrival Your players need to adequately warm up before a game, so you should instruct them to arrive 45 minutes before game time to go through the team warm-up (see the "Warm-Up" section on page 195). You can designate where you want the team to gather as they arrive at the field. Consider making a team rule stating that players must show up 45 minutes before a game and go through the complete team warm-up, or they won't start.

Facilities, Equipment, and Support Personnel

Although the site coordinator and officials have formal responsibilities for facilities and equipment, you should know what to look for to ensure that the game is safe for all players (see the "Facilities and Equipment Checklist" in the appendix on page 216).

You should arrive at the field 50 minutes before game time so you can check the field for potential hazards, check in with the site coordinator and officials, and greet your players as they arrive to warm up. If the officials don't arrive before the game when they're supposed to, you should inform the site coordinator.

Unplanned Events

Part of being prepared to coach is to expect the unexpected. What do you do if players are late? What if *you* have an emergency and can't make the game or will be late? What if the game is rained out or otherwise postponed? Being prepared to handle out-of-the-ordinary circumstances will help you if unplanned events happen.

If players are late, you may have to adjust your starting lineup. Although this may not be a major inconvenience, you should stress to your players that being on time is important for two reasons:

1. Part of being a member of a team is being committed to and responsible for the other members. When players don't show up, or show up late, they break that commitment and burden the entire team, because replacements must then be found for them.

2. Players need to go through a warm-up to physically prepare for the game. Skipping the warm-up risks injury.

An emergency might cause you to be late or to miss a game. In these cases, you should notify your assistant coach, if you have one, or the league coordinator. If notified in advance, a parent of a player or another volunteer might be able to step in for the game.

Sometimes a game will be postponed because of inclement weather or for other reasons such as unsafe field conditions. If the postponement takes place before game day, you must call every member of your team to let them know. If it happens while the teams are on the field preparing for the game, you should gather your team members and explain why the game has been postponed. Make sure that all your players have a ride home before you leave—you should be the last to leave.

If you are asked to decide between putting your players at risk or canceling a game, your decision will have a far-reaching impact. Your win–loss record is not the most important criteria in judging your coaching contributions. No youth coach has ever been selected to head up a Division I or NFL team. Always put your players first.

Communicating With Parents

The groundwork for your communication with parents will have been laid in the parent-orientation meeting, where the parents learned the best ways to support their kids'—and the whole team's—efforts on the field. You should encourage parents to judge success based not just on the outcome of the game, but also on how the kids are improving their performances.

If parents yell at the kids for mistakes made during the game, make disparaging remarks about the officials or opponents, or shout instructions on which tactics to use, you should ask them to refrain and to instead support the team through their comments and actions. These standards of conduct should all be covered in the preseason parent-orientation meeting.

When time permits, as parents gather at the field before a game (and before the team has taken the field), you can let them know in a general sense what the team has been focusing on during the past week and what your goals are for the game. However, your players must come first during this time, so focus on your players during the pregame warm-up.

After a game, quickly come together as a coaching staff and decide what to say to the team. Then, if the opportunity arises, you can informally assess with parents how the team did based not on the outcome, but on meeting performance goals and playing to the best of their abilities. Help parents see the game as a process, not solely as a test that is pass or fail, or win or lose. Encourage parents to reinforce that concept at home.

GAME DAY

Warm-Up

Players need to both physically and mentally prepare for a game once they arrive at the field. Physical preparation involves warming up. Conduct the warm-up similarly to practice warm-ups, focusing on practicing skills and stretching. Making sure your players are properly warmed up before the game can help reduce the potential for injury during the contest.

Develop the warm-up so that players practice techniques and tactics that will occur in the game, such as blocking, running the football, passing the ball, receiving the ball, kicking the ball, tackling, and covering receivers. You should also include the drills you use in your daily warm-up. However, this doesn't mean that extensive time must be spent on each skill. Limit the repetitions and then finish the warm-up period by having your offensive team run plays against the defensive team with little or no contact. At this time, you should also have your special teams run through a change of units—from punt team to field-goal team—in order to check personnel substitutions. Keep the warm-up sharp by running drills and plays quickly and keeping your players moving. Take time during the warm-up period to individually ask players questions about their assignments and to review with them the focus of the game plan.

During the warm-up, you should also do the following:

- Remind players of the techniques and tactics that they've been working on in recent practices, focusing on their strengths and the things they've been doing well.

- Remind players of the team tactics you focused on in the previous practice in preparation for this game.

- Focus players' attention on performing the tactics and skills to the best of their individual abilities and on playing together as a team.

- Remind players to play hard and smart—and to have fun.

During the Game

Throughout the game, you must keep the game in the proper perspective and help your players do the same. You should observe how your players execute tactics and skills and how well they play together. You will need to make tactical decisions in several areas. You must model appropriate behavior on the sideline, showing respect for opponents and officials, and you should demand the same of your players. You must also watch out for your players' physical safety and psychological welfare in terms of building their self-esteem and helping them manage stress and anxiety. Let's first focus on how you can help your team keep the proper perspective, and then we can focus on the tactical decisions for game-day performance.

Proper Perspective

Winning games is the short-term goal of your football program; the long-term goal is helping your players learn the skills and tactics and rules of football, how to become fit, and how to be good sports in football and in life. Your young players are "winning" when they are becoming better human beings through their participation in football. Keep that perspective in mind when you coach. You have the privilege of setting the tone for how your team approaches the game. Keep winning and all aspects of competition in proper perspective, and your young players will likely follow suit.

Tactical Decisions

As mentioned, you don't need to be a great military strategist; however, you will need to make tactical decisions in several areas throughout a game. You'll make decisions about who starts the game and when to enter substitutes, about making slight adjustments to your team's tactics, and about correcting players' performance errors or leaving the corrections for the next practice.

Advanced discussions and decisions by the staff can aid in tactical decisions during a game. When meeting with the staff to implement the game plan, you should discuss questions such as the following:

- Will your team be able to win with basic play calling because you have equal or better players than your opponent?

- Is there any phase of the game in which your team can dominate this opponent?

- Does this opponent have more talent than your team? Will your team need to create some momentum by blocking a punt, running a double-reverse pass, or gambling on fourth down?

One coach should be responsible for calling the offensive plays, one coach for calling the defensive plays, and one coach for making special-teams decisions. In all of these areas, the head coach should be able to add input. On small staffs, individual coaches may have to assume responsibility for more than one area.

COACHING TIP During the game, when a particular segment of the team is on the field, the focus should be on what is happening on the field and how to prepare for the next call.

Starting and Substituting Players

You should make sure that everyone on the team gets to play at least half of each game (you may need to adjust your strategy for playing time based on league rules). This should be your guiding principle as you consider starting and substitution patterns. We suggest you consider two options in substituting players:

1. **Substituting individually.**

Replace one player with another. This offers you a lot of latitude in deciding who goes in when, and it gives you the greatest combination of players throughout the game. With this method, keeping track of playing time can be difficult, but this can be made easier by assigning an assistant or a parent the task of charting the number of plays that each player has participated in. Be aware of the exact number of plays that your league's rules require each player to play.

When using individual substitution, you have the option of substituting players by series. You may tell players before the game that they will play two offensive series and then the substitute will play the next two series. Players will then know in advance when they should be on the field.

2. **Substituting by quarters.**

The advantage of substituting players after each quarter is that you can easily track playing time and that players know how long they will be in the game before they will be replaced. When substituting by quarters, you still need to keep track of the actual number of plays that each player is on the field.

At the youth level, every player deserves a chance to participate. Allowing each of your players to experience competing in the great game of football is a worthy mission.

Adjusting Team Tactics

For players aged 11 and under, you probably won't adjust your team tactics significantly during a game. Rather, you'll focus on the basic tactics, and during breaks in the game, you'll emphasize the specific tactics your team needs to work on. However, coaches of 12- to 14-year-olds might have reason to make tactical adjustments to improve their team's chances of performing well and winning. As the game progresses, assess your opponent's style of play and tactics, and make adjustments that are appropriate—that is, those that your players are prepared for. You may want to consider the following examples when adjusting team tactics:

- Does your opponent have slow or less skilled defensive backs? If so, you might want to emphasize your passing game.
- Does your opponent have skilled running backs who could break open long runs? If so, you might want to shift your defensive alignment to put more players on the line.
- Does your opponent always run on first down? If so, you might want to stack the line on first downs.
- Does the opposing quarterback tend to make poor decisions and rush passes when under pressure? If so, you might want to put more of a rush on the quarterback to try to create turnovers.

Knowing the answers to these questions can help you formulate a game plan and make adjustments during a game. However, don't stress tactics too much at this time. Doing so can take the fun out of the game for the players. If you don't trust your memory, you should carry a pen and pad to note which team tactics and individual skills need attention in the next practice.

COACHING TIP Have someone record every offensive and defensive call and the result of the play. Then, when that segment of the team is off the field, review the call sheet, noting successful plays and defenses. Repeat these calls until the opponent makes adjustments.

Correcting Errors

In chapter 6, you learned about two types of errors: learning errors and performance errors. Learning errors are those that occur because players don't know how to perform a skill. Performance errors are made not because players don't know how to execute the skill, but because they make mistakes in carrying out what they do know.

Sometimes it's not easy to tell which type of error players are making. Knowing your players' capabilities helps you to determine if they know the skill and are simply making mistakes in executing it or if they don't know how to perform it. If they are making learning errors—that is, they don't know how to perform the skills—you should note this and cover it at the next practice. Game time is not the time to teach skills.

If they are making performance errors, however, you can help players correct those errors during a game. Players who make performance errors often do so because they have a lapse in concentration or motivation, or they are simply demonstrating human error. Competition and contact can also adversely affect a young player's technique, and a word of encouragement about concentration may help. If you do correct a performance error during a game, do so in a quiet, controlled, and positive tone of voice during a break or when the player comes to the sideline after his series on the field.

For those making performance errors, you must determine if the error is just an occasional error that anyone can make or if it is an expected error for a youngster at that stage of development. An encouraging word and a coaching cue (such as "Remember to follow through on your passes") may be just what the player needs. Knowing the players and what to say is very much a part of the art of coaching. If a player seems down or frustrated when you are correcting such errors, remind the player that even the great professional athletes began their careers by correcting and improving their skills.

COACHING TIP Designate an area on the sideline where players gather after coming off the field. In this area, you can speak to them either individually or as a group and make necessary adjustments.

Coach and Player Behavior

Another aspect of coaching on game day is managing behavior—both yours and your players'. The two are closely connected.

Coach Conduct

You very much influence your players' behavior before, during, and after a game. If you're up, your players are more likely to be up. If you're anxious, they'll take notice, and the anxiety can become contagious. If you're negative, they'll respond with worry. If you're positive, they'll play with more enjoyment. If you're constantly yelling instructions or commenting on mistakes and errors, it will be difficult for players to concentrate. Instead, you should let players get into the flow of the game.

The focus should be on positive competition and on having fun. A coach who overorganizes everything and dominates a game from the sideline is definitely not making the game fun. So how should you conduct yourself on the sideline? Here are a few pointers:

- Be calm, in control, and supportive of your players.

- Encourage players often, but instruct during play sparingly. Players should focus on their performance during a game, not on instructions shouted from the sidelines.

- If you need to instruct a player, do so when you're both on the sidelines, in an unobtrusive manner. Never yell at players for making mistakes. Instead, briefly demonstrate or remind them of the correct technique, and encourage them. Tell them how to correct the problem on the field.

You should also make certain that you have discussed sideline demeanor as a coaching staff and that every coach is in agreement on the way the coaches will conduct themselves on the sideline. Remember, you're not playing in the Super Bowl! At this level, football games are designed to help players develop their skills and themselves—and to have fun. So coach in a manner at games that helps your players do those things.

Player Conduct

You're responsible for keeping your players under control. Do so by setting a good example and by disciplining when necessary. Set team rules for good behavior. If players attempt to cheat, fight, argue, badger, yell disparaging remarks, and the like, it is your responsibility to correct the misbehavior. Initially, this may mean removing players immediately from the game, letting them calm down, and then speaking to them quietly, explaining that their behavior is not acceptable for your team—and that if they want to play, they must not repeat the action.

You should consider team rules in these areas of game conduct:

- Player language
- Player behavior

- Interactions with officials
- Discipline for misbehavior
- Dress code for competitions

Physical Safety

Chapter 4 is devoted to player safety, but it's worth noting here that safety during games can be affected by how officials call the rules. If officials aren't calling rules correctly and this risks injury to your players, you must intervene. Voice your concern in a respectful manner and in a way that places the emphasis where it should be—on the players' safety. One of the officials' main responsibilities is to provide for players' safety. Both you and the officials are working together to protect the players whenever possible. Don't hesitate to address an issue of safety with an official when the need arises.

Player Welfare

All players are not the same. Some attach their self-worth to winning and losing. This idea is fueled by coaches, parents, peers, and society, who place great emphasis on winning. Players become anxious when they're uncertain whether they can meet the expectations of others or of themselves—especially when meeting a particular expectation is important to them.

If you place too much importance on the game or cause your players to doubt their abilities, they will become anxious about the outcome and their performance. If your players look uptight and anxious during a game, you should find ways to reduce both the uncertainties about how their performance will be evaluated and the importance they are attaching to the game. Help players focus on realistic personal goals—goals that are reachable and measurable and that will help them improve their performance while having fun as they play. Another way to reduce anxiety on game day is to stay away from emotional pregame pep talks. Instead, remind players of the tactics and plays they will use, and remind them to play hard, to do their best, and to have fun.

When coaching during games, remember that the most important outcome from playing football is to build or enhance players' self-worth. Keep that firmly in mind, and strive to promote this through every coaching decision.

Opponents and Officials

Respect opponents and officials. Without them, there wouldn't be a competition. Officials help provide a fair and safe experience for players and, as appropriate, help them learn the game. Opponents provide opportunities for your team to test itself, improve, and excel.

You and your team should show respect for opponents by giving your best efforts. Showing respect means being civil to your opponents. Don't allow your players to "trash talk" or taunt an opponent. This behavior is disrespectful to the spirit of the competition and to the opponent. Immediately remove players from a game if they disobey your orders in this area.

> **COACHING TIP** You should keep your demeanor even and positive on the sidelines. Conduct your game responsibility the same way regardless of the score, help correct your players' errors in a positive manner, and continue to offer encouragement to each player.

Remember that officials at this level are quite often teenagers—in many cases, they may not be much older than the players themselves—and the level of officiating should be commensurate to the level of play. In other words, don't expect perfection from officials any more than you do from your own players. Especially at younger levels, officials may not make every call, because to do so would stop the game every 10 seconds. You may find that the officials for younger teams only call the most flagrant penalties, those directly affecting the outcome of the game. As long as the calls are being made consistently on both sides and the flagrant penalties are being addressed, most of your officiating concerns will be alleviated.

After the Game

When the game is over, join your team in congratulating the coaches and players of the opposing team, then be sure to thank the officials. Check on any injuries that players sustained during the game, and inform players on how to care for them. Be prepared to speak with the officials about any problems that occurred during the game. Then, hold a brief meeting or "team circle" (described later) to ensure that your players are on an even keel, whether they won or lost.

Reactions After the Game

When celebrating a victory, make sure your team does so in a way that doesn't show disrespect for the opponents. It is okay and appropriate to be happy and celebrate a win, but do not allow your players to taunt the opponents or boast about their victory. Keep winning in perspective. Winning and losing are a part of life, not just a part of sport. If players can handle both equally well, they'll be successful in whatever they do.

Players are competitors, and competitors are disappointed in defeat. If your team has made a winning effort, let them know this. After a loss, help them keep their chins up and maintain a positive attitude that will carry over into the next practice and game.

> **COACHING TIP** Immediately after a game, regardless of the outcome, you must stay positive. When the players arrive at the next practice after a game, make certain that you let the previous game go, make needed corrections, and focus on the next opponent and game.

Postgame Team Meeting

After the game, gather your team into a team circle in a designated area for a short meeting. The players can sit on the ground or kneel on one knee, and they may take off helmets and shoulder pads. Before this meeting, decide as a coaching staff what to say and who will say it. Be sure that the coaching staff speaks with one voice after the game.

If your players have performed well in a game, compliment them and congratulate them. Tell them specifically what they did well, whether they won or lost. This will reinforce their desire to repeat their good performances. Don't use this time to criticize individual players for poor performances in front of teammates. As Theodore Roosevelt once said, "In the battle of life, it is not the critic who counts. . . . The credit belongs to the man who is actually in the arena." Help players improve their skills, but do so in the next practice, not immediately after a game.

The postgame team circle isn't the time to go over tactical problems and adjustments. The players are either so happy after a win or so dejected after a loss that they won't absorb much tactical information. Your first concern should be your players' attitudes and mental well-being. You don't want your players to be too high after a win or too low after a loss. This is the time you can be most influential in keeping the outcome in perspective and keeping players on an even keel. Remember, too, that although the final outcome of the game may be extremely important to you, the staff, and some of the parents, for young players the biggest concern may be whether or not they will get pizza. You need to realize that the majority of your players are playing the game to have fun. Understand that their desire to go out together for something to eat rather than relive the game is not a reflection on their desire to play well. Stay positive, allow the players to be kids, and avoid making too much over the outcome of the game.

Finally, make sure your players have transportation home. Be the last one to leave in order to ensure full supervision of your players.

We hope this book has been helpful to you and that you've learned a lot from it: what your responsibilities are as a coach, how to communicate well and provide for safety, how to teach and shape skills, and how to coach on game days. But game days make up only a portion of your season—you and your players will spend more time in practice than in competition. You will be teaching young people more than just the game of football, and you will be doing so at a stage in their lives when they form their values.

Do Your Research

Do your research to maximize the time with your team. During the football season, coaches must organize certain practices differently based on the following factors:

- Time of year
- Equipment available
- Weather and field conditions
- Injuries to players

When planning practices, you will divide them into preseason practices (with and without pads) and regular-season practices, depending on the time of year. You will vary both your preseason practices and your in-season practices depending on whether or not they fall before scrimmages or games. Later in the chapter, we look closely at practice plans and provide examples you can use during the various times of the year.

When you are developing your season plans before the start of the season, be sure to take inventory of practice equipment and look over the fields you will use for your practice sessions. Remember that equipment may vary from one practice facility to another. For example, your practice field may be unmarked, so you will need to provide tape or cones to mark the line of scrimmage and the boundaries of the field. Or, you might lack goalposts on your practice field for your placekicker, but you can still hold kicking practice. Handheld lightweight blocking dummies that are easily transported from practice to practice are also useful. Make sure to include in your individual practice plans whatever equipment you will need for each practice.

Regardless of the time of year, you should be aware of the weather conditions that could force you to shorten or even eliminate a practice session. This is especially true in the preseason when heat might force you to adjust the length of your practice. In this case, you should shorten each segment of your practice schedule, include more water breaks, and make sure that your players are not overheating. You must also be aware of lightning during severe weather. If lightning is nearby when the players are on the field, quickly get them to shelter.

Because injuries are unpredictable, you cannot plan for them. But they will occur, and you may need to make on-the-field changes to your practice plan when certain players are unavailable because of injury or sickness. At these times, you need to be flexible and understanding. Have a plan for adjusting your practices so that you can accomplish the most and can prevent avoidable injuries.

Season Plans

Before the first practice with your players, sit down as a coaching staff and write down each practice and game date on a calendar. Then go back and number your practices. Those practice numbers will become the foundation of your season plan. Now you can work through the season plan, moving from practice to practice to create a quick overview of what you hope to cover in each practice.

To create a season plan, simply list the practice number, the purpose of the practice, the main skills you will cover, and the drills you will use during the practice. While developing this plan, keep in mind the research that you gathered earlier. Also keep in mind the various skills that your players must learn. Be sure to cover those skills in your season plan (see chapters 7, 8, and 9 for descriptions of basic skills). Your season plan provides a snapshot of the entire season. See the "Sample Season Plan" below for an idea of what this overview looks like.

COACHING TIP Many players have a dream position that they would like to play. The early preseason is the time to let them find out if they have the skills to play the position and how they compare to their teammates.

Sample Season Plan

This sample provides a glimpse of a season plan for 8- to 14-year olds. It includes a quick overview of the first 10 practices in the season. The plan lists the practice number, the purpose, the main skills to be taught, and the drills to be used. More detailed practice information is listed in the "Practice Plans" section (page 209).

Practice 1 (no pads and noncontact)

PURPOSE
This practice gives every player a chance to try out for any position and helps you find the players on the team who have the best natural skills required to play specific positions.

TECHNICAL SKILLS AND TACTICS
Throwing (page 108), punting (page 173), receiving (page 111), and kickoff (page 174)

DRILLS
Open throwing drill, open punting drill, open receiving drill, open kickoff drill, and interception drill

> continued

> *continued*

Practice 2 (no pads and noncontact)

PURPOSE
This is a continuation of the first practice. Give every player a chance to try out for any position, and find the players who have the best natural skills required to play specific positions.

TECHNICAL SKILLS AND TACTICS
Throwing (page 108), punting (page 173), receiving (page 111), and kickoff (page 174)

DRILLS
Open throwing drill, open punting drill, open receiving drill, open kickoff drill, and interception drill

Practice 3 (no pads and noncontact)

PURPOSE
Begin assigning positions to players and teach them basic defensive, offensive, and special-teams concepts. Drills are performed on air and without contact.

TECHNICAL SKILLS AND TACTICS
Offensive stance (page 88), throwing (page 108), receiving (page 111), drive block (page 94), cutoff block (page 96), defensive stance (page 139), backpedal (page 148), and kickoff (page 174)

DRILLS
Round the clock drill (page 130), tap and go drill (page 130), man-to-man coverage drill (page 164), and punting drill (page 186)

Practice 4 (no pads and noncontact)

PURPOSE
Continue refining the positions of the players and their alignments. Begin to run basic offensive plays, defenses, and special-teams plays.

TECHNICAL SKILLS AND TACTICS
Pass tree (page 120), man-to-man defense (page 149), zone defense (page 150), and punt return (page 178)

DRILLS
Pass protection–blocking drill (page 126), tap and go drill (page 130), quarterback three- and five-step drop-back drill (page 132), pass rush drill (page 159), filling your gap responsibility drill (page 167), and punting drill (page 186)

Practice 5 (no pads and noncontact)

PURPOSE
This is a continuation of practice 4.

TECHNICAL SKILLS AND TACTICS
Pass tree (page 120), man-to-man defense (page 149), zone defense (page 150), and punt return (page 178)

DRILLS
Pass protection–blocking drill (page 126), quarterback three- and five-step drop-back drill (page 132), pass rush drill (page 159), contain drill (page 160), tip drill (page 163), and punting drill (page 186)

Practice 6 (pads)

PURPOSE
Begin working players against one another and introduce the idea of contact on a limited basis.

TECHNICAL SKILLS AND TACTICS
Tackling (page 142), cross block (page 96), double-team block (page 98), receiving (page 111), and pass tree (page 120)

DRILLS
Breaking- and receiving-points drill (page 129), cross-blocking drill (page 125), double team–blocking drill (page 127), and cutback runner technique drill (page 161)

Practice 7 (pads)

PURPOSE
This practice builds on practice 6. Continue helping players become comfortable with contact, and begin developing the competition between offense and defense.

TECHNICAL SKILLS AND TACTICS
Front-on tackling (page 143), angle tackling (page 144), zone blocking (page 98), pass tree (page 120), pass protection (page 100), and pass rush (page 145)

DRILLS
Front on–tackling drill (page 159), angle-tackling drill (page 161), zone-blocking drill (page 128), quarterback three- and five-step drop-back drill (page 132), pass protection–blocking drill (page 126), pass rush drill (page 159), contain drill (page 160), and cutback runner technique drill (page 161)

> continued

> *continued*

Practice 8 (pads)

PURPOSE
This is a continuation of practices 6 and 7.

TECHNICAL SKILLS AND TACTICS
Front-on tackling (page 143), angle tackling (page 144), zone blocking (page 98), pass tree (page 120), pass protection (page 100), and pass rush (page 145)

DRILLS
Front on–tackling drill (page 159), angle-tackling drill (page 161), zone-blocking drill (page 128), quarterback three- and five-step drop-back drill (page 132), pass protection–blocking drill (page 126), pass rush drill (page 159), contain drill (page 160), and filling your gap responsibility drill (page 167)

Practice 9 (pads)

PURPOSE
This practice prepares the team for the following day's scrimmage.

TECHNICAL SKILLS AND TACTICS
To be determined based on where the team is at this point

DRILLS
To be determined based on where the team is at this point

Practice 10

PURPOSE
Hold a scrimmage that simulates a real-game experience. Substitute all players according to a substitution plan dedicated to giving all players equal playing time.

TECHNICAL SKILLS AND TACTICS
All skills could come into play.

DRILLS
Not applicable

Use your season plan to begin developing individual practices. You may need to adjust your season plan throughout the season, and that is okay. The plan is meant to serve as a guide that can be revised and adjusted. You can adjust the plan if you and the staff believe the team needs extra work in certain areas or if injuries or equipment issues force you to change your plans.

Practice Plans

Coaches rarely believe they have enough time to practice everything they want to cover. Therefore, you must set and agree on priorities concerning how the practices will be conducted and the actual amount of time to allocate for each part of a practice. Although your practice structure will vary slightly depending on where you are in your season, each practice plan should include the following sections:

- Purpose
- Equipment
- Plan

The purpose section focuses on what you want to teach your players; it outlines the main theme for the practice and should be drawn from your season plan. Equipment sections note what you need to have on hand for each practice. Plan sections are the core of what you will do during practice. Plan sections consist of the following basic elements: warm-up, introduction, individual period, group period, special-teams period, team period, and cool-down.

All but the warm-up and cool-down of the plan section will vary both in structure and in content depending on where you are in the season. See page 210 for more details.

If you have players who play both offense and defense, you may need to organize your practice schedule so that one day is an offensive day and the next is a defensive day. Players playing both offense and defense can then focus on one phase of their preparation on each day. Inform players what the emphasis will be before the warm-up period at the start of practice.

Practice Types

As discussed earlier in this chapter, you will vary your practices based on where you are in your season. The main parts of the season are the preseason and the regular season.

Preseason Practices

League rules will require that a certain number of practices at the beginning of the season be conducted without pads. Use the first two practices to introduce individual techniques, work on conditioning, and establish practice organization. These two practice sessions should be devoted to giving every player a chance to try out for any position and to finding the players who have the best natural skills (throwing, catching, running fast, punting, and kicking) required to play specific positions. For an example of this type of practice, refer to the "Sample Plan for the First Two Preseason Practices," begining on page 211.

Plan Section

WARM-UP (5 TO 10 MINUTES)
During the warm-up, the entire team is arranged in predetermined rows and positions. This type of setup lets you see easily who is absent from practice. Use brisk running to raise the core temperature of each player during this period.

INTRODUCTION (5 MINUTES)
This period can be used to introduce a new offensive play or a new defense depending on the focus of the day. This introduction should be short and to the point.

INDIVIDUAL PERIOD (15 MINUTES)
During this period, teach individual techniques to the various groups. The size of your coaching staff will determine the number of groups. An optimal number of coaches is six, because this allows every unit to have the benefit of a position coach. With four coaches, you can split up the team into an offensive backfield, offensive line, defensive line, and defensive backfield. With less than four coaches, you can simply divide the team up into an offensive and defensive unit. Keep the drills short, teach one technique in each drill, and allow each player the maximum number of repetitions.

GROUP PERIOD (20 MINUTES)
Use this time for groups to play against one another. The drills that you use will vary from one practice to the other. The following are examples:

- Passing drills with the receivers running routes against defensive backs
- Pass protection drills with the offensive line working against the defensive line
- Half-team assignments against half defenses
- Techniques in the one-on-one drills and assignments in the half-line drills

SPECIAL-TEAMS PERIOD (10 MINUTES)
Focus on one or more of the special-teams segments that you need for the game. Try to work on corresponding parts of the kicking game. For example, work on the kickoff team and kickoff return team at the same time.

TEAM PERIOD (20 MINUTES)
Work the entire offense versus the entire defense. During the offensive segment, the defense acts as the opponent by running the opponent's defense (and vice versa during the defensive segment). The major focus should be on timing, assignments, and working as a unit.

COOL-DOWN (5 TO 10 MINUTES)
Use the cool-down to bring the team together and run offensive plays down the field or run team pursuit or interception defenses against the air. This is a conditioning period using a football activity that players perform as a group, followed by a short stretching period with players in groups.

Sample Plan for the First Two Preseason Practices

The first two practice sessions of the preseason should be run without pads.

PURPOSE

To give every player a chance to try out for any position and to find the players on the team who have the best natural skills required to play specific positions.

EQUIPMENT

Players should wear mouth guards, helmets, T-shirts, shorts or football pants, socks, and football shoes. They should also bring water. Coaches should provide five or more footballs, a whistle, a clipboard, forms for recording notes on players, a kickoff tee, a field-goal tee, water, and a basic first aid kit with a cell phone.

WARM-UP (10 MINUTES)

Each player lines up for the start of practice. The order of the player lineup can be identified at the first preseason practice. Once the order is determined, explain that players should line up in this order at the start of each practice and for pregame warm-ups. Keep a chart so that you can easily look out and see who is missing. Once the players are lined up, conduct a short stretching period, a set of 10 push-ups, and a set of 10 sit-ups. Then have the players run strides across the field to raise their core temperature for practice.

OPEN THROWING DRILL (15 TO 20 MINUTES)

All players who want to try out for quarterback should have the chance. With very young players, you could substitute a softball for a football. Have players throw for accuracy to their right and their left to players running slant routes and then hook routes; then have them throw deep on up routes. Have two quarterbacks throw at a time, and keep the lines moving. Evaluate natural arm strength and accuracy without coaching. Always keep a written record.

OPEN PUNTING DRILL (15 TO 20 MINUTES)

Any player who wants to punt should be given the opportunity. Allow each player to take five punts. Evaluate natural leg strength and accuracy without coaching. Always keep a written record. Arrange the other players in two lines to try to catch punts.

OPEN RECEIVING DRILL (15 TO 20 MINUTES)

All players who want to be wide receivers should be given the opportunity. The other players can fill in at the tight end positions. Explain and demonstrate the three pass routes that will be run. Spread four lines across the field and have two coaches throwing the ball. The two lines closest to the quarterback run routes for tight ends, and the two wide lines run routes for wide receivers. Start with a slant and look-in route combination, an all-hook combination, and then an up route by the wide receivers and a post route by the tight ends. Evaluate the natural ability of each player without coaching. Always keep a written record.

> *continued*

> *continued*

OPEN KICKOFF DRILL (15 TO 20 MINUTES)

Any player who wants to kick off should be given the opportunity. Allow each kicker to take five kicks. Evaluate natural leg strength and kicking skill without coaching. Always keep a written record. Arrange other players in two lines to try to catch kicks.

INTERCEPTION DRILL (15 TO 20 MINUTES)

Divide the team into four groups. Spread the team into four lines across the field, 10 yards down the field from the coach and facing the coach (one coach is on each side of the field). The coach points the ball at the first player in line. The player runs in place, and the coach throws the ball; the player makes the interception and runs the ball back to the coach. Evaluate the natural ability of each player from a defensive position without coaching. Always keep a written record.

COOL-DOWN (10 MINUTES)

Finish the practice and bring the team together in their original positions. Lead cool-down stretches and explain what will be done in the next practice session. After the practice, evaluate the players based on your records and on watching them perform. Begin to determine where players will be best suited to play.

The practices that follow these first two practice sessions can be used to condition your team; to introduce the players to your practice schedule, offense, defense, and special teams; and to prepare players to practice in pads later in the season. Practices without pads at the start of the year are a good time to get players lined up properly on offense, defense, and special teams and to focus on teaching individual techniques against the air. Move the players into different positions to give them experience playing those positions and to help you evaluate where a player should line up. A template is provided in the appendix (see "Preseason Practices [No Pads]" on page 223) that you can use to guide you when designing practices for this part of your season.

After your required practices without pads, you will begin your preseason practices with the players in full uniform. Some coaches require only helmet and shoulder pads if the team will not be scrimmaging. Do not allow players to practice without hip, thigh, and knee pads, because this makes players vulnerable to bruises and injuries of the lower body. Always require helmets for any practice where running plays are involved. Use the practices with pads at the start of the year to introduce your base offense, defense, and special teams. Focus on teaching the individual skills needed to play each position. Then begin bringing the players together so that they can start to function as an 11-player unit and can get used to contact. These practices can be broken into small groups; the number depends on the size of your staff. A template is provided in the appendix (see "Preseason Practices [Pads]" on page 224) that you can use to guide you when designing practices for this part of your season.

During the preseason, you will also need to plan practices with pads that occur the day before a scrimmage. In these practices, you should prepare the team for the scrimmage by reviewing how players will line up for stretching, where they will go, and what they will do to warm up. Review all the substitutions for offense, defense, and special teams during this practice. Eliminate all but half-speed contact from this practice. Do not run the players excessively; keep their legs and minds fresh. A template is provided in the appendix (see "Preseason Practice Before First Scrimmage [Pads]" on page 225) that you can use to guide you when designing this type of practice.

Regular-Season Practices

You will conduct your regular-season practices with pads according to your practice plan once the regular season is under way. If you have a limited staff or if several players play both offense and defense, you may want to designate one practice as an offensive day and the next practice as a defensive day. This method is especially well suited to introducing the walk-through, the individual period, and the emphasis during the group and team segments of your practice. A template is provided in the appendix (see "Regular-Season Practices [Pads]" on page 226) that you can use to guide you when designing practices during this part of your season.

In regular-season practices with pads before game day, you should prepare the team for the game by reviewing how they will line up for stretching, where they will go, and what they will do for a warm-up. Review all the substitutions for offense, defense, and special teams during this practice.

Another good idea is to do a surprise call for a unit to take the field at an unpredictable time during this practice. For example, yell out for the field-goal team and ask that the unit line up and kick a field goal in less than 25 seconds. Or, while the team is practicing offense, call out for the defensive unit, checking the substitutions as they take the field. This will help prepare the team to respond to gamelike situations.

Eliminate all but half-speed contact from this practice. Do not run the players excessively during a practice right before a game. Keep their legs rested and their minds fresh. A template is provided in the appendix (see "Regular-Season Practices Before Game Day [Pads]" on page 227) that you can use to guide you when designing this type of practice.

Fun Learning Environment

Regardless of where you are in your season, you must create an environment that welcomes learning and promotes teamwork. Following are seven tips that will help you and your coaching staff get the most out of your practices:

1. Stick to the practice times agreed on as a staff.
2. Start and end each practice as a team. Visualize a victory to conclude practice (count off the seconds).
3. Keep the practice routine as consistent as possible so that the players can feel comfortable.
4. Be organized in your approach by moving quickly from one drill to another and from one period to another.
5. Tell your players what the practice will include before the practice starts (and tell them when the practice will end).
6. Allow the players to take water breaks whenever possible.
7. Focus on providing positive feedback, such as "Atta boy," "Nice job," "You're the man," "Oh yeah," or "Hooya!" Praise or reward players when they do something outstanding.

COACHING TIP Including games in each practice will not only make practices more enjoyable for the players, but will also keep the players' attention level high.

You may also want to consider using games to make practices more fun. In chapter 5, you will find a number of gamelike drills. During your season, it may be fun to use the games toward the end of the week to add variety to your practices. Modify games so that there is no contact when you are holding practices without pads.

Appendix

Related Checklists and Forms

This appendix contains checklists and forms that will be useful in your football program. All checklists and forms mentioned in the text can be found here. You may reproduce and use the forms indicated as needed for your football program; these forms may also be found at the following Web site: www. HumanKinetics.com/CYFootball5E/ExtraPoints.

Facilities and Equipment Checklist

Field Surface

❑ Sprinkler heads and openings are at grass level.

❑ The field is free of toxic substances (lime, fertilizer, and so on).

❑ The playing surface is free of debris.

❑ No rocks or cement slabs are on the field.

❑ The field is free of protruding pipes, wires, and lines.

❑ The field is not too wet.

❑ The field is not too dry.

❑ The field lines are well marked.

Outside Playing Area

❑ The edge of the playing field is at least 6 feet (183 cm) from trees, walls, fences, and cars.

❑ Nearby buildings are protected by fences or walls from possible damage during play.

❑ Storage sheds and facilities are locked.

❑ The playground area, including ground surface and equipment, is safe and in good condition.

❑ The fences or walls lining the area are in good repair.

❑ Sidewalks are without cracks, separations, or raised concrete.

Equipment

❑ Goalposts are held together securely.

❑ Players' equipment has been checked as specified in the Player Equipment Checklist.

From *Coaching Youth Football, Fifth Edition*, by ASEP, 2010, Champaign, IL: Human Kinetics.

Player Equipment Checklist

You must be sure to keep your player equipment safe. Use this checklist to frequently check the equipment of your players.

❑ **Shoulder pads**   Body padding should not extend beyond the tip of the shoulder; the pads should fit snugly in the neck area when the arms are extended overhead.

❑ **Helmet**   The helmet must fit snugly around the head and in the jaw section; the head should be in contact with the crown suspension when the front edge is approximately 1 inch (2.5 cm) above the eyebrow.

❑ **Clothing**   The jersey should fit close to the body and should always be tucked into the pants to hold the shoulder pads in place; the pants should hug the body to keep the thigh and knee guards in place.

❑ **Mouth guard**   The mouth guard should fit properly.

❑ **Girdle pads**   The girdle, or hip, pads must cover the point of the hip and give proper protection to the lower spine.

❑ **Thigh and knee pads**   Thigh and knee pads must be the proper size and must be inserted properly in the lining of the player's pants.

❑ **Shoes**   Cleats should be inspected regularly to ensure even wear and stability; proper width is very important; the upper should never overrun the outsole.

From *Coaching Youth Football, Fifth Edition*, by ASEP, 2010, Champaign, IL: Human Kinetics.

217

Medical Clearance Form

Association name: _____

Medical Clearance Form: Must be dated after January 1st of the current season.

I, hereby my signature below, do certify that I am licensed by the state and am qualified in determining that (Child's Name) _____
is physically fit, and I have found no medical or observable conditions which would contraindicate him/her from participating in youth flag football, tackle football, cheer, dance, step, or athletic activities. I am therefore clearing this individual for athletic participation.

Please print or use office stamp here:

Signature: _____

Print name clearly: _____

Date: _____

Office address: _____

(Must be dated after January 1st of the current season)

PLEASE NOTE: If this medical clearance is voided by injury, accident, or illness, it will be the responsibility of the parent/legal guardian to notify the participant's coach and league officials. It will also be the responsibility of the parent/legal guardian to obtain WRITTEN permission from his/her physician to resume participation. A "Doctor's Resume Participation Medical Clearance Form" is available from the league, or you may have the doctor supply his/her own WRITTEN clearance as long as it is on the doctor's official stationary and includes the following statement: "(Participant's Name) is physically fit and I have found no medical or observable conditions which would contraindicate him/her from participating in youth flag football, tackle football, cheer, dance, step, or athletic activities. I am therefore clearing this individual for athletic participation."

This statement must be supplied by the physician attending to the injury, accident, or illness.

This form can be modified or substituted ONLY to comply with local and/or state laws or due to medical practitioner regulations.

NOTE: This form, as with any and all forms used by your association, should be reviewed by your local counsel for compliance with any state or local statutes. This form should be kept on file for a minimum of seven years, longer in the event of an injury. Please confer with your local attorney for advice as to the appropriate maintenance and storage term for this and all such forms.

Courtesy of American Youth Football, Inc. Source: www.myayf.com.

Minor Waiver or Release

Release of Liability for Minor Participants

READ BEFORE SIGNING

IN CONSIDERATION OF _____, my minor child/ward ("my child"), being allowed to participate in any way in the _____ (name of organization) program and in related events and activities, the undersigned acknowledges, appreciates, and agrees that:

1. The risk of injury to my child from the activities involved in these programs is significant, including the potential for permanent disability and death, and while particular rules, equipment, and personal discipline may reduce this risk, the risk of serious injury does exist.

2. FOR MYSELF, MY SPOUSE, AND MY CHILD, I KNOWINGLY AND FREELY ASSUME ALL SUCH RISKS, both known and unknown, EVEN IF ARISING FROM THE NEGLIGENCE OF THE RELEASEES or others, and assume full responsibility for my child's participation.

3. I willingly agree to comply with the program's stated and customary terms and conditions for participation. If I observe any unusual significant concern in my child's readiness for participation and/or in the program itself, I will remove my child from the participation and bring such to the attention of the nearest official immediately.

4. For myself, my spouse, my child, and on behalf of my/our heirs, assigns, personal representatives, and next of kin, I HEREBY RELEASE FROM LIABILITY the other participants, sponsoring agencies, sponsors, advertisers, and, if applicable, owners and lessors of premises used to conduct the event ("releasees"), WITH RESPECT TO ANY AND ALL INJURY, DISABILITY, DEATH, or loss or damage to person or property incident to my child's involvement or participation in these programs, WHETHER ARISING FROM THE NEGLIGENCE OF THE RELEASEES OR OTHERWISE, to the fullest extent permitted by law.

5. For myself, my spouse, my child, and on behalf of my/our heirs, assigns, personal representatives, and next of kin, I HEREBY INDEMNIFY AND HOLD HARMLESS all the above releasees from any and all liabilities incident to my involvement or participation in these programs, EVEN IF ARISING FROM THEIR NEGLIGENCE, to the fullest extent permitted by law.

I HAVE READ THIS RELEASE OF LIABILITY AND ASSUMPTION OF RISK AGREEMENT, FULLY UNDERSTAND ITS TERMS, UNDERSTAND THAT I HAVE GIVEN UP SUBSTANTIAL RIGHTS BY SIGNING IT, AND SIGN IT FREELY AND VOLUNTARILY WITHOUT ANY INDUCEMENT.

_____ _____ Date: _____
(PARENT/GUARDIAN SIGNATURE)   (PRINT NAME)

Understanding of Risk

I understand the seriousness of the risks involved in participating in this program, as well as my personal responsibilities for adhering to rules and regulations, and I accept them as a participant.

_____ _____ Date: _____
(PARENT/GUARDIAN SIGNATURE)   (PRINT NAME)

NOTE: This is a SAMPLE WAIVER FORM only. Final wording should be as directed by the insured's counsel but must observe the principles represented within the above.

Injury Report Form

Date: _____ Time: _____ a.m. / p.m.

Player's name: _____

Type of injury: _____

_____

Anatomical area involved: _____

_____

Cause of injury: _____

_____

Extent of injury: _____

_____

Person administering first aid (name): _____

First aid administered: _____

_____

Other treatment administered: _____

_____

Referral action: _____

_____

Person administering first aid (signature): _____

Date: _____

Emergency Information Card

Player's name: _____ Sport: _____

Age: _____ S.S. #: _____

Address: _____

Phone: _____

Provide information for parent or guardian and one additional contact in case of emergency.

Parent's or guardian's name: _____

Address: _____

Phone: _____Other phone: _____

Additional contact's name: _____

Relationship to player: _____

Address: _____

Phone: _____Other phone: _____

Information

Name of insurance company: _____

Policy name and number: _____

Medical Information

Physician's name: _____Phone: _____

Is your child allergic to any drugs?   *Yes   No*

If so, what? _____

Does your child have any other allergies (e.g., bee stings, dust)? _____

Does your child have any of the following?   *asthma   diabetes   epilepsy*

Is your child currently taking medication?   *Yes   No*

If so, what? _____

Does your child wear contact lenses?   *Yes   No*

Is there additional information we should know about your child's health or physical condition?   *Yes   No*

If yes, please explain: _____

Parent's or guardian's signature: _____Date: _____

From *Coaching Youth Football, Fifth Edition*, by ASEP, 2010, Champaign, IL: Human Kinetics.

221

Emergency Response Card

Be prepared to give the following information to an EMS dispatcher. Note: Do not hang up first. Let the EMS dispatcher hang up first.

Caller's name: _____

Telephone number from which the call is being made: _____

Reason for call: _____

How many people are injured: _____

Condition of victims: _____

First aid being given: _____

Location: _____

Address: _____

City: _____

Directions (e.g., cross streets, landmarks, entrance access): _____

_____

_____

_____

Preseason Practices (No Pads)

Purpose

Equipment

Warm-Up *(5-10 minutes)*

Offensive Period 1 *(20 minutes)*

Defensive Period 1 *(10 minutes)*

Special-Teams Period *(20 minutes)*

Offensive Period 2 *(20 minutes)*

Defensive Period 2 *(20 minutes)*

Cool-Down *(5-10 minutes)*

From *Coaching Youth Football, Fifth Edition*, by ASEP, 2010, Champaign, IL: Human Kinetics.

223

Preseason Practices (Pads)

Purpose

Equipment

Warm-Up *(10 minutes)*

Introduction of New Plays *(10 minutes)*

Individual Period *(20 minutes)*

Special-Teams Period *(10 minutes)*

Group Period *(15 minutes)*

Offensive Team Period *(20 minutes)*

Defensive Team Period *(20 minutes)*

Conditioning *(10 minutes)*

Cool-Down *(5 minutes)*

From *Coaching Youth Football, Fifth Edition*, by ASEP, 2010, Champaign, IL: Human Kinetics.

Preseason Practice Before First Scrimmage (Pads)

Purpose

Equipment

Warm-Up *(5-10 minutes)*

Individual Period *(15 minutes)*

Use this time to cover the individual warm-up to be used at the scrimmage.

Sideline Substitution Review *(20 minutes)*

Use this time to practice all substitutions for offense, defense, and special teams by having players run on and off the field.

Kicking Review *(20 minutes)*

Use this time to review all phases of the kicking game.

Offensive Review *(20 minutes)*

Use this time to review the first 10 plays that the offense will run.

Defensive Review *(20 minutes)*

Use this time to review base fronts and pass coverages for defense.

Cool-Down *(5-10 minutes)*

Use this time to review the time structure and location of the scrimmage. Be positive and emphasize that the scrimmage is a learning situation.

Regular-Season Practices (Pads)

Purpose

Equipment

Warm-Up *(5-10 minutes)*

Introduction of New Plays *(5 minutes)*

Individual Period *(15 minutes)*

Special-Teams Period *(10 minutes)*

Group Period *(20 minutes)*

Offensive Period *(20 minutes)*

Defensive Period *(20 minutes)*

Cool-Down and Conditioning *(5-10 minutes)*

   From *Coaching Youth Football, Fifth Edition*, by ASEP, 2010, Champaign, IL: Human Kinetics.

Regular-Season Practices
Before Game Day (Pads)

Purpose

Equipment

Warm-Up *(10 minutes)*

Individual Period *(10 minutes)*

Sideline Substitution Review *(10 minutes)*

Kicking Review *(20 minutes)*

Offensive Review *(20 minutes)*

Defensive Review *(15 minutes)*

Cool-Down *(5 minutes)*

From *Coaching Youth Football, Fifth Edition*, by ASEP, 2010, Champaign, IL: Human Kinetics.

227

Glossary

audible—A vocal signal at the line of scrimmage to change the play previously called in the huddle.

backfield—Players who are 1 yard or more behind the scrimmage line when the ball is snapped, including the quarterback, running backs, and wingback.

blitz—A play in which the defense commits extra players, in addition to linemen, to rush the passer.

chains—The 10-yard length of chain used to measure the distance required for a first down.

cross block—A block in which two linemen block defenders who are diagonally opposite the blockers' own starting positions; one of the blockers, usually the outside blocker, goes in front.

defensive formation—An alignment of defensive linemen, linebackers, and defensive backs positioned to stop a particular offense.

downs—A series of four consecutive charged scrimmages allotted to the offensive team; to retain possession, the offense must advance the ball 10 yards during these four downs.

eligible receiver—Any offensive player who is legally in the backfield or any player on either end of the line of scrimmage.

end zone—The area bounded by the goal line, end line, and sidelines.

extra-point conversion (or PAT)—In youth football, a play in which the offense successfully runs or passes into the end zone to score an additional point after the touchdown. To encourage the development of kickers, most youth football leagues will award a team two points after the touchdown for kicking the ball from a tee through the uprights and over the crossbar of the goalpost.

fair catch—An unhindered catch by a member of the receiving team of any kick that has crossed the kicking team's line of scrimmage or free-kick line, provided that the proper signal (one hand and arm extended above the head and moving from side to side) has been given by the receiver.

field goal—A placekick or dropkick from scrimmage that goes over the crossbar and through the uprights of the goal without touching the ground first. Three points are awarded for a field goal.

first down—The first of four allotted downs the offensive team receives, occurring when the offensive team gains 10 or more yards within its allotted four downs.

forward pass—A pass that strikes anything beyond the spot from which it was thrown; a pass in the direction of the opponent's goal.

fumble—Losing possession of the football by means other than passing or kicking it.

goal-line defense—Defensive alignment used near the defensive team's own goal line; this defense features defensive players driving for penetration through the gaps and has all defensive players close to the line of scrimmage in an attempt to stop the offensive team from scoring a touchdown.

goalpost—A structure located on each end line; attempts at field goals and extra points must pass over the crossbar and through the goalposts to be successful.

handoff—The action of handing (not passing or throwing laterally) the ball from one player to another. The quarterback usually executes a handoff to a running back, but a running back might also execute a handoff to the receiver on a reverse.

hash mark—The line running the length of the field and bisecting the yard lines. The ball must be placed inside the hash marks when a play is to begin.

I-formation—The offensive formation in which a fullback and tailback are positioned in a line directly behind the quarterback; the center, quarterback, fullback, and tailback form the letter I.

illegal use of hands—With possession of the ball established by either team, a player's using the hands to grasp and impede an opponent who is not the ballcarrier.

ineligible receiver—A player on the line of scrimmage (with at least one other player on either side of him) who cannot legally catch a pass or, on a pass play, be downfield before a pass is thrown.

interception—The action of gaining possession of the ball when a defender catches a pass thrown by the offense.

kickoff—A free kick initiating each half of a game; it also occurs after the scoring of a field goal or a touchdown and extra-point attempt. The ball is kicked from the kicking team's 40-yard line; the ball is either placed on a kicking tee or held by a player on the kicking team. All players on the kicking team must remain behind their 40-yard line until the ball is kicked. Once the ball travels 10 yards downfield, either team can establish possession.

kickoff return—The action of a team receiving a kickoff to establish possession of the ball and to attempt to advance the ball upfield.

late hit—An infraction occurring when a player hits an opponent after the play is over.

lateral pass—A pass in which the ball is tossed or thrown backward. (If it is dropped, it is considered a fumble.)

line of scrimmage—An imaginary line running perpendicular to the sidelines. The offensive and defensive lines of scrimmage are located on either end of the neutral zone and mark the ball's position at the start of each down.

man-to-man coverage—Defensive pass coverage in which defenders are assigned specific receivers to cover; the defenders cover those receivers no matter where they run their routes (they only leave their receiver when he blocks, when the ball is thrown, or when the ballcarrier crosses the line of scrimmage).

neutral zone—The length of the football that spans the width of the football field. Neither team (other than the snapper on a scrimmage down or the holder and kicker on a free-kick down) can be in the neutral zone before play begins. The offensive line must be behind the back point of the ball, and the defensive line must be beyond the front point of the ball.

offensive formation—The offensive team's lineup, or the offensive players' locations before the snap of the ball.

onside kick—A play in which a kickoff is deliberately kicked short so that the team kicking off has a chance to gain possession of the ball.

option—An offensive play designed to give the ballcarrier, usually the quarterback, the opportunity to carry the ball up the field, hand the ball off, or pass it to a teammate.

pass rush—A defender's attempt to tackle or hurry a member of the offensive team attempting to pass the football.

passing route—The path a receiver takes in an attempt to get open to receive a pass (or to serve as a decoy).

placekick—An action in which the ball is kicked from a tee or from the hold of a member of the kicking team; used for field goals and kickoffs.

play-action pass—A play in which a fake handoff precedes a pass attempt; this play is designed to pull in the linebackers and defensive backs and to slow the pass rush (by making the defense think the play is a run).

possession—Having control of the ball.

punt—Kicking the ball after dropping it and before it reaches the ground. Offensive teams who have failed to cover 10 yards in their first three attempts often punt on the fourth down.

punt coverage—The action of the players of the punting team running downfield when the ball is punted in an attempt to tackle the opponent who has fielded the punted ball (if the opponent has not called a fair catch).

punt return—The action of the player who has received a punted ball in trying to advance it.

quarterback sneak—A play in which a quarterback runs or dives over the line of scrimmage.

roughing the passer—An infraction that occurs when a defensive player hits the quarterback after the ball has been released. The official must decide whether the defensive player had time to stop after the ball's release.

sack—The action of a defender tackling the quarterback behind the line of scrimmage on an attempted pass play.

shotgun—An offensive formation in which the quarterback is lined up in the backfield 4 to 6 yards behind the center.

snap—The quick exchange of the football from the center to the quarterback to put the ball into play.

T-formation—An offensive formation in which the fullback is positioned 2 to 4 yards behind a quarterback who is positioned immediately behind the center. One halfback is on either side of the fullback, and the fullback and the two halfbacks are in a line parallel to the line of scrimmage.

time-out—A brief period during which the clock is stopped at the request of a player from either team. In general, each team is allowed three time-outs during each half of a game.

touchback—Occurs when the ball is kicked through the end zone or is downed in the receiving team's end zone. Play restarts on the receiving team's 20-yard line.

trap block—A technique in which offensive linemen pull laterally from their original position on the line of scrimmage and block an unsuspecting defender elsewhere down the line or in the defensive backfield.

wishbone—An offensive formation in which the quarterback is under center (direct snap), a fullback is directly behind the quarterback, and two halfbacks are behind and to the sides of the fullback.

zone coverage—Defensive pass coverage in which defenders are assigned specific areas to cover; the defenders focus on the quarterback and react to the area of the field where the ball is thrown.

About the Authors

The **American Sport Education Program (ASEP)** has been developing and delivering coaching education courses since 1981. As the nation's leading coaching education program, ASEP works with national, state, and local youth sport organizations to develop educational programs for coaches, officials, administrators, and parents. These programs incorporate ASEP's philosophy of "Athletes first, winning second."

American Youth Football (AYF) is an international nonprofit youth football organization founded in 1996 to promote the wholesome development of youth through their association with adult leaders in the sport of American football. AYF invites all youth programs to join and participate, without restricting weights or sizes of participants, leagues, financial abilities, or any other biases.

With 700,000 participants, 90,000 coaches, and 40,000 administrators, AYF has become the largest football organization on any level of the sport.

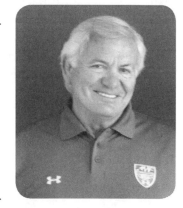

Joe Galat serves as the president of AYF. He is also employed by FieldTurf Tarkett as vice president of sales and dean of the FieldTurf Sports Science Institute. Joe's leadership began early as captain of the Harvey High School (Painesville, Ohio) and Miami University (Ohio) football and wrestling teams. At Miami University, he was elected president of the Varsity Letterman's Club and was named Outstanding Student Athlete in his senior year. Playing honors included selections to the All-Ohio All-Star High School Team and All-Mid-American Conference.

Joe's football experience was honed by some of the game's greats: Bo Schembechler, Carm Cozza, and John McVay. When Pro Football Hall of Fame coach George Allen was owner of Montreal, he appointed Joe to be his head coach. Joe then went on to become head coach and general manager of the British Columbia Lions of the Canadian Football League. He coached college football at Miami University, Yale University, University of Kentucky, and Youngstown State University.

In 1982, Joe was inducted into the Miami University Hall of Fame. He was also inducted into the Painesville Harvey High School Hall of Fame (along with the NFL's winningest coach, Don Shula). After his coaching days, Joe was national color commentator for CBC-TV Sports. This experience gave him the distinction of having held every position in organized football (player, coach, manager, broadcaster, and youth executive). Joe has participated in youth football clinics in the United States, Canada, and Mexico, and throughout Europe and Russia. Joe was also honored as a Kentucky Colonel by Governor Wendell Ford.